MAMA'S DIAMONDS

Memories of a young girl

EMCIE DAY

Printed in USA
Published by: Lulu.com

ISBN 978-0-557-02915-0

First Edition

Day, Emcie
    Mama's Diamonds,
    Memories of a young girl

R8d

Book design and layout by Donald F. Day
Cover design by Patrick J. Day

To my mother, Helen Louis Grogan

For her years of love and devotion to her children

To my brother, William Grogan

For his love and his untimely sacrifice

And to my husband Don

For his loving support and help in completing this book

To Wanda —
Best BB Q in AZ
Emcie Day

All Children of The Field

The earth is still, the stars are gone,
    the birds have fled in fear.
Man is angry once again,
    a storm is drawing near.

The brave, the young and in between,
    do what's expected now.
It must not come. Hold it back,
    hold it back... but how?

People say it can't be done,
    once started rain must fall.
But hold it back they will because
    they answer freedom's call.

The raging field holds much despair,
    see in the flashing glare
the look of death on every face,
    reflecting nerves so bare.

Some will fall, but rise again,
    to carry out the deed.
Some will fall, become the earth,
    to nurture morrow's seed.

Then easy as the morning light
    when thunder is no more,
the morning dawns and brings a peace
    that men have struggled for.

The battle's won, but left behind,
    such devastation here.
What keeps the hand of God in check?
    Instead He sheds a tear.

The dove's return brings to man
    hope and life, and song.
But who will heed the message,
    and for just how long?

Heavy hearts beat slower now
    longing to be healed.
Make pledge this day, forget them not,
    All Children of The Field.

       M. Day

CHAPTER 1
No Greater Sacrifice

Strange, it never sounded like that before. Kali O'Brien had spent all of her sixteen years within earshot of train whistles, but tonight from the outskirts of town came the wail of a lost soul. Tomorrow another train will come to town, a special train that has kept the O'Brien's waiting for three long months. Soon the waiting will be over for the family, and the coffin making the journey. Bells in the Lutheran Church nearby are striking twelve. A relief from train whistles but not enough to ease the apprehension. If Kali's mind could rest long enough, perhaps sleep would come. Three trains had passed through since Kali climbed into bed hours ago. Although the trains have moved swiftly through town, each one has left its mark, adding a little more to the frustration. One more toss and turn in the bed and her pajamas will be worn thin. Angrily, she kicks at the sheet that has tangled around one of her legs. Pausing, she looks at her sister, Mary, who shares the bed with her. Mary is undisturbed.

A silence fills the room leaving the air around her heavy with bothersome thoughts again. Mulling over the happenings of the past weeks have been no help to answer the nagging questions. Some may have none at all, but there is a need for answers now. What will it be like not to see someone again that you have known and loved for so many years, and what about Helen, her mother? It seems that Helen will never be as she was before. Not to share another song or story with her mother would be as though two people had died, not just one.

It was only a year ago that Helen found herself unable to dissuade her two oldest boys, Joseph and Andy, from joining the service, knowing that Korea had become an obvious threat to peace. Her fears have become a reality. Tomorrow one of them returns to her in a coffin. Why should it take such a thing as death to make Kali's father stop drinking? Since moving into the new house, Bob appears contented, faithfully coming home after work each day. There have been no arguments, no flares of temper to shatter the reason for the new house. Still, losing a family member is such a high price to pay for her Dad's improvement. The thought is upsetting. One life isn't supposed to be sacrificed for another. It's not right. Why would God permit it? Yet, it has happened.

Unable to cope, Kali leaves the bed, tiptoes down the stairs, and out onto the porch. The warm breeze feels good, better than a stuffy bedroom. Approaching the railing, she embraces one of the posts like an old friend. Her moist cheek presses tenderly against it. The post feels smooth, and smells of fresh paint. Staring for a moment at a full moon, that is playing peek-a-boo with her from behind the big maple; she thinks, "Mama is right, blowing leaves do rustle like party dresses." The chatter of the katydid is next to catch her attention. "Our very own katydids," she muses. The new glider swing at the far end of the porch beckons to Kali. This is what she needs. The rocking of the glider will ease the unsettled feelings. A calm embraces her as she cuddles in the corner of the glider and soon she surrenders to this softer world of stars, maple trees and katydids.

"This has been such a hard time, once the funeral is behind us it will be different … it has to be. How many people will meet the train tomorrow? It's kind of weird. One minute you feel you aren't important at all, and the next you're on the front page of the newspaper. Will people look at us differently from now on? Dad has never been the friendliest person in town. His friends are the same comfortable few for years, flocking around the bars together, but 'most everyone likes Mama. Why should it take such a sacrifice to make life better for us? I hope it's not my fault with my secret desire to live here, up on the hill. Could I be the cause of the way things turned out?" Her thoughts don't come with anger and confusion, but in her guilt, she reaches out for answers from the days that used to be:

Growing up here in Chipwey, there have been times tough enough to squeeze every bit of pride from us, but there were good times too. Some people think living in a small town is boring and dull; and maybe there is some truth to that. I don't think that's been so for us O'Brien's. Mama and Dad were both born and bred here in Chipwey. For the past ten years, we've become known as one of its poorer families trying to scratch out an existence, and Dad's drinking problem has been anything but a secret around town.

Chipwey, cradled in this lush green valley in upper New York State, isn't more than a mile long. On the North hill, homes are scattered up the gentler slope that runs east and west on three different levels above the park. The South side hill is the same as it was when Chipwey was first settled because the incline is too steep and rocky to build on. It's earned the reputation for being every mother's nightmare. Mama says it's the work of something sinister to put apple trees and berry bushes up there to attract the young and foolhardy. One misplaced footstep on the rocky surface could end in a deadly landing on the railroad tracks below.

One section of the South hill juts out to form a high cliff that looks out over railroad tracks and the town's industrial section that produces everything from dresses to bicycles. The railroad tracks have always been a measuring stick of a family's wealth in Chipwey; the nearer to the tracks, the poorer the family is. Who would want to hear the constant noise and deal with the soot of trains every day? Most of our town's people living near the railroad are the factory workers. The North side is where a privileged few live, putting as much distance as possible between themselves and the tracks.

Those fortunate enough to live there, have homes handed down from one generation to another. Built after the Civil War, these homes stand three and four stories high. Large porches, fancy cornices and shutters give them a look of elegance. They stand like giant sentinels on the street surrounding our largest park. Sprawling green lawns keep these homes more than a good distance from the curious. It's as though some entity watches over them, making sure they remain strong and pleasant to the eye. They never seem to grow old.

The higher the North hill rises the smaller and more practical the homes become. Over the years, more of the "not doing bad" kinds of people have built homes here. The hill developed into an area of houses that are distinctively different from one another, is "the" place to live; far from the hustle, bustle and soot of downtown Chipwey.

As a young girl, my mother, Helen Louise Desmond, lived in a modest, but attractive home on the highest street of the North hill. Behind her home, sprawled out for acres, is a wooded area that Mama played in as a child. Being the youngest of six children, life was good for Mama through the efforts of her Irish-born parents. Grandma was a good Catholic woman who worked hard every day for her family. Grandpa was a carpenter and worked in a furniture factory in nearby Morgan. There was always food on the table, and adequate clothes to wear. He and Grandma made sure there was a healthy mixture of religion and propriety for all the Desmond children.

When Mama was in here seventeenth year, all of her brothers and sisters had been married off. She was left behind to live a life very much as an only child until meeting Dad in the fall of 1928. A Halloween dance was the occasion. Dad had attended the affair, expecting nothing more than to be entertained by the array of imaginative costumes.

Dressed like a Geisha Girl, and with her naturally almond shaped brown eyes, Mama was much in character with the help of a little makeup. The charming girl in Oriental style dress caught Dad's eye right off. What a delight was the slender figure that gracefully moved about the dance floor. It was some time before Dad was given the opportunity to dance with her, but when he did, there was an irresistible urge to study her face at close range. Unaware that she had fooled him completely, she grew uncomfortable under Dad's steady gaze.

"Can I ask you something? Are you really, a … I mean … are you a for real Oriental?"

"Why, … yes I am."

"Aw come on."

Not able to continue the deception, Mama's laugh gave her away. For the rest of the evening the tall, lanky young man with dark wavy hair danced with her as often as he could. Mama's lighthearted personality was infectious, and without even trying, she had spun a web around Dad's heart. Mama said the first thing she noticed about Dad was how different he was from the younger boys that she was used to. There was no clumsy conversation to deal with, and Dad didn't speak in three different octaves. His air of self-confidence made it easy to get to know him. Being five years older, his attentions were very flattering.

Six months later Mama planned to drop out of school. There was talk of marriage. Marrying Dad was what she really wanted. Grandma and Grandpa objected to her marrying so young, and may have thought that with time, her new love would burn itself out, but that wasn't to happen. Dad had the gift of a good Irishman, a persuasive tongue. He vowed to take care of her, saying that he planned to build a home for her one day. He boasted of his position as head electrician at the bicycle factory. Dad started at the factory hand striping bicycle frames, and fenders. Gradually the job evolved to where he was often in the company of the maintenance man. Dad learned the principles of electricity from this man who taught him with the patience of a father. With the desire to learn more, he acquired a fair knowledge of electricity. Soon he was being called on to help with some of the electrical repairs. Being a strict Catholic, Grandma was appalled that Dad had never been baptized, and had no religion at all. Dad overcame that objection too. He became a "convert" before he and Mama married. With Dad becoming a Catholic only one objection was left, one he could never change … his background.

Mama and Dad married on June 27, 1929. A picture in the family album of Mama sitting on a rock by the side of a stream tells how happy she was. Her thin sleek body is draped in a pink chiffon dress. She is holding a pink wide brimmed hat. Her short wavy brown hair is full around he face. It was a good beginning. Within a few weeks, a different side to Dad's personality began to show. He kept track of Mama's day even when he wasn't at home. If Mama planned to visit her mother that day, he would tell her, "Wait until after supper. We'll go together," For a while Mama took this as his desire to be with her. After a time it was obvious that this behavior fenced her in as surely as barbed wire.

Mama told me that, when Dad took her to one of the clubs he belonged to, he would set her on the most remote barstool he could find; the last one on the end was always isolated. Then he would buy her a glass of ginger ale, as one might pacify a child with an ice cream cone. Once he had Mama taken care of, he would begin his ritual of visiting everyone in the room, deserting her in the process. Mama, safely mounted on the bar stool like a prize trophy, was supposed to be out of reach from everyone. It wouldn't be wise for any man to sit next to her, and commit the unforgivable sin of friendly conversation.

"What the hell's going on here?"

"Sit down Bob, have a drink."

"Drink bullshit. Why don't you keep moving?"

"Come on Bob. Sit down."

"Listen, keep your drinks. Give 'em to your own wife. Leave mine alone." Dad would already have Mama by the arm leading her out of the club, socializing for that evening was over.

The ruckus that Dad created would turn every head in the place. Mama couldn't leave fast enough, and that wasn't the end of it. On the way home, a further scolding not to talk to that son of a bitch again because he was one of the biggest womanizers in town.

"Maybe he's justified in reacting this way," she reasoned. "He is more worldly, more experienced in these things."

For a time, she trusted the instincts of her new husband; certain he had her best interests at heart. She tried to give him the benefit of the doubt, but couldn't brush everything away. If this was true, why was there always the feeling of embarrassment? How could it be, every man who spoke to her had a devious nature? Soon she stopped trying to figure it out and turned down any suggestion to go to the club. She knew what would happen. Their social life was diminished to going for walks or to the movies. It was easier on her nerves.

Three months into the marriage, Mama became pregnant; being in a family way only added to her feelings of being tied down. The desire to enter the grown-up world was all she longed for in the eighteenth year of her life. Well, now she was there. Troubled by the questionable behavior of this man, and a new baby on the way, Mama spent much of her time trying to sort it all out. Living apart from her family for the first time, and Dad working five days a week, Mama found herself alone for so many hours. Who would have thought it possible to be homesick for home when home was less than a mile away? As the pregnancy progressed, the lonely figure of a girl in the window became an everyday event. The little apartment was on the lower part of Main Street. The view of this new world of hers, so depressing and hateful, was distorted even more through her tears. Instead of her beloved woods, green lawns and graceful trees, she was buried alive in a world of cement and brick. Across the street were apartment buildings and next to those, small shops, everything from grocery stores to garages. That was the worst of all, the noisy hammering and banging of that auto mechanics shop.

Most times, there was an active stream of cars moving up and down Main Street, but none brought someone to visit her. Yet, she could handle everything she would tell herself; except for the baby. Being her first it was a scary thing, and it would have been consoling to talk to someone. There were a million questions to be asked. All of her education on the subject would come from a book. A job would have helped to pass the time, but Mama would learn through the years, that would never be allowed. Though their main source of entertainment was a Sunday movie at the Rialto, Dad did take Mama up on the hill for an occasional visit with her parents. This had to be done with tact and timing. Too many trips might give the impression she was lonely and discontented. It may have been true, but it could never show; there were too many objections to her marrying to start with. Married such a short time, there still had to be the glow of a new bride. Riding the highs and lows of confusion she tried to console herself with, "After the baby is born life would be different. It's been years since Bob had a family. The baby is what he needs."

When Bob was 12 years old, his father, Robert O'Brien Sr. was snatched from him with no warning. A happy, good-natured man, Robert worked hard for his pay hauling wagonloads of coal around town. It wasn't a very profitable way of life, but in 1917, it was a common way to earn a living for men of little education.

The O'Brien's occupied a small shanty of a house that was less than adequate for a family of three. The house had a kitchen, and two bedrooms. Some distance from the house a building resembling a coffin standing on end was their bathroom. The family, the house, the horse and wagon were all of Robert Sr.'s earthly attachments. Factories lined the railroad tracks just across the way from the little shanty. Grandma had her hands full trying to keep it clean. Between the strange smells that were spewed into the air, and the train soot that seemed to have the power to ooze through walls, life must have seemed impossible at times.

Robert Sr., a true Irishman, was a lover of the cool brew. He and his friends believed that the best way to wash the dusty impurities from a parched throat would be with a frosty mug of ale. Many a night he returned home with an unsteady swagger after washing the impurities from his throat.

The Ol' Shillelagh Tavern was Robert's last stop before going home almost every night. One night as he left for home he gave everyone his usual good-by. "God be with ya all," he calls back to the few holdouts. A wide brimmed hat is swung onto his head as he makes his way to the dirt road. His coveralls are well worn but far from soft. They rustle like paper from the coal dust that has worked itself into the fiber.

Robert climbs on to the wagon. The weary old horse, patiently waiting where he was left hours ago, knows he'll soon be back in his stall where young Bob has set out fresh hay and water. Dark leathery hands give a feeble snap to the reins, but the horse still responds. The wagon moves slowly off into the night leaving the lights of the tavern fading behind. The old horse had made that trip home so many times he could do it blindfolded, a handy talent on such nights. Hauling heavy wagonloads of coal all over town had a way of making a man and his horse much older than they really were. Who could deny Robert time to unwind after a hard day at work? He was better off than the rest; at least the horse and rig belonged to him.

A layer of clouds drifting across the moon and the smell of moisture in the air predicts there'll soon be rain. It goes unnoticed as Robert rides along with his eyes closed. The rhythmic clop, clop of the horse's hoofs, and the creaking bowed wooden planks of the old wagon, are the only sounds breaking the silence of the deserted road. Under the spell of the alcohol, he nods off. The wide brimmed hat that keeps the summer sun from his head will keep the rain away too. With his head bowed, the hat completely blocks his view of the road, but no matter, the horse knows where he's going. It won't hurt to catch a few winks until he gets to the other side of the tracks.

The breeze is turning a bit cooler now, as it begins a gentle dance with the first delicate drops of rain. Little notice is taken beyond pulling his collar up. Robert's face is buried deeper into his clothing. As the rig continues to plod along, there may be only a vague awareness of an oncoming train. Working and living near the tracks has a way of conditioning a man to the sound, sometimes not conscious of it at all until the train roars by. It's of little concern, if any. The horse begins to cross the double sets of tracks. Neither man nor animal is aware there is not enough time. As the train rounds the bend, the condemned wagon is still moving slowly over the crossing. The engineers are horrified; that wagon isn't going to try to make that crossing! The whistle blares out several times. The old horse is startled. There's a pause, then a drawing up in fright, then a desperate lunge forward. The engineers have been applying the brakes for what seems an eternity. The night echoes a chilling screech of metal on metal. When the train finally comes to a stop, the engine is heaving gusts of hot steam into the wet night. Excited voices can be heard. Lighted lanterns bounce and wag in the darkness as shadowy figures move quickly to help.

Edith was still a good-looking woman despite the hard life she and her family lived. As a widow in her mid-thirties, and after twelve years of being a wife, mother and homemaker, she was unprepared to face the world alone. Her husband left no insurance. The horse and rig lost in the accident had dwindled finances down, creating a critical situation. There were no relatives to lend a helping hand. The house and her son were all Edith had left, and Bob had only his mother for security. A few months later Edith took to entertain men in her home, choosing the wrong path for both of them. Her reputation soon became known around town like a secret that respectable folk pretended not to know of. Only, everyone did know. Bob hated what she had done to herself … and to him.

He knew the reason for his mother's clients tossing him a quarter along with a strong suggestion to go to the movies. He understood when some came after dark and didn't leave until morning, that the little gray house was no longer his home, but his mother's place of business. He had no parents at all now. Sometime in his future, he would live in the upper part of Chipwey, and leave everything else behind, even his mother. Eventually Grandma O'Brien did marry again, but by then Dad had made an art out of hiding his feelings of being inferior to everyone else. His happy nature turned solemn and quiet. When Dad was fifteen years old, he left home, striking out on his own. Although he remained in Chipwey, he never lived in the little house again. Cutting all ties with his past was the easiest way. Now, nine years later, he was married. His time had come to build a life the way he wanted to live. His new beginning wouldn't come easily.

The newspaper came off the press early that day, blaring out the news that the stock market had crashed. Mama was four months along in her pregnancy when, on the 29 day of October 1929, our country collapsed into an economic depression. The mass selling of stock sent the economy into a tailspin that spread panic over the country like a disease. Banks and businesses of all kinds closed by the hundreds causing unemployment for millions of people. Many a proud father in Chipwey looked to the city for help, which wasn't much once spread over those in most need. How was the head of the household to keep a roof overhead and food on the table when jobs disappeared overnight?

Dad's plan was to take the RCA radio correspondence course, and open a radio shop of his own. The depression had closed the bicycle factory, but Dad was kept on for a few hours a week as an overseer for the deserted factory. It was better than nothing. Unfortunately, words of encouragement that layoffs wouldn't last too long were all the men had to take to the bank; but empty bellies couldn't be filled on promises. Each man had to find his own way during this time. With a practical knowledge of electricity gathered at the factory, and his curious tinkering with radios, Dad already had a head start in understanding how the radio worked. It was a good plan, having the classroom came to Dad by mail allowing him to stay at home with Mama.

Once Dad had his diploma from RCA, he lost no time opening a radio shop of his own. There was plenty of time to devote to the small shop. The big display window that looked out on Main Street would tell everyone that this was a serious place of business. Making use of his talent with a striping brush, Dad put the lettering on the big window himself. He used gold leafing to enhance the words Chipwey and RCA. It read:

CHIPWEY RCA
RADIO SALES AND SERVICE

Dad was very opinionated and confident in his new line of work. His reputation for repairing anything electrical made him well known around town. He never turned down the chance to fix something. The biggest achievement Dad had was repairing a pipe organ. The organ belonged to Mr. Windecker, Dad's boss at the factory. Over several weeks, many repairmen had done their best. Still no one was able to figure it out. They all agreed that it would take an organ specialist, the closest being in New York City, for accurately diagnosing the ailing beast.

One day Mr. Windecker asked Dad to take a crack at the problem. Within a day, the organ was piping out in good voice. Very pleased, Mr. Windecker shook Dad's hand in disbelief. Dad told us later the solution was almost ridiculous. The trick was troubleshooting the problem to start with. All it took was something called a "cotter pin" bent in a special way, to repair it. "I may not be a big wheel," Dad said, "but I'm one of the spokes." That was the day Dad proved he was a fixer of all things. If the patient couldn't be brought to the shop, he was willing to go to it.

Dad's radio shop helped close the gap left by the ailing economy. It was strange that, in this time of stress Dad found he was a little better off than a lot of his friends. He was showing everyone that, although not lavishly, he could give his family shelter and food.

Joseph William O'Brien was born on April 4, 1930. Mama says, "Grandma always thought he was too pretty to be a boy." Joseph's rosy red cheeks, and sandy brown curly hair, gave him an angelic look. His eyes were such a dark brown they looked like two ripe olives. A picture of him at the age of two shows an expression of wisdom beyond his years. Grandma and Grandpa Desmond cared for Joseph many times. He loved visiting them in the old homestead on the hill.

At last, Mama's life was full. The lonely days of that first year were fast fading from her memory. With the hardest part behind her, Mama looked forward to being a good wife and mother. Eventually Dad moved Mama and Joseph out of the apartment on Main Street. The move to the outskirts of the residential part of town was one of great joy for Mama. Being in a duplex it could still be considered a kind of apartment, but here they were on a street with trees and green lawns, a good place to raise a family.

Andrew Terrance, born on November 17, 1932, was second in the O'Brien line. There were no sandy colored ringlets for Andy. Instead, he was a bubbly mass of energy, with dark brown hair straight as a string, and a glint in his eye that told the world, he wasn't going to miss anything if he could help it. Joseph and Andy were good buddies, and had Mama and Dad's sole attention until I arrived on the 4th day of May, three years later. As my brothers before me, my christening was at St. Michael's Church; my name, Kathleen Marie. I was called Kali for short.

It took another five years, but the day did arrive when Dad fulfilled his promise to Mama. He rented us a cozy little house that placed us well in the residential part of town, and though it wasn't ours outright, it couldn't have felt more like our own. Mama fell in love with it from the moment she saw it. A backyard big enough for a garden of flowers and vegetables was the most pleasurable pastime for Mama and me. By late afternoon, shade from the horse chestnut tree in the front yard would engulf the whole house with its enormous branches.

Mr. Milliner, a neighbor who lived to the right of us, grew several pear trees enclosed behind a fence; looking at that ripened fruit was too tempting. Many boys in the neighborhood including Joseph and Andy would steal over the fence and climb the trees. Sometimes the raid was made easier when the gate to the yard was left open. When that happened, I was able to follow into the yard with them. "Psst, here it comes," would be followed by a piece of the hand grenade shaped fruit dropping straight down landing at my feet. Pears they picked for themselves were stuffed into the boy's shirtfronts.

Mama was upset with us when she found out that we had robbed the trees again. "Asking for permission would save you a lot of heartaches." Although it was the right solution, our way was more exciting, heartaches or not.

Mr. Milliner didn't catch us every time anyway. When he did, he'd yell at us in a raspy voice, "You boys get out of my trees." I'd be the first one to run, because I was already on the ground. The boys would scamper down the trees and dart through, or over, the gate. Hitting the sidewalk like a handful of marbles dropped to the cement, they'd scatter and disappear. With shirts bulging from pears tucked inside, they looked like misshapen creatures running for their lives. We'd all meet behind a garage belonging to one of the boys, and sit around chomping on the forbidden fruit, out of sight from Mama.

Although life was good, Dad continued to treat Mama like his prize possession. Still very jealous of her when another man was around, it was a twist of fate that between working at the factory and his radio shop Dad spent more time away from home. This pattern became a way of life for Dad, and gave Mama freedom to go for an occasional visit, or shopping without explanation. Everything seemed to be falling in a comfortable, relaxed order until the day our new neighbor, Leo Fahey, came into her life.

The Faheys were aware of the arguments that popped up between Mama and Dad. The closeness of our two houses made it impossible to miss them. Mae, his wife, never brought the delicate subject up when she and Mama talked, but Leo had no trouble saying right out that Dad didn't appreciate her. His visits at our front door increased as the days went by.

Mae was aware that her husband had a wandering eye, and pretended not to notice his admiration for Mama. Having been in this position before, Mae knew Leo would come to his senses as he had done so many times before. Confident that Leo's infatuations would eventually fizzle out, Mae had only to wait it through, and be there to welcome him back.

In the beginning, Leo's drop-by chats seemed innocent enough. Mama was polite and took time for the conversations. Leo wasn't hard to like. He was always dressed neatly, and no matter what he had on, he wore a cap in a matching color to go with his shirt. He had only to smile and his whole face lit up, creating little wrinkles at the corners of his eyes. He was indeed a charmer, and according to Mama, that wasn't a false characteristic but part of his true personality. Soon Mama felt uneasy. Was there something more going on here? He had become quite critical of Dad every chance he got, but Mama would jump to Dad's defense every time. It didn't matter. Leo spoke out about how he felt, "Bob doesn't appreciate you. If you were my wife I'd treat you a whole lot better than that."

Mama thought the solution was going to be easy, just avoid him. She even changed her daily routine. A simple task such as sweeping the front sidewalk would immediately bring her admirer out of his house. The best time for this chore was while Leo was sleeping. Leo worked a late shift at a local factory, and slept most of the morning away, but he was awake by afternoon. This odd sleeping schedule gave Leo free hours to visit Mama, hours that Dad and Mae were sure to be at work. For Leo, this was quite a convenience, for Mama, an annoyance.

What disturbed Mama most; Leo didn't care if his visits were timed right or not. If Dad was at home, Dad was the likely one to answer the knock at the door. If Leo called, Mama would duck out of sight into another room, but, craning his neck to see around Dad, would holler out, "Hi in there Helen, it's just me, Leo." Mama would call back was a stiff "hello." If Dad knew how many times these visits took place when he wasn't home, now he would be justified in getting angry.

Mama worried that one day it was bound to happen; a confrontation between the two men. She made up her mind not to open the door to Leo again. These gabby visits would stop here and now. Let him knock until his knuckles turn blue. One of Mama's plans for out-maneuvering Leo was to retreat. When the familiar knock came to the front door, she would go out the back door. Hiding out in the backyard, she'd wait until he gave up and went home; it was a short-lived solution. He soon caught on and would look for her in the backyard.

One day Mae paid Mama a call with a strange request. "While you're having supper, will you please pull your kitchen shade down?" Mae wasn't angry, but she was serious.

"Why?"

"Because when you're all at the table Leo can see you through your window. He gawks over here until you move out of sight."

"I'm sorry Mae, but I can't do that. Pull your own shade down. Tell Leo to look at something else."

Mama knew Dad would see right away that the kitchen was being zipped up tighter than a sardine can. It would bring unwelcome attention to the problem. After that disturbing conversation, Mama sat in a chair and looked through our kitchen window; sure enough, when positioned at the right angle one could look from Mae's dining room right into our kitchen. Mama maneuvered the table around, just enough to do the trick. Dad may not even notice the slight adjustment of the table. It would have been worth anything to see Leo's expression when he found out the next time that he would be gazing into Dad's lovable face.

A quiet week passed. Mama thought maybe Mae had persuaded Leo to knock it off. Mama was breathing easier for the first time in two months. Then like the return of a bad dream, a familiar knock. Mama slammed the spoon down into the bowl of cookie dough, and abruptly approached the door. This time she was going to face him, and tell him to stop bothering her or she would have to do something drastic. In her anger Mama pulled the door open so fast, a swirl of barbershop perfume almost took her breath away. Leo's face beamed under the peak of a brand new cap. In his arms, he held odd shaped bundles wrapped in brown butcher paper.

"Helen I know you can use these, we're going to move, can't take 'em with us … your family can use 'em." Leo pushed by Mama heading for the kitchen. He continued to talk a mile a minute as he shoved the little bundles into our icebox.

"What are you putting in there?"

"Meat."

"I don't want your meat!"

"Yes, now you take it. You have a big family. You can use it." Still wearing the wide smile Leo patted the top of the icebox, and left the house.

It wasn't more than an hour later that Mama heard another knock at the front door. This time it was Mae, trying her best to smile. She was clearly embarrassed.

"Helen, did Leo bring our meat over here?"

"I told him I didn't want it, but he said you were going to move, and … "

"Oh, that man! Maybe it is time we did call it quits," she said with a wave of her arm. "Helen I've got to have it back. We're not moving. He's going to Buffalo to stay with his brother for a while."

Mama led Mae to the icebox where the meat rested inside on the big chunk of ice. "I know why he did this, you know. Flowers or candy was out of the question. Meat can hardly be called a personal gift." Mae's last remark was so sarcastic it made Mama uncomfortable.

Mama heaped the bundles in the cardboard box and Mae left without a word. Later that day, returning from a trip to the grocery store, Mama hardly had time to unlock the front door when she heard Leo call to her from behind. Mama stayed outside talking to him. He was asking Mama to go to Buffalo with him.

"Meet me under the clock on the bank corner. If you're not there by eight ... "

"Don't wait for me there or any place. I can't believe you'd think I could desert my family."

"Oh, you don't have to desert your kids. Bring them with us. I promise I'll treat ya-all good."

"No! No! Leo, you have a good trip. I have to go in now."

Reaching out, he took Mama's hand. It was the first affectionate gesture Leo had attempted during these months of his unrequited love for her. He just squeezed her hand tenderly, tipped his cap, turned and walked away. The only thing missing was the beaming smile and the little wrinkles at the corners of his green eyes. Mama felt so guilty. She rubbed her hand hard against her dress as though she could rub off the guilt. Then Leo gave one final reminder, "Remember, I'll be waiting." Quickly Mama scurried into the house and locked the door.

That was the last time she saw Leo. A month later, Mae put the house up for sale. She didn't stop to talk to Mama anymore. A polite greeting was all the two women exchanged. As far as Mama knew, Dad had never caught on to Leo's mad desire for her; that was no less than a small miracle.

With the Fahey's gone Mama's life was normal again. No more feeling trapped like a rat in her own home. Things appeared to be working out. The little radio shop was doing as Dad planed. We weren't living in the lap of luxury, but we never went hungry. Dad was aware of what some people had gone through trying to keep body and soul together during the depression. He was a "good ol' boy" during that period; releasing repaired items with a promise of payment next week would be his downfall. If he didn't get paid right away, chances were he wouldn't get paid at all. It was hard to demand payment from a man who had all he could do to feed his family. Despite the gruff exterior Dad cloaked himself in, he had a soft heart. This softhearted way of doing business, however, was defeating. It undermined how fully successful the radio shop could have been. Dad had set a standard that he either was unable to, or didn't want to change.

On the fourth day of August in 1940, Mary joined our growing family. With four of us kids to support, Dad had to keep his nose to the grindstone. The factory, operating at full speed again, took up eight hours of Dad's busy day. The radio shop dominated the remainder. After supper, Dad would return to the shop, and work until long after we kids were fast asleep. We all knew Dad enjoyed a glass of beer at home at times, but Mama could see he was drinking more. Between the two jobs, it took all of his efforts to keep us going. When Mama voiced her concern, Dad's answer was the same, "I work hard all day. There's nothin' wrong in havin' a drink or two, 'n relax with my friends."

The fifth year of my life I was going to school for the first time, had a new baby sister and we were entering the month of the Christmas holidays. Unaware of the problems my parents were trying to cope with, my brothers and I never suspected that this would be the last Christmas spent in our house on the hill.

There were wonderful sights, sounds and aromas that filled every room at Christmas time. A fragrance of flowers coming from a present under the tree is probably perfume for Mama. A dish of Christmas candy and a bowl of nuts are on a table by Dad's chair. The silver nutcracker, and the long sharp things used to dig the nuts from the shells are there too. On one side of the tree is a table set aside for the Christmas manger. Christmas Eve we hung our stockings by the imaginary chimney to wait Santa's generous gift of Christmas candy, nuts, an apple and an orange.

First came Christmas Mass. Then after breakfast, Mama would start preparations for our Christmas dinner. As the day wore on, the smells of turkey and spicy pumpkin pie filled the kitchen, already tempting the taste buds. On our cast iron stove is a mass of steam pouring from pots cooking the meal of celebration. A favorite of the whole family is Mama's special celery stuffed with cream cheese and little pieces of walnuts. Mama makes this special treat only for Christmas, and we usually end up fighting for the last piece on the dish.

After the presents are opened and we have feasted on our Christmas dinner the best is yet to come. Evening with the glow of the Christmas tree lights and the lighted wreaths in the windows, the room feels like an enchanted land. Mary is tucked into bed for the night. I sit close to the tree surrounded by the soft colorful light, holding my new baby doll close. Dad is sitting in his easy chair, Mama is on the couch, and Joseph and Andy are sprawled on the floor. We are listening to Christmas programs on the radio. Everyone is in the right mood for the happy day that it is. Mama always gives the impression she is the happiest person she could be, but at Christmas she is almost childlike happy. She is an important singular part of every holiday, very much like the secret ingredient that makes the recipe just right.

Four months after Christmas, we kids were made aware that the decision had been made. The rent on our house and the rent on the shop had become a strain. The house was a luxury we couldn't afford. Moving to an apartment was the only solution. Sure, it would relieve the pressure on our budget, but sure to break Mama's heart.

The location of our new home would draw us into the busiest part of downtown. The quiet streets, green lawns, gardens, our big chestnut tree, all left behind. Our new home would be on Gardner Street, a half a block from Main Street, a block and a half from the railroad tracks. We were going to be in the heart of the shopping district, in a world of cement and brick.

Helen's mood was reflected in the gray skies that greeted the O'Briens on the morning of moving day. Full of energy and excitement Joseph, Andy and me made a game of filling the car with smaller items. Helen never let anyone see her true feelings, but even she had no way of seeing into the future. Moving wouldn't be a temporary setback, but the first step down. Not only would we surrender our little house, but would in time resign our dignity and pride as well. Change would come slowly, leading to feelings of discontentment and a need to escape.

CHAPTER 2
A Not So Secret Confession

*G*ardner Street was a typical downtown street; the only hint of any greenery was two stilted geranium plants on an apartment windowsill. A jewelry store wrapped itself around one corner of the street, and Hunt's Cigar and Candy Store occupied the opposite corner. In the middle of the block there was an active barbershop, and some empty storefronts that told of once being thriving businesses before the depression. Two of the more prominent buildings used to be popular hotels. One hotel languished in slow ruin. The second had been converted into apartments. Twenty-six years ago The Hotel Lafayette was a desirable hotel for the wealthy. To the O'Briens, for the next five years this would be home.

I couldn't wait to look out of the bulging bay windows in the front room of our new home. Hanging out from the third floor, they were like box seats at the movies. Laced down the building's center was a mesh of bars and ladders. They looked like iron porches to me. "Porches hell," Kali's father said. "If there's a fire we'll use 'em, otherwise stay off 'em." Each apartment was laid out like a string of pearls. To get from the kitchen to the front room meant passing through a dining room and two bedrooms. A small entrance hall separated the second bedroom from the front room. Entering the apartment by way of the entry hall allowed us to entertain company in the front room without disturbing the privacy of the bedrooms. When the building was converted to apartments, the bathrooms were left untouched in the hallway. We were able to come in from play and use the bathroom without stepping one foot into the apartment. Mama said this was the only place she knew of where the bathroom was in the hallway and the hallway was outside the apartment. Not only was this different from living in a house, but different from any other apartment house in Chipwey.

We had shuffled up and down the stairs any number of times on moving day, and now nearing the supper hour, smells of different foods flooded the hallways in a sickening mix, but it did remind us we were getting hungry. In the apartment, Dad was putting beds together while Mary dozed in her crib. Joseph and Andy were beginning to wear down and paused for a moment as they passed Mama and me on the stairs.

"Boy … don't know about these stairs, Mama," Joseph said catching his breath.

"Yeah … where's the elevator?" Andy breathed heavy as he bent over the banister.

Mama was sympathetic and spoke softly, "Take a minute and rest."

"Can't, Mama, gotta help Dad with beds now."

Mama and I continued to unload the last few items from the car. It was our last climb up and as we reached the top of the first flight of stairs, a gangling old man stepped from the shadows of the hallway into the light. He was thin and frail. His trousers, held up by suspenders, hung on him like baggy clown pants. His slippers made a swooshing sound with each sliding step he took, and the sparse hair on his head lay like the wisp of a cloud crowning some far off mountain. Standing with a slight stoop, he steadied himself with a shaky hand resting on the banister. Sunken cheeks didn't leave much to the imagination as to the shape of the skull beneath his wrinkle skin, and as if this wasn't enough, the empty stare of his wide lifeless eyes completed the spectral picture. He was definitely a left over fragment from Halloween. Though he faced in our direction, unblinking eyes never looked our way. We crossed the landing, and continued up the second flight of stairs with me a little closer to Mama. Entering the kitchen, I was bursting with curiosity.

"His name is Mr. Hollick. He's blind."

"He can't look at anything?"

"He can't see."

"What happened to 'im?"

"He's pretty old. Sometimes old people can't see good."

"How'd he get out there?"

"Blind people use their hands to feel their way. He may be hard of hearing too. You just stay away from him."

"But what if …."

"Just stay away."

Our kitchen, the hub of the household, was a generous size. Mama was pleased with the working space it offered. Our stove and a second hand refrigerator had to be carried up those mountainous stairs by several men that Dad hired. This would be our first electric refrigerator, putting the old icebox to a well-deserved rest. For the first time we had a dining room. Mama's treadle sewing machine was stored in one corner, but that new addition to our fine eating, a dining set, dominated most of the room. It was the most unsightly table I had ever seen. Dad bought it for next to nothing. To me, it was clear why he got such a good deal; what an eyesore. At such a tender age I could not be considered proficient in judging dining room tables, having no interest in tables at all except for the good eats that were on them, still this table, with fat stumpy elephant-looking legs, was the ugliest of the ugly. Its massiveness and gruesome dark color reminded me of the giant's table in Jack and the Beanstalk. For sure, if anyone was able to talk a giant into selling his table cheap, it was Dad. This hideous creation from some tortured mind, proved to be a challenge to the three men who wrestled it up two flights of stairs. Too bad, it couldn't walk by itself with those gigantic legs. This wooden mastodon would serve us only on big holidays. Covering it with a tablecloth allowed us to get through a meal without having to look at its depressing color. This was especially true for we shorter people, whose faces were closer to it when sitting down.

Next to the dining room was Mama and Dad's bedroom where Mary's crib occupied a corner. My brothers and my room came next. Because there were only two bedrooms, I had to bunk with Joseph and Andy. The door in our shared bedroom led out into the little entry-hall, and on the other side of the entry was the front room with the beautiful bay window. The ceilings were extremely high in all the rooms; more than half way up, a decorative ledge encircled the living room walls. Mama said, "They put that there so the ceilings don't look so high." One time, looking up at that fancy border, as I walked across the room, I fell over Andy sprawled on the floor reading one of his comics. "For crying-out-loud come back from Cloud-cuckoo-land, watch where you're going." He barked.

The first time Andy used that term, "Cloud-cuckoo-land," I ran to Mama highly insulted.

"Andy said I was cuckoo."

"It doesn't mean what you think."

"What then?"

"Well, it means someone is off in a place of daydreams … someone with their head in the clouds … in a world of their own." Mama made it sound so good that I came away thinking that I was doing a wondrous thing without even knowing it. There would be other trips to my Cloud-cuckoo-land in the years to come.

It was impossible to get to know many of the families in the building because some moved in and out so fast. Three families did remain our neighbors during our five years there. One of them was a Polish family; a mother, father, son and daughter, who lived across the hall from us. Although Leona was six years older than I, we enjoyed walking to school together. For some reason Leona's mother didn't agree with that plan, and as we climbed the last few stairs, she would scold Leona in Polish. That strange language couldn't hide what she was saying. What did she disapprove of? Where was the harm in walking to school together?

On the First Friday of the month, everyone in school was encouraged to go to Mass and Communion. This meant getting up about an hour earlier than for school, and walking the distance in the pre-dawn darkness. By the time Mass ended it would be light outside, but now we would have to race home, eat breakfast, and hurry back to school before the last bell rang. One such morning I caught up with Leona and together, we hurried along so we wouldn't be late for Mass. We weren't too far from the Church when Leona stopped and announced, "Oh, I swallowed some water this morning brushing my teeth. I can't go to Communion. I'm going to school early."

That was the hardest rule to keep when one went to Communion. It was a strict fast from midnight the night before until after you received Communion the next morning. Not even a drop of water was to pass your lips. Leona turned, and with a wave of her hand, walked toward the school doors. I wondered how she was going to get into school because the doors to all classrooms were locked until after Mass. After I entered the church and knelt down in a pew, Leona slipped in through a side door and sat on the far side of the church. I knew, her mother's disapproval of me made her do this mean thing. I felt sorry for Leona and after that day stayed away from her ... I only got her in trouble. I was thankful that everyone didn't feel as Leona's mother did, and anyway, there was bound to be any number of different kids to walk home with after school. With Alice Baker, a new girl in my class at school, I was sure of an entertaining walk home. She carried the conversation the whole way, talking like a Magpie about her past adventures. Her energetic gab kept me laughing, although I doubted everything she said was true. Alice had moved to Chipwey from Albany and considered herself a big city girl compared to me.

One day on the way home, Alice suggested that we stop at St. Joseph's Church for a quick prayer. St. Joseph's Church was a Catholic Church that we past everyday on our way home. It was much smaller than our cathedral-like St. Michael's. Mother Superior was constantly warning us at school to stay away from there because the church belonged to the Italian community. Our taking up the limited space in the church on Sunday wasn't fair to the people who were meant to be there. Unless the language was understood, going to Mass at St. Joseph's wasn't really the best way to fulfill our Sunday obligation, the Mass and the sermon was said in Italian. When Alice suggested we go into St. Joseph's for a visit, it sounded innocent enough. The Italian God most certainly would be smart enough to understand English prayers too. Entering the empty church, Alice immediately took off to one side and walked up the aisle. Looking into each pew, she scanned the floor as she ambled along. I had no idea what she was doing. Then she stepped into a pew and bent down picking something up from the floor. I walked a few steps behind her. There, she did it again … and again.

"What are you doing?" I whispered. She said nothing, but opened her hand to me and grinned. In her palm were two nickels and a penny. "I'm not through with this side yet. Do the same over there." She pointed to the opposite side of the church.

"We're not supposed ta, are we?"

"Why? I do it all the time. It's money dropped by accident, belongs to nobody. No different than finding it on the street."

Reluctantly I began strolling down the other side of the church, but found that my side was not as profitable as hers, only three pennies. When Alice finished her search, she walked to the Altar rail and stood in front of the rack of votive candles. Reflected in the soft glow of the candles, her face appeared innocent and spiritual until she held out one hand palm up, into which I dropped the three pennies. She had just lit one of the candles and I knew she hadn't put an offering in the slot. Then she handed me the wick for lighting the flame. "Light a candle say a prayer and we'll go," she said. I was spineless and did as she said. When we left the church, we headed straight for Mrs. Hunt's candy store.

Mrs. Hunt was a spry little woman who moved around the confines of her little shop with ease. She looked businesslike with a pencil poked into a round knob of gray hair, but otherwise could have been the grandmother of anyone of us. She wore a wrap-around apron, was friendly, and made kids feel as though they were in her kitchen rather than her store. Even so, she demanded the best behavior, no roughhousing.

This would be a busy time for Mrs. Hunt because any kid with a penny or two in his pocket was certain to stop off at her store for an after school treat. Today the store seemed to be unusually crowded. Alice and I stood on tiptoe trying to peek over the shoulders of kids standing three deep. Choosing favorites from the display of so many different candies came quickly to some, while others couldn't make up their minds. Being knee deep in tempting confections, along with the excited chatter in the store, guilty feelings were cast aside.

Finally, Mrs. Hunt had cleared everyone out leaving Alice and me lingering over final decisions. "Hi there Kali," Mrs. Hunt sang out. "Must be you've come into some money." There was a serious tone to her voice. My face burned from a blush. Maybe Mrs. Hunt saw us coming out of the church; she knows. My nerves were getting the best of me. "I'll wait for you outside." I said. Alice didn't question why, but calmly began calling out our choices. "We'll take two cents worth root beer barrels … two pieces of bubble gum … two boxes of dots."

Once outside, I stood with my nose pressed against the store's window watching as Mrs. Hunt drops the candy in a little brown bag. When Alice joined me, we stood on the corner dividing the spoils then parted promising to, "See ya tamarra."

My first experience acquiring candy money this way was bothersome enough by day, but worse during the quiet hours of night. A very effectual conscience tugged at me, but was pushed aside. The real problem was, I didn't know what was allowable and what wasn't, I argued to myself. We continued to violate St. Joseph's Church for weeks. We were quick and thorough, never missing one pew in our search for God's mislaid money, and never left without saying a prayer at the altar. I came to think of that prayer as a just trade for the coins we took. Our daily raids on St. Joseph's Church kept Alice and me constant companions, and each time my conscience started on another nagging spree my life of crime was buried a little deeper.

One day Alice began walking home with someone else. She had found another girl to walk with and didn't even take the same way home as she had with me. Without Alice around, my conscience came to the surface and would grant me no peace. I was left with a guilty feeling that grew bigger and bigger. There would be only one way to get this bothersome weight off my mind. Confession. Saturday afternoon, I stood in the shadowy church waiting in line to empty my soul of these reprehensible deeds. I was in line to go to Father Feeney because he was every kid's choice. He was a very young-at-heart priest, and as far as anyone knew, never hollered at a kid for committing sins. I rehearsed over and over what I'd say; I fought with my brother three times and in the middle of everything I'd slip in the 20 times that I had stolen, then follow it up with disobeying mother once. The stealing sin could get lost in the middle. Finally, it was my turn to enter the confessional. I was always nervous going into the confessional box and disappearing behind the dark green curtain that covered the little doorway, but when I knelt down and the little light inside went off it was like falling into a dark hole until my eyes got used to it. Father slid the little window open and was already saying the Latin prayer. It was time for me to begin.

"Bless me Father …" After itemizing my gross sins, I felt all went as planned. It was time to breathe again; at least that part was over.

"What have you stolen?" Father asked.

"I took money from under the pews, and lit candles without putting money in the coin slot."

"You shouldn't take money out of the church. If you do find money in church it should be put in the poor box."

"Yes Father," I said humbly.

"Now, why did you light candles, for fun?"

"Sometimes, but mostly I prayed for my father."

"Is your father sick?"

"No. He drinks a lot, but he's been getting better." I couldn't believe what I was saying. Where did that come from? That wasn't planned. Why did I say that?

"Oh, I see," Father Feeney said, "that's all right. Maybe someday you can put an extra something in the Sunday collection basket."

"Yes Father."

After receiving absolution and a minimal penance, I left the confessional with my knobby knees quivering. Unburdened from my heavy load, I attended Mass Sunday morning as light as a feather. Seated with my classmates at the children's Mass I was very pleased with myself. Father Feeney climbed the steps to the pulpit that stood several feet above the floor, putting him into full view of everyone; it was time for him to read the Gospel, and then there would be an ear-grabbing sermon from him. What Father delivered at our Sunday Masses were stories rather than sermons. Father brought the lessons of good and evil down to the level where all of St. Michael's students could understand. Father Feeney stood silently for a few seconds waiting for everyone to settle in the pews and focus on him. His timing in his Sunday talks would rival any actor's. "Yesterday afternoon as I was leaving the church," his voice boomed out over the speakers, "I met a young girl about six or seven years old. She asked me a very unusual question."

That first sentence was a strong delivery designed to pull any wandering mind back into line. I was ready for an entertaining story. "She wanted to know if it was a sin to light candles without putting something in the coin slot." Here Father injected one of his tactful pauses. "I told her it depended on the reason for doing such a thing. If it was just for fun, it would be the same as stealing. 'Have you been doing this'? I asked her. Yes, she had."

"Gee, I wouldn't have guessed that another kid would have done the same thing as me."

Father continued: "When I asked her why she was asking such a thing, her answer startled me." Not even a cough could be heard now. "I've been praying for my father … that he will stop drinking." He fed the last few words slowly to a stone silent audience. My face began to feel the warmth of a blood rush as I recognized what he was saying. Was this part of my penance, to be the Sunday sermon? Father talked on about the pure faith and prayers of a little girl for her weak father. This was a serious sermon. This was pure agony. Sneaking a look around to see if anyone was looking my way, there was a feeling of sitting there with not a stitch of clothes on. Alice sat at the opposite end of the same pew, but continued to look straight ahead. The words Father spoke didn't seem to bother her a bit.

When Mass was over I headed for home contemplating what had happened. Suddenly it struck me. I was like a celebrity now. A nameless celebrity, but maybe this was God's plan. I was meant to blurt it out about Dad's drinking. Maybe that sermon had a purpose, and I was the instrument that started it all. A very special feeling touched my very soul. I told Mama of my confession being the Sunday sermon. "Don't tell anyone else about this. Confession is a private thing between you and God." It was a disappointment to hear those words until she added, "It wouldn't be smart telling the world about your father drinking too much, either" I hadn't thought of that. If Dad got wind of it ….

The first adult neighbors to befriend my family were Larry and Reeg Mills, a young couple who occupied an apartment on the first floor. Almost every evening after supper Larry would come outside, sit on the big step of our apartment building, and talk with Joseph, Andy and me. Spooky old Mr. Hollick was seen more often than anyone. He lived with his unmarried daughter, but she was never home in the daytime because of her job. Many times throughout the day, we'd see him scuffing long the gloomy hallway outside his apartment. This private hallway was lit for all the other apartments but his.

"Where's his light, Mama?"

"He doesn't need it. He's blind."

"We do. When we talk to him, we can't see him very good."

"You don't have to see him to answer hello. Stay away from him."

Anyway, the fright he gave me that first day had worn off after seeing him there so often. Mama's fear of one of us running into him and knocking him down was nothing to worry about. It soon became apparent he wasn't hard of hearing. He could tell after that first summer of standing on his landing and listening, which one of us was on the stair. He would call out a feeble hello, greeting us by name. My brothers were a convenience for Mr. Hollick. Alone all day, and unable to go to the store himself, Joseph and Andy often ran errands for him. The old man would give them a dime or nickel for their effort. I envied them being asked to go on errands. It was a good way to earn spending money. When I asked my brothers why he never sent me on an errand, "too little," was the answer. Besides, I wasn't to run errands for Mr. Hollick. "Let the bigger boys run the errands," Mama said, "You stay away from him." I was sure everyone was just being mean. I had run errands for Mama many times. How different could this be?

Mama's youngest brother, Uncle John, remained in Chipwey where he and Aunt Hannah chose to raise their family. Because we lived downtown, we saw Uncle John often; he worked for the city. He would always be driving a city vehicle of some sort. There was always a wave and smile from him when he was near our apartment. In the winter, we saw him on the plow keeping the streets clear, but the best times were seeing him drive the big street sweeper in the spring, summer and fall. The sweeper was a massive piece of machinery that Joseph and Andy had suitably named, "The Sherman Tank." We couldn't help feeling proud when we saw him driving it. The sweeper had huge brushes in the rear, sprayed with water to hold the dust down as it moved along the gutters. I was baffled by how that big hulk could turn on a dime. Joseph and Andy explained how a small pivot wheel underneath the machine was the magic. The next time the sweeper passed by, I wanted to see for myself what a pivot wheel was.

"Hey you dumb cluck, get up," Andy yelled as the sweeper swished past my head pressed to the sidewalk.

"You'll end up with rocks in your head." Joseph warned.

It was big news to tell Mama we had just seen Uncle John driving the sweeper. The three of us would stampede upstairs with shouts of "I'm gonna tell Mama first."

Uncle John and Aunt Hanna lived in a small but comfortable home up on the hill. They had three children, our cousins Johanna, Carol, and John Jr. Johanna was the oldest and the first to get married, but Carol and John Jr. became close friends of mine. Carol was a gifted piano player, and talked often of plans to become a concert pianist one day. This wasn't just a trip to Cloud-cuckoo-land for Carol. She had taken piano lessons for six years at St. Michael's. When playing a solo at any of the school recitals, Carol always stood out over the rest.

One time, pretending that John Jr. and I were her audience, Carol played the *Saber Dance* for us. It was the piece for her next recital, and she would settle for nothing but perfection in her performance. When Carol finished playing her serious music she would put the classics away and play songs that we could all sing. At least once or twice during summer vacation, Carol would invite me to her house. Sometimes it would be just for an afternoon, or if on the weekend, it could mean sleeping over. I loved to go with Carol because it always meant we would have peanut butter and jelly sandwiches, and being where the flowers grew, and trees were tall and thick with maple leaves. They reminded me of the little house we used to live in.

When my invitation included sleeping over, the three of us spread blankets on the floor of the porch, and with a couple of pillows to make us comfortable, we'd experience a kind of a poor-man's camp out. Once settled down on the blankets, we'd take turns telling our best ghost story. Carol had to be paid for her story. A simple act of tickling by lightly running our fingers up and down her arm. I'd take the first shift, and tickle her arm as she extended it over my stomach. When I grew tired John Jr., who was on the other side, would take over. Because Carol was in the middle, she got to have both arms tickled, but when we told our story, we would get only one arm tickled. We didn't catch on to that trick of hers for a long time. It was so good to be there at all I would have scratched her back too.

When our nonsense dragged on longer than it should have, Aunt Hanna would call down from her bedroom window, "It's late. Try to sleep now." We only got sillier, giggling into our pillows to keep from being heard, that made us giggle even more, trying to make quiet noise.

We were never aware of exactly when, but suddenly our energy was gone. We would slip into a quieter time, a time for listening. I was never afraid, even if I was the last to drop off to sleep. The chorus of katydids singing out of turn, the quick flashes of the lighting bug, and the breeze rustling the bushes beside the porch were all friends. Carol and John Jr. lived in this beautiful place every day of their lives; they were so fortunate. How was it that everyone else managed to live here on the hill but us? Had some wicked witch cast a spell on us for doing something bad, and was this banishment the penalty? The punishment was hard enough to bear, but not knowing our crime was even worse. There is no chance to make things right, when you didn't know what to *make* right.

No matter how hard we tried to hold on to those three months of summer freedom, time had the last word. Then, the day came when our porch camp-out days were over forever. Carol had reached a turning point. She was no longer excited with sleeping on porches because she was growing up, and with growing, came new interests. Life was changing again, leaving only memories.

CHAPTER 3
Lessons From A Bee

Getting ready for school in September dredged up warm memories of a house I had thought would always be home. The oatmeal making, bloop-bloop sounds as it cooked on the stove, and the smells of a wood burning fire were familiar things attached to another place, not this apartment. Joseph and Andy handled it all so well, how come change was such a worrisome thing for me? I should have known. Things never stayed the same for long. There always seemed to be a new worry waiting in the wings. Maybe that was God's plan: get a new worry and the old one is forgotten.

The latest worry for me was to stay out of Dad's way in the morning. My habit of being an early riser got me in trouble. Dad didn't want anyone else except Mama in the kitchen while he shaved, cleaned up, and had breakfast. My intrusion on his early morning hour brought cross words down on her head, because she let it happen. "What's she doing up already?" dad would bark.

Mama would whisper, "Go back to bed."

Being sent back to bed so many times, finally drove the message home. I learned to stay in bed and wait to hear the closing of the door, footsteps out in the hallway and down the stairs. He's gone. Drinking coffee and reading the newspaper, Mama is enjoying a few minutes of peace and quiet. Mary will be stirring at any moment, starting Mama's busy day. Joseph and Andy are the last ones out to the warm kitchen. Clothed only in their union suits, they'll hang around that warm old stove like flies around a picnic table. After gulping down an oatmeal breakfast, scrambling around for a lost belt or shoe, and giving Mama a peck on the cheek, we're on our way.

Walking in the crisp fall air, we'd be wide-awake by the time school was in sight. Though Joseph and Andy didn't mind me tagging along, the time wasn't far off when I'd feel out of place walking to school with boys. Mary wouldn't be old enough to start school for four more years, and then we would have each other to walk with. I barely had time to console myself about this problem when, true to form, another change was already blowing in the wind.

Aunt Mildred and Uncle George lived forty miles away. Because Mildred could drive a car, she was able to make the trip a couple of times a year to visit us. Mildred never had children of her own, but she liked children, and she liked being asked to care for her nieces and nephews. Knowing exactly how a child should be raised, these short visits helped satisfy her motherly instincts. Mama was going to have her hands full with Mary, who was now one year old, plus another new baby on the way. There was also the matter of the six days Mama would be in the hospital. With Mama's day of deliverance only a few weeks away, Mildred predictably came to her rescue. Normally our caring aunt would stay with the family she was helping. It was less upsetting for the smaller children not to be taken out of their own homes. Mildred was an outspoken woman and didn't mince words about what was on her mind. She wasn't comfortable in our apartment on Gardner Street, and she didn't get along with Dad. She and Dad had battled each other before and it was always the same argument. She openly disapproved of his drinking.

There was only one solution. Mary would go home with Mildred for a few weeks, maybe a month, only long enough for Mama to get back on her feet again. Dad wasn't happy about turning one of his kids over to Mildred nor was he happy about spending six days under the same roof with Mildred. There was no denying, we needed someone to help.

Reluctantly he agreed to let Mary go. The day Mildred came to take Mary was a happy visit, until the moment of departure came. Then Mama's mood changed from light to heavy-hearted, finding the moment of separation painful. Joseph carried the brown paper bag with Mary's clothes inside, down to the car. Mama carried Mary, hugging and kissing her all the way. I think it wasn't until we saw Mary seated in the car that we realized she was really going away. Mama watched through wells of tears as the car disappeared around the corner with her baby.

"How long is Mildred going to keep Mary?" We asked.

"Not long." Mama dabbed her eyes with a handkerchief. "Just a couple of weeks."

So. It was all right we told each other. We'll see Mary again in just a few weeks, and in the meantime, Mary will have the best care anyone could have. Even Dad had to admit Mary was in the best of hands. It would be only a short-lived change. No question, this plan made everyone happy. Mildred was the answer to Mama's prayers, and this fifth addition we were to welcome into the world played right into the hands of our kind benefactor. Mildred would have the opportunity to care for a child in her home for quite an extended time; the answer to her prayers.

One early November morning, Mama readied herself to go to the hospital. Richard, a name Mama had chosen weeks before, was about to join the O'Brien family line. While Mama was in the hospital, Dad came home after work each night to make sure everything was okay. We all had to pitch in and help with meals and dish washing. Joseph washed, Andy dried, and I was given the job of cleaning the table and sweeping the floor. As efficient as we had become, we were glad to see Mama when she returned six days later. The little bundle Mama held in her arms captivated me. For all of us, our new baby brother was a distraction from the vacant spot Mary left.

Christmas of 1941 there were now five young O'Briens, but one of us was tucked away in Hartford. A Christmas joy that we hadn't counted on until we saw it, was the un-obstructed view of the Main Street corner, decorated with lighted garlands. Looking out from the bay window of the warm living room, we could see the stream of people and cars milling back and forth under the colorful lights. We had seen these decorations every year, but never so close. Stretching across the road all the way down Main Street, the garlands formed a colorful canopy. This magical transition each year was no doubt Uncle John's handy work. Not everyone could say they had an uncle that was Santa's Helper.

Speakers on street light posts poured Christmas music into the streets. Pressing an ear close to the icy window, every note could be heard. At night when the crowds began to thin out and the traffic became lighter, the music was crisper and clearer. At night the lights were at their best too, throwing off their frosty spikes of color into the cold air. For now, this was acceptable compensation for giving up our house on the hill: a box seat for a spectacular show.

Standing on the snowy corner of Main Street, I'd watch people rush from store to store scurrying around like little elves. Christmas wasn't far off when beautifully wrapped packages passed by in such haste. Occasionally, a shopper would lose a package in the snow. That was my cue to help, placing it back into their jam-packed arms. Many times my reward was a handful of change. Not wasting a second, my course was set for the five and dime store to buy a gift for someone in the family. With my newly bought treasure in hand, I headed home convinced this was truly the season of good will toward men.

Although we had exchanged the cozy front room we once had in our little house for a front room with all the intimacy of a dance hall, we could now have a Christmas tree as tall as a building. Waiting until Christmas Eve to buy a tree would become the usual thing to do. They were always cheaper then, sometimes even free. It was murder waiting for Dad to come home on Christmas Eve, but when he did, we knew the fun would begin. It didn't make any difference that he smelled of beer, we didn't mind, he brought Christmas excitement with him. In some ways, Christmas on Gardner Street would be the same as when we lived on the hill. All the good feelings were still with us.

It was Dad's job to stand the tree in place and string the lights. The smell of pine spread throughout the room as the teeth on the saw cut into the moist trunk of the tree. After the stand was nailed in place, and the lights distributed, Dad placed our beautiful evergreen in the bay window for all to see.

When Dad came home, he brought unexpected treats with him that someone had been thoughtful enough to give us. A bag full of apples and some holiday candies were only a part of his surprises. Nearly hidden by the large bag he carried was a shopworn looking box. When the excitement of trimming the tree was almost over, Dad brought out the mystery box and opened it up. We saw twelve miniature cups in individual compartments, no handles. Only a hole in the bottom, that made no sense at all until Dad took one out of its snug compartment, placed it over a light socket and screwed in one of the colored lights. The cup was a tiny lampshade. With the light shining through, we could see figures from one of our favorite Sunday comic strips, and now they were part of our tree decorations. We chattered with delight as Dad showed Joseph and Andy how to put them on the strings of lights, being sure to match the color of the shade with the color of the bulb. "Now be careful." Dad said gruffly, "Don't get tinsel in the empty socket unless yer looking to get yer hair curled. Kali, leave this to the boys. You just hand 'em out."

Later that night, Mama and I gathered the empty decoration boxes strewn around the living room. She was mine alone during this time. A prisoner with no escape from my wagging tongue about Santa, and how soon the generous old man would be paying us a visit. Mama didn't know that I had been bothered for weeks about a vicious rumor that had spread through first grade faster than a virus. It began as a murmur and had escalated to an out and out debate. Had someone attacked the credibility of the Easter Bunny, it wouldn't have mattered at all, but when it was said that mothers and fathers were Santa Claus, and that's where all the presents came from, well, that was too much. Although we staunch believers turned a cold shoulder to such a sacrilegious idea, a trace of doubt remained like the after taste of cod liver oil. The seed of doubt had been planted. I had to test this new theory on Mama, and if this was true, maybe she would come clean and confess everything.

"You think I'll get a doll from Santa?"

"If you've been good."

"Well, if I stayed on the couch all night, really still, would I see him?"

"Santa won't come until you're asleep. You know that." Mama seated herself on the couch. "Did I ever tell you what happened to me when I was a little girl and poked my nose in where I shouldn't have?" Shaking my head no, I sat on the floor in front of her, my mouth watering with anticipation. The smell of a story was in the air, and it was a perfect night for it.

"I was just about your age," Mama began. "My mother had closed the two big sliding doors to our parlor. Sometimes if a room was freshened up for company, mother would keep it closed off until they came. One afternoon mother did have a visitor, a lady friend she knew. They both went into the kitchen, where mother busied herself making tea. I wondered restlessly through the house. The parlor doors being closed didn't mean I couldn't go in. I wasn't going to mess anything up, just look out of the window at the snowfall. I opened the doors and went in. As I knelt on the couch, and leaned over the back to push the window curtains aside, I looked down and saw a long white box. Crouched down behind the couch, I carefully opened the lid and pushed away the tissue paper. Lying in that box was the most gorgeous doll I had ever seen, a beautiful princess doll. Her dress was a satiny white gown, and she wore a sparkling tiara was on her head."

I interrupted mama's story, "What's a ... tera?"

"A tiara is a small crown with diamonds in it. Women of royalty wear them. Of course, these weren't real diamonds, but they sparkled just the same. "Well," I thought, "this certainly has to be for me," being the youngest and the only one still getting dolls for Christmas. My heart was jumping for joy. Then it occurred to me; what had I done? Quickly I pushed the tissue paper back into place and closed the lid. I hurried from the room and closed the doors behind me. I could still hear mother talking to her friend in the kitchen."

"Phew, no one saw you, huh mama?"

"I didn't think so," she replied. "For days all I could think of was the wonderful present I was going to get on Christmas morning. I was so sure the big box would be under the tree it nearly brought tears to my eyes when I didn't find it. I never saw it again."

"Why not ask Grandma where it was?"

"Oh, I couldn't. I was too ashamed to admit I had snooped into a Christmas gift that was hidden. So be careful if you don't want to lose your best present."

"Did that really happen?"

"Cross my heart," Mama made a cross over her heart and pointed up to heaven, a very serious oath. Mama's experience was enough for me. I went to bed with no fuss.

When I rushed into the front room on Christmas morning the first thing that caught my eye was a big white box under the tree. Joseph and Andy were already on hands and knees looking for their gifts, when Joseph hollered up at me, "Hay Kali. Look what you got"

"Don't stand there, dummy ... open it up ... see what's inside." Andy said with a grin.

I walked closer and stared down at the box in disbelief. From behind me, a soft quivery voice said, "Go ahead Kali, it's for you." Mama was standing in the doorway, smiling. I slumped to my knees, tore the ribbon off and shredded the Christmas wrap; the lid pulled off easily. Gently I pulled the tissue paper away. There, smiling up at me was a lovely doll wearing a diamond tiara and a pink gown; she was almost as big as me, a lovely Princess doll.

The extra money that Dad gave Mama to spend on our Christmas didn't all go to buy toys. It was expected that we receive some clothing too. Though money was becoming more of a stranger to us, our big Christmas dinner never suffered for it. Andy would get some boy type things, like glider airplanes, or Lincoln Logs, perhaps a sled, or a cap pistol. Joseph was the steady patient kind. His favorite was airplane models that came in a box with zillions of pieces. He had to have the patience of a saint to cut and glue the tiny pieces together that transformed the pile of odd-looking junk into the graceful airplane. He would spend weeks on a model to make it perfect. When his beautiful creation was completed, it was hung from the ceiling of the bedroom with the others; a good place to keep away careless hands.

The cutting and gluing was too much for Andy. A string of models left for Joseph to complete was proof of that. Andy would rather be flying them than building them. Even his headgear in wintertime reflected his choice. An old worn flyer's hat, with its matted fur on the inside, and it's cracked leather on the outside, was strapped under his chin from the first snow fall till spring. Then, the strap was pulled up over the top of the hat and buckled into place. Andy would wear it for as long as it he could. Keeping warm would be no small task during the bitter cold weeks ahead. We would have a coal fire burning in the stove constantly from now until the end of winter. As Chipwey was drawn tighter in winter's clutches, we'd close bedrooms off during the daytime. The high ceilings may have been great for an elegant look, but they didn't make heating the rooms easy. Richard's bassinet was moved into the dining room where he would be warm and undisturbed.

Many times Joseph, Andy and I would pull our chairs in front of the stove and prop our feet into the big mouth of the toasty oven. Some evenings, after the smallest O'Brien was tucked into bed, Mama would sit with us, making believe we were seated in front of a fireplace. She would read stories to us from books she owned since she was a little girl. These books had enough fairy tales in them to feed our imaginations. Most of the stories we had heard a dozen times or more, but we never tired of them. This was a special time, not only did we have Mama all to ourselves, but the three of us were quite contented in each other's company. Those evenings, spent huddled around that old stove, wouldn't be easily forgotten, but easy to draw warmth from in years to come.

When catching colds were at its peak, Mama would give each of us a teaspoon full of cod liver oil every day. "It's good for you," she'd say. Whoever invented that stuff was trying to liquidate us kids along with the cold. To help the horrible tasting concoction stay down, Mama would give us a piece of coconut candy, or whatever she had on hand that could be called a treat. Something sweet was supposed to take the awful taste away, but nothing completely camouflaged the smell before, or the taste after. The candy became an acceptable bribe. Sometimes, if there was no candy, we'd have to settle for a teaspoon of peanut butter. Joseph and Andy would bow to the compromise. It wasn't something they'd rave about, but better than nothing. To make it more interesting the boys would roll the spoonful of peanut butter into a ball making it looked like a piece of candy, not a shapeless glob of peanut butter. The substitute was more than satisfying for me. I could never get enough peanuts to satisfy me.

This lust for peanut butter, one day, got me into an embarrassing situation. Mama was busy in the kitchen washing diapers for Richard. A small tub placed on the utility table next to the kitchen sink held hot soapy water. After the diapers were washed, they were tossed into the sink full of rinse water. From the pile of diapers that had been lying on the utility table, a small, brownish colored ball had rolled out. Busy with all the washing and tossing to notice, Mama continued working. It didn't take but a split second after I entered the room for me to draw a bead on the little brown ball, concluding that someone had abandoned a peanut butter treat. "Finders Keepers" was my motto, and I was about to put it into action. Mama had no idea what was about to happen as I came, I saw, and popped into my mouth said brown ball. The waxy feel of it sent out an immediate message from my brain; "Beep, beep … this ain't no peanut butter ball you jerk." I began spitting and sputtering as the little sphere was ejected from my mouth. Whizzing through the air like a pellet from an old musket, it hit Mama in the ankle.

"You didn't put that in your mouth, did you?"

"I thought it was peanut butter."

Grabbing my arm Mama lifted me up to the sink. "Wash your mouth out good."

I had put something poison in my mouth. I was surly going to die. Choking from sucking in the water too fast, I coughed and gagged a million times. Good grief! I found something that was worse than cod liver oil. Mama lowered me back to the floor, water dripping from my hair. Her look was one of concern at first. When the realization of what had happened sank in, her expression softened. With a towel in hand, she patted the moisture from my face. A faint smile crossed her lips, then a giggle, then a full-blown laugh, while I was close to tears, embarrassed by the whole ordeal. Mama said it was a good lesson to remember; things aren't always what they seem to be.

Sniffing out good things to eat took a back seat only to the promise of going sledding with Joseph and Andy. We had only one sled, it had to be shared. Occasionally my brothers felt sorry for me and permitted me to go along. The park that we went to provided a clear shot from the top of its gentle slope to the bottom. When the three of us piled on the sled, my place was in the middle. Andy and Joseph would scout out the path to be taken, and choose certain places to heap snow across the trail. Packing it down, they made some king size jounces that would actually make us airborne for some distance. That was as close to flying as Andy was getting then. After each ride, Andy would pace off the distance to see if we had flown through the air farther than the time before. Our short flights through the air made us laugh. We always ended up spilling over, and dumping ourselves face first in the snow. The rougher it got, the more we liked it. When it was over, we'd head for home with boots full of snow, clothes with little balls of snow clinging to them, and our mittens soaked. "You smell like a bunch of wet dogs," Mama would say.

It was Dad's rule was that we were to be home before dark, and winter days had a sneaky way of becoming night. With a yell of, "Crimernetly the street lights are on," we would take off like the devil himself was after us. In a way, that wasn't too far from the truth, at least from our point of view. If Dad got home before we did, we would get his famous loud tongue-lashing, or a cuff along side the head if we were more than just a little late. Dad had a booming voice that petrified us. We were on guard all the time not to get him mad at us. As added incentive, just in case we were tempted to push our luck, there was always that old piece of cowhide hanging on the kitchen wall to be reckoned with. Although we counted on Mama not to let Dad hit any of us with it, we weren't willing to take the chance. As time passed, things changed. Dad spent more, and more of his after work hours between the radio shop and Danahey's Bar, sometimes not even showing up for supper.

Any kid who has ever lived through the long months of snow and ice would agree, that around February winter was becoming old stuff. By then, repair jobs on our tired old sled would have frustrated Andy to no end. The sled would have been fixed with enough orange crate wire to fence an acre of farmland. Mittens wore out fast, so we were lucky to have Aunt Katie to help with our mitten problem. She was really our great aunt, and the sister of Grandma Desmond. Aunt Katie lived in Chipwey too, and was known for her talent with crochet and knitting needles. It was good to go all winter with new mittens and colorful toboggans, thanks to Aunt Katie.

It was mysterious to me the way the seasons knew when to change. The transition was a day-by-day affair, and without being conscious of it, the time would come when only a few traces of snow lingered hear and there. The thin cover of ice on the melting snow in the gutters was the last touch of winter. As we walked to school, the three of us would race to see who could crack the most ice, giving way beneath our feet like the sound of breaking glass. The whole school was giddy as we cast aside the bonds of winter. Each day did bring spring's promise closer and closer, but spring fever wasn't the only way to make our hearts lighter. The anticipation of spring break overshadowed all other thoughts. When the dismissal bell rang, it sounded the end of a long day for the nuns as well as students. For me, getting up mornings when there was no school was much easier than any other morning. Knowing that the hardest thing the brain had to do was figure how to keep entertained for the day. With the job of breakfast clean up out of the way; my dash for the door was a one-man stampede.

"I'm going out now, Mama."

"Okay. Don't go far. Stay in front so you can hear me if I call."

Starting down the first flight of stairs, my sights were on the doorway at the bottom of the second flight. A bright sunny day waited for me. When I reached the first landing, Mr. Hollick called out my name. "Kali, that you?" I didn't see him at first as he stepped forward from the darkness to the edge of the muted light. With his dark clothes and the dimly lit hall, it was hard to make him out. I answered.

"Yeah, Mr. Hollick, we don't have school today."

"Here!" Slowly, without thinking, I walked toward him. He was holding a coin out to me. I had to walk even closer to reach it. Maybe he wants me to run an errand for him; earning spending money is a great way for a six-year old to start the day.

"It's for you ... here, for you."

I took the nickel and smiled up at him, though I knew very well Mr. Hollick couldn't see. My desire for that nickel made me as blind as he was. He put his hand on my shoulder and drew me nearer to him. This sudden show of affection was a little troubling, but it did seem that he liked me. Then my body was backed up against him. With his left hand on my left shoulder, he said something about, "Pretty little girl." His shaky right hand traveled down the front of my dress, then between my legs. What is he doing? Although he didn't go into my panties, he was feeling me through them. This was a strange way to show that he liked me. Mr. Hollick wouldn't do anything to hurt me; even so, I dislike what is happening.

A noise from the entryway below caused Mr. Hollick to release his hold on me. Someone entering the building banged out a few steps, opened a door and slammed it shut. Mr. Hollick faded into the depth of his hallway. He was swallowed up in the gloom that was familiar to him alone. What had happened was wrong. No one should touch me there.

With the nickel buried in my fist, I ran up stairs as fast as I could. The safety of home was all I wanted. I charged into the kitchen and slammed the door behind me. Startled, Mama spun around to see who had come in. A trace of a scowl lined her face. She waited for me to say something. In a haste to flee the devil behind me, I hadn't thought of what I'd say to the angel in front of me.

"Uh ... look what I got." I held the nickel up like a trophy.

"Where did you get that?" The sharp tone sent chills up the back of my neck.

"Mr. Hollick."

Mama grabbed a towel and wiped her hands as she walked toward me. "Kali, you've been told to stay away from that old man. I *do not* want you taking money from him. *Do you understand?*"

A slight nod was my answer.

"Why did he give you a nickel? You haven't been gone long enough to run an errand."

I shrugged my shoulders; "He just gave it to me."

Scared to death that she would question me further, I continued to stare at the nickel rather than look her in the eye. Showing indifference to the money, I handed it to her. "You take it. I don't want it." Maybe giving the nickel up will be punishment enough. Mama took the nickel and placed it on the windowsill above her washtub. Richard stirred in his crib, distracting Mama. She took a baby bottle from the refrigerator, placed it in a pan of water on the stove, and lit a gas jet. I slumped into a kitchen chair. Then Mama said, "You can go outside and play now, but stay in front." Her face wasn't as hard looking as it was a few moments ago, but it didn't matter, the desire to leave the apartment was gone. "I think I'll stay in." I headed for my bedroom. My bedroom, reeking with the stinky smell of Joseph's freshly glued airplane and clothes strewn about the unmade bed, was a safe and welcome haven for me.

It was a relief to go back to school. Chances were I wouldn't get into trouble there. Everyone was entering school laughing and talking; I envied them having no problems. Distracted by the familiar flow of my day at school, my recent experience with Mr. Hollick gradually settled to the back of my mind.

It was almost time to go home. We worked quietly, printing words in a workbook. Sister Magdalene sat at her desk writing. A soft breeze from an open window breathed a warm gust of air across the room, occasionally moving a paper from a desk to the floor. This was the first day that the window had been opened since the snow left us. The tree's branches were full of the little bumps that would soon turn into spring's new crop of leaves. Then without warning the room around me turned to chaos. Kids were sliding out of their seats, their voices full of squeals and giggles, as they tried to avoid something in the air. "A bee, a bee!" It flew close to, first this kid, then that. He was so agile that with a little imagination you could almost hear him laugh, "What a wonderful game." Books and papers were swinging through the air, but he gracefully dodged every one. For someone who had entered the room so silently, he certainly found a way to make his presence known. The many arms and notebooks lashing out at him had turned the game from a playful skirmish into a dangerous battle. He knew he was out numbered. In a flash, he headed for the window. My seat was in the row directly across from his only avenue of escape. I sat very still not daring to move. Mama told me the best way to avoid a curious bee, was to stand perfectly still, and if I had to move at all, to move very slowly.

The buzzing sound grew louder as he approached my side of the room. He zoomed straight for me, hovered for a second, then with the softness of a feather landed gently on the pencil in my hand. My classmates gasped with astonishment; why had he picked such a strange place to land? At first, the fear of being stung was all I thought of, and then I realized, he was probably as frightened as I was. Besides, I couldn't help admiring his ability to balance himself on that tiny eraser. However, with his wings held away from his body, it did seem he was prepared to take off at a moment's notice. Had he chosen me to help him? Holding the pencil tightly in my hand, I slide to the edge of the seat. Rising slowly, I turned to the open window, the pencil at arm's length in front of me. My hand wasn't fully through the opening when the little bee spread his wings and disappeared into a more acceptable outside world.

I could hardly wait to get home and tell Mama what happened. Mama was always busy with something or other when we got home from school, but she never failed to take time to listen to our day's experiences. "Guess what happened?" Bubbling over with excitement, my story began before the door closed behind me. I have interrupted Mama stirring something on the stove, probably chili con carne that required hours of simmering. Covering the pot of chili with the big lid, Mama sat on a chair as straight as an arrow, her two hands in her lap.

"What?" Her voice dripped with animated excitement. "What happened?"

"There was a bee in school today."

"A bee, how'd a bee get in school?" I leaned into her knees. Mama is trapped. My prisoner, until she's heard the story of the bee.

"Well, you did the right thing. I told you if you move slow you won't get stung."

"I did. I stood up very slow. Sister Magdalene told me 'thank you,' when I let the bee out the window."

"Good for you!"

I chattered on for a few minutes more until Joseph and Andy burst into the room. "What's cooking?" Andy asks as he drops his schoolbooks on a chair by the door. Andy could be ten miles away, but could always smell food cooking. It had become a family joke; no matter where he was, when Mama was baking cookies, after the first batch was out of the oven Andy would come bounding in the door. She was always tickled with his perfect timing. Joseph, on the other hand, with his easy quiet manner, lifted the lid from the cooking pot, leaned into the gush of steam and sniffed. "Mmmmm, chili tonight."

The next morning, I felt sure that Mama and Dad had finished breakfast. There were no voices to be heard, only soft music coming from the radio in the kitchen; that radio was always on. I peeked around the doorway. There was Mama reading her paper and drinking coffee. Dad was gone. It was okay to get up now. I entered the kitchen and with a running jump landed on the nearest chair.

"Why are you up so early? You can sleep this morning remember? It's Saturday."

"I don't know." I had more interest in the last piece of toast on the dish then answering Mama.

"Here, let me get you a glass of milk to go with that." Mama took a can of evaporated milk from the refrigerator, poured a small measure of it into a glass, and filled it with hot water. A spoonful of sugar, a quick stir, and breakfast was ready.

We had stopped buying bottled milk because of Richard's allergy to whole milk. He could tolerate the caned milk so Mama switched all of us to evaporated milk. As it turned out, evaporated milk was cheaper and could be stored in the cupboard along side the string beans and corn. We all had to get used to drinking it. Our protests over drinking this flat tasting milk fell on deaf ears.

"It's the same as bottled milk. The water has been removed that's all," Mama said.

"But they took the sweet taste out with the water," We'd argue. The few grains of sugar we were allowed to put back in made it a little better.

Since the attack on Pearl Harbor, certain things, like meat, butter and sugar, had become scarce in grocery stores. Many other items, like gasoline and rubber tires were hard to come by as well. They were being considered first for the war effort, and then for those of us at the home front. This was part of our sacrifice to help the fighting forces overseas.

To make sure everyone across the country received an equal share of the hard to get supplies, the rationing stamp was initiated. The scarce items could be bought only with the proper stamp. As a kid, it was easy to do without tires or gasoline; not so for sugar. If the sugar bowl became empty too soon and Dad had none for morning coffee, Mama would never hear the end of it. Times had not only changed, but were getting worse. Now our sugar bowl would be monitored closely. Sugar could only be bought one pound at a time, and we needed those little stamps to get it. Poor Mama went crazy trying to catch us slipping two spoonfuls into our milk. She didn't raise her voice to us often, but this abuse of the sugar bowl would definitely do the trick, "That's all the sugar we'll have for another week!" Getting nowhere with that line of reasoning, she was forced to change her tactics. "You're gonna get sugar diabetes, if you didn't stop using so much!" It worked for a while, but Andy was the first one to challenge that statement. It was all an idle threat. He would go for two scoops every time he could. When I caught him breaking the rule, seconds later Mama knew about it. I wasn't all that innocent and would give in to temptation too, but ratting on Andy gave a heightened sense of satisfaction.

"Mama, Andy is going to get sugar bideetus."

"Andy! Only one spoonful!"

"Kali, mind your own bees wax. Nobody likes a blabber mouth." With that he'd move away from me grumbling low,

"… can't even say the word right." Mama finally hit on the perfect solution. A special portion was stashed away for Dad, and if we used all that was left in the bowl then we were the ones to do without.

Since it was Saturday, Joseph and Andy had already left for the park with a small gas motor mounted on a Flying Tiger model they were impatient to launch on its maiden voyage. Mama and I had finished the dishes and Richard was back in bed for his morning nap. I was free to go outside and play. As I started down the first flight of stairs, the sound of my shoes hit each step with an entertaining echo in the otherwise quiet hall. I had gotten almost to the bottom of the first flight, when a voice broke the stillness. Not a loud voice, but one so soft that it was hard to understand what was said. I pause straining my ears to listen. There it is … again.

"Kali, that you?" Mr. Hollick was standing in the darkened part of his hallway. I said nothing to let him know it was me, I held my breath.

"Kali?" He called again.

I peeked down at him through the banister slats. He was tilting his head to hear. Then his slippers made the familiar swishing sound as he took a few sliding steps. The frightened feeling I had the first day that I saw him returned with that sound. He was someone I didn't trust or like. My reaction was to stand very still. He may go back into his apartment. No, he moved to the bottom of the stairs, and held on to the big knob on the banister post. He knows it's me. I won't answer. What should I do? Stand here forever? Go back up stairs to Mama? None of these seemed to be the thing to do. Going back up would only bring out the problem of the other day. Taking that nickel from Mr. Hollick I had deliberately disobeyed. What if Dad found out? If that happened, I may as well take poison. There was no other way. Pass that old man. Just walk by him. It should be easy. What could he do anyway? As my foot reached for another step down, I heard him again.

"Kali, I've somethin' for you. Come down." What if he reached out for me as I pass by? His ears are very sharp. He would know when I was near. Looking back up the stairs trying to find an answer, my mind was jammed in its search.

"Maybe I should … no … keep going down, but how? I'll run. He won't have a chance to grab me. I can be fast, when I want to be." Then it came to me, the frightened bee. Yes, do like I did with the bee, don't be afraid, and move slowly. It was worth a try. Moving from Mr. Hollick's side of that wide staircase to the other side put me farther away from him. Each step I took fell with the softness of a feather, one step after another. Reaching the first landing Mr. Hollick was but six short steps away; again,

"Kali … that you?" His voice is softer as he moved another step forward. Reaching out a hand, a coin is held out to me. I stiffened, not daring to move.

"Now! Cross the landing. Get down the stairs," I thought as I glared back at him, feeling angry and scared at the same time. He remained motionless, holding on to the banister knob. His eyes had their usual wide, lifeless stare, but this time not looking down at the floor, but in my direction.

He called my name again, "Kali?"

The steps moved beneath my feet, one, two, three … four. "I've gotten by him! I've gotten by… " Not worried anymore about what was behind me, my feet have wings and carry me down the stairs, and out into the beautiful bright sunlight.

Mr. Hollick wasn't seen much after that dreadful day. He still shuffled back and forth as always, but kept pretty much to himself. Even the errands Joseph and Andy once ran for him had stopped. I was always on my guard when passing his landing, and remained cautious until the day an ambulance came to take him away. As it happened he never did return, but it wouldn't have mattered. If ever he did come back, I knew what to do; treat him like a bee.

Mama never found out about Mr. Hollick. This shameful secret would be mine forever. I felt quite good about handling the problem myself, but there was still a hard road to travel before being grown up.

CHAPTER 4
The Alleyway Theater

The radio was our only family entertainment during the week, but the Saturday matinee at the Rialto was something special to look forward to for us kids. Just as peanut butter helped with the cod liver oil going down, a movie on the weekend helped the coming school week to go down. Joseph and Andy were beyond relying on Dad for spending money. They had learned how to raise their own. As for me, getting a dime for the movies could be very exhausting. I'd wait until Dad was relaxing in his recliner before attempting to ask him for spending money. Besides, it was somehow easier to talk to him when he was look helpless.

"Dad, can I go to the movies?"

"I don't care. It's up to your mother."

Running from the front room to the kitchen, I'd head for Mama. "Dad says I can go."

"Did he give you money?"

"No."

"Well I don't know where you're going to get it. I don't have it."

Back again to the front room, hopeful Dad would come across.

"I don't know what you're going to do then. I don't have it."

Back again to the kitchen. Things don't look too promising.

"Mama, Dad doesn't have it either."

On bad days, I would end up out of breath trying to get my dime. Then there were the good ones when Mama would reluctantly take a precious nickel from her coin purse. "If Dad can give you another nickel you'll have enough to go, but no money to spend for candy."

Back again to Dad, "Dad do you have a nickel? I only need one more."

"No, I don't."

Back again to Mama. "Mama, do you think Dad would let me take one of his empty beer bottles back to the store. I'd have enough then."

"Ask him. I can't give one to you."

Back again to Dad, stammering and a little fearful of reprisals for asking, the words choked out a bit tongued-tied. "Dad … can I … uh … have one of your bickel nottles … I … I … mean, I mean nickel bottles."

His look of irritation was enough to make me want to jump out of the beautiful bay window, but you never could figure Dad. "Only one."

Phew, that was close. I finally had the price of a ticket but was almost too pooped to get myself to the movies.

On Saturday mornings, Joseph and Andy started out early collecting bottles for their deposits or running errands, to raise spending money. If I was lucky, they might earn enough to take me with them, a less strenuous way of getting to the movies. During the summer, the Rialto would have special shows, silly movies and a raft of cartoons to tickle the funny bone of any kid. It did more for me than that; it was like reaching into a well-stocked cupboard for my choice of food. Today the Rialto was showing the Bowery Boys, The Three Stooges, and an Our Gang Comedy. The Our Gang movies impressed me more than the others. Kids, like me, were doing something I didn't think was possible for kids to do. Spanky and his gang were act for the movies; still the idea of kids putting on a talent show was fascinating. What a visit to my Cloud-cuckoo-land this would be, not only for me but for my friends as well.

Rosie moved to Gardner Street a year after we O'Briens did; we were best friends. Our other friends on Gardner Street were two other girls who lived in the neighborhood, Jean and Jackie. I was the youngest of the group, but we all got along well. The idea of putting on a talent show put a spark in Rosie that I didn't think she was capable of. Rosie was always trying to convince the world she was a singer, and took every opportunity to practice. Rosie even sang in the bathroom as she sat on the throne. She liked singing there best because of the echo. If desire were all that was necessary to be a star, she would have been another Alice Fay. Unfortunately, Rosie's voice rivaled the sound of two rocks scraping together. Mama said, "Believing in yourself is the important thing in anything you want to be."

The day Rosie and I asked the others about putting on a musical as Spanky did, Jean was alive with ideas. Before we knew it, we were headlong into a high-spirited discussion of how to put it together. I couldn't believe we were really going to do it. Jean and Jackie took dancing lessons from the same dancing teacher. Jackie took tap dancing while Jean specialized in aerobic dancing; Jean could sing too. There was just one problem. Jean had an alto pitched voice that was pleasant enough, but she also had an awkward abundance of saliva to deal with when she sang. About midway through her song, she sounded as though she was trying to keep up with a fast melting Popsicle on a hot day. I was just the opposite. Always so nervous, my mouth was drier than one of Dad's empty beer bottles. Mama had taught me many songs that she knew from her childhood. We sang together often as we worked around the apartment. What made my performance, wasn't my singing, it was what I sang. Songs like, "Little Red School House," "Baby Sister Blues," and "Won't You Be My Playmate." Those songs, that the other girls didn't seem to know, worked for me. It was quite a good feeling being original. In spite of ourselves, we were really developing into a real variety show.

Between our apartment building and Rosie's was an old alleyway. Years ago, the alley had been used for deliveries when our building was a hotel; wide enough for a horse and wagon to drive through, it resembled a train tunnel. The front end opened on to our street, and the back emptied into a small courtyard. Many years had passed since it was used for this purpose, and because of it was cool in there during hot summer days, we kids used it like a clubhouse. For our musical, it was ideal. Our open-air theater buzzed with activity. The dust flew as we swept the train soot from the old cobblestone floor of the ally. Seats for the kids were cardboard boxes turned upside down, and supported wooden boards were used for the adults. It took days for us to scramble around town and collect material for the seating arrangement.

Two of the most artistic in our group were called on to make colorful crayon signs on pieces of cardboard. Main Street being the busiest Street was the most desirable for getting the word out. The posters were placed inside the windows of grocery and other stores that would cooperate. Our steadfast friend, Woolworth, was one of our best supporters with six windows.

Crepe paper, a most important prop for our show, was used for our colorful decorations and costumes. A ten-cent package was just enough to make a costume, but scrapping up those ten cents for everyone was a challenge. We'd spread out in all directions to do errands, smash piggy banks, and scout around for those ever reliable empty bottles. When we all had a dime tight in our fists, we lost no time heading for Woolworth's, chattering like a bunch of chickens. You'd have thought we were going to the best clothing store in town. We never let up on our fast pace until we reached the counter where the crape paper was displayed. The array of colors dazzled our eyes. From the second we started out for the store Jean made sure we knew the red color was reserved for her. We turned many a head as its usual calm atmosphere vibrated with our squabbling over the remaining colors. The bickering was short-lived. Each of us would leave the store totally satisfied that they had gotten the most beautiful color.

The better part of our crape paper was used for our skirts and top. The final touch was to make the ruffles. Stretching the edges of the crape paper, as one would flute a piecrust, the paper stayed puckered giving it the frilly look of real clothes. Oh the ruffles, they were the most fun part to do.

Rehearsals lasted but two days; then, finally we were ready. The old sheet hanging by a rope was the curtain, separating the audience from the players, intending to build suspense. I knew this to be true from my visits to the movies. When the huge curtains at the Rialto peeled back, it's was as though a magician had thrown his cape open, giving life and breathe to his wondrous illusions. We would try giving this feeling to OUR audience. The seats were filled with friends and family. Dad was never there, but Mama always was, holding the current youngest O'Brien on her lap. Our audience came from blocks away; sometimes seats were filled with kids and even adults we didn't know. The time had come for us to reap the harvest for all our efforts. We charged three cents a ticket for big people and one cent for kids, and shared equally in the profits. With every show, I received something more lasting than a few pennies. Hypnotized by the excitement of opening afternoon, the rustle of crepe paper costumes, the smell of lipstick and bubble gum, I was hooked on performing. It would be a whole year before we'd put on another show … a long time to wait.

When the weeks of togetherness ended, we'd separate seeking our pleasures in other ways. The past weeks were all that the older girls could take of us. Jean Ann always had other fish to fry, and it didn't include a small fry like me. While we were putting on that first musical show, I had a feeling that Rosie wasn't fully accepted by the others. It wasn't until the following year while planning our second show I knew I was right and that nothing had changed. Jean had gotten some of her dance school friends to join our troupe. They were squeezing Rosie out. When Rosie and I showed up for practice they said, "Sorry, we don't need another singer." When I asked if Rosie could be announcer they said, "We have an announcer already. Tell her she can come to the show for free." It reduced Rosie to tears. She wanted to be part of the show, not the audience. I wasn't comfortable around people when they cried. I had seen Mama cry at times when she had a bad argument with Dad, and those tears made me feel sad and helpless.

When I was sure Rosie was not going to be allowed to perform, I returned home, and found her sitting on her front stoop. Her long blond hair almost completely covered her face as she leaned into her lap, sniffling the tears backs. I didn't know what to say to her. Then she raised her head, and said, "Oh God, nobody wants to play with me." One of the meanest hurts I knew was there in my friend's words. It was a wound not easily healed, rejection.

"I do. I'm … somebody." I said hesitantly. She smiled a weak smile, and we both broke out laughing. I was taken back when, with no warning, she threw her arms around me. Neither of us was in the show that year. That was when we became special friends.

I have to admit Rosie was always a little different, and though we had good times together, there seemed to be an underlying sadness about her in spite of the laughter. Some secret deep inside wouldn't loosen its grip … her pretty, blue-gray eyes never completely seemed to reflect the smile she wore. I didn't question the way she was, a quiet soul, except those times she fancied herself a singer. Her fair skin was the perfect setting for her blond hair that I admired so much. Her thin frame and the dark shadows around her eyes gave a wrong impression of her being a delicate type, which was true only in how easily her feelings could be hurt.

One day I realized it was happening again, another change was creeping up on me. While Rosie's mother was at work, chores at home kept Rosie confined more and more. Since I couldn't be with her every day, Andy and I had become a team, resorting to prowling the back allies to find empty beer or soda pop bottles for their precious deposits. Dad's three or four empties standing along side the refrigerator was a constant temptation. His bottles were quart sized, and would bring a five-cent deposit; not like the two cents we got from the smaller bottles. The only problem was Dad wanted his empties and counted on them to all be there when he took them back to the bar to buy more beer. Occasionally there would be four or five of them lined up by the side of the refrigerator. Out of desperation, we'd hike one back to the store. I would think that Dad wouldn't miss just one … not so, Dad kept track of them very well, yelling at Mama for the missing bottle. In an act of self-preservation, she would scold us, "Don't even look at those bottles." In our search for those transparent trophies, we would occasionally find ourselves in the possession of a bottle that none of the local stores would claim as theirs. It made us crazy having a perfectly good bottle, and not able to collect a cent on it. Maybe it would take a week or so, but Andy would eventually find a store somewhere in Chipwey that would put claim to it. He was good at the game of survival. No one was better than Andy.

Joseph and Andy traveled much farther from home than I did. Sometimes they'd walked for miles out of town to Arrowhead Creek to fish. During the summer, frogs multiplied in great numbers there. The boys came home with a fair catch of frog's legs, a great delicacy I was told. It was horrible, what they did to those poor things. "Do they die when you do that to them?" I asked as they washed a stinky batch of legs in the sink.

"Naw," Joseph assured me, "they're frogs. They'll grow two more legs in a couple of days." It was suggested more than once that I try one of their deep fried tasty delights, but even if they could grow two more, I was never convinced that one should eat the legs of a frog. When fish or frog's legs weren't running, Joseph and Andy went down to the railroad tracks and harvest milkweed. The weed got its name from the milk-like substance that flowed from inside when it was snapped in two. It thrived in the soot-laden earth along side the railroad tracks. Aunt Katie had taught the boys how to choose the youngest plants because the young tender weeds had the best flavor. They could easily collect enough to fill a large grocery bag. This wide leafed green plant had a similar taste to spinach. On the plus side, it didn't cost the boys a cent. On the minus side, they could spend the next twenty-four hours running to the bathroom.

At first, one might say this was a good way for two growing boys to spend their summer, but it had a deeper meaning than that. It had become harder for Mama to stretch the few dollars she was given to buy food. Those fishing trips the boys took became a necessity to feed their growing appetites. I doubt that Dad knew how necessary those trips to Arrowhead were.

By now the back room of Dad's shop was his bar away from bar. The bicycle factory was operating full time. After a full day there, Dad continued to work his radio shop each night although it would be hard to say how much or that time was spent on business. Dad's close bevy of friends was there every night with him. Even though Danahey's Bar was a few steps away, meeting in the radio shop had become a sort of private club.

I remember the day I found out how successful Dad's RCA home course had been. Helping with the cleaning chores was my responsibility. The task of tidy up the front room was not a difficult a job. A brown overstuffed couch and chair hardly filled the spacious room. A table in front of the bay window was the resting place for our precious radio. A dark blue recliner was Dad's reserved spot to relax in and read his electronic books. Next to his chair was a small table that held his books and a round pipe stand with odd-shaped pipes. Dad didn't smoke the pipes anymore; he was a cigar man. We had been told repeatedly that the contents behind the two doors in the table were of interest only to Dad. The books, papers, and remains of one broken pipe were all that the doors could reveal. I had the stubborn idea we weren't being told everything; besides, nothing peaked my imagination more than to be told that something was off limits.

There was a piece of dried cowhide on the kitchen wall. Dad hung it as a warning about breaking house rules … or anything else. There's a lot of respect for this dirty brown strap and it's power to reduce us to a shivering mass of gelatin. We knew this sightless spy was just waiting for the moment when one of us would step out of line. A low diabolical laugh could be heard when passing the thing.

"I should dust inside the table to … to do a thorough job," I thought. Despite the warnings and old animal hide, today I was going to uncover the secret of the two doors. Kneeling down I opened one of the doors. "Please, don't squeak!" Then the second door, a quick glance behind me, did Mama hear? Is she standing there wearing a cross expression? Something told mothers to be at the right place at the right time, I must be careful. A quick tour of the inside was short of my expectations, nothing but a stack of papers. No deep, dark family secrets at all. Not even one of the National Geographic books with pictures of the other countries showing life in the raw. I was right about one thing; a fine settling of dust covered everything inside. I lifted a wad of loose papers permitting the bottom layer to drop into my lap. With one eye on the papers and the other on the doorway, I tried to pick them up as fast as I could, when something caught my eye. One of the pages had the number 98 on it. It wasn't just a number, there was a percentage mark after it underlined in red pencil. On the top left corner of the paper was Dad's name, Robert J. O'Brien. Could that be a grade mark? I separated the papers to get a good look; there's another one marked 94%. Another marked 98%, and another and another! The figures and squiggle lines drawn on them are strange. Are they exam papers from some school? It was an amusing thought, Dad going to a school. It was true, it was a school called "RCA."

Those grade marks were all in the nineties. The ones marked 100% really impressed me. "He's got to be so smart to get marks like that," I thought, "and I never knew." How impressive … school up to then had been difficult for me. I scooped the papers up, and returned them to the wooden tabernacle. It was clear why Dad kept them tucked away like treasure. My deliberate act of disobedience replaced a self-righteous attitude with a feeling of guilt, which was short-lived, giving way to a feeling of pride and a whole new respect for my father. **Reverently closing the doors, a firm promise was made never to invade this hallowed place again.**

Dad's drinking increased during our years on Gardner Street. Unlike his father before him, Dad wasn't always a happy drunk. Maybe he was at the bar, but when he came home, it was a different story. We never knew which of his moods we would be faced with. My newly acquired ability to study a situation carefully came into good use during these times. From the moment Dad entered the apartment, my brothers and I would grow silent, shrinking to the background until we knew what we were in for.

Sometimes Dad would open his butcher-paper wrapped salami and pass it out to us with unsuspecting generosity. There were times when he'd be moved to hand out a few dimes or quarters to us. Other times he would come home hardly able to keep his eyes open, and offer us nothing. When he fell asleep sitting at the table, we had another problem, we'd have to move around the kitchen like shadows. A sudden noise could arouse the sleeping lion, putting us at the mercy of his anger. Should one of us kick the leg of a chair we knew the resulting noise could be the starting signal. Dad would awaken already wearing the frown of agitation.

"What the hell's goin' on?"

"Nothing. I just bumped the chair." Mama would volunteer.

Topping off the glass of beer, Dad takes a sip. "What happened to all the salami?"

"You ate it."

"Ate it hell, there was a half pound of meat there."

"Oh, so *we* ate it?"

"Well *I* sure as hell didn't."

One by one, Joseph, Andy and I would ease toward the dining room doorway. It was better to be in the front room, as far away from the kitchen as we could get. Huddled around the window looking out on to Main Street, we would silently stare out, as the argument in the kitchen grew in anger and volume. There was little to be thankful for when the argument finally gave way to a time for sleep when we knew the dawn of a new day would bring a continuation of the this episode. He'd rise up the next morning already swinging his next punch.

"Where the hell's my money."

"You gave some to the kids last night."

"Gave it to the kids." Dad mocks Mama as he jerks his chairs out and seats himself for breakfast. He stirs his coffee and slams the spoon down.

"You gave it to the kids." Mama repeats.

"Ya come home with a couple'a drinks under your belt and everybody takes advantage of ya." Dad drinks the coffee, but hardly touches the eggs and toast. Still, no matter how angry he was, kissing Mama good-bye was never overlooked.

There were other times that he wouldn't have any money when he came home. Maybe it was a lost bet on the fights, or maybe a bad night playing cards. All we were ever sure of was something hadn't gone well for him, putting him in a thunderous mood. Dad fancied himself an expert on so many things he seemed to think he always had to come out number one. He was never a graceful looser. With all the betting on horses, boxing matches, and card games, there was no guessing about his state of mind.

Dad was paid every Friday at the bicycle factory, and the small amount of household money Mama was given was far from sufficient. As good as Mama was at stretching each dime, the food supply would always give out before another Friday came around. From Friday to Sunday, there was enough food to go around. As the week went on, the meals would became more meager. Thank God for potatoes. They were cheap and it wasn't unusual if they were all we had for supper, home fried, French fried, even sometimes raw. By Friday, Joseph and Andy would go fishing. We all had good appetites, right down to Richard who wasn't eating baby food anymore. Growing up fast was an important trait to be an O'Brien.

In summer when the days grew longer, we'd go outside after supper and play for a longtime before dark. My two brothers, Rosie, and I made up the usual group to play. Larry Mills was a married man who also lived in our building would join us in a game of hide and seek occasionally. Whenever Larry played with us, the game was more fun because he was an adult. Even though he was much older, because of his short stature it was easy to accept him as one of the gang. He acted more like a seventeen-year old than someone in his late twenties. Larry was fast on his feet, and gave challenge to the game. It wasn't easy out-running him when he discovered where you were hiding. He enjoyed the thrill of the finding us, and flushing us out of our hiding places. It seemed to give him such pleasure. His blue eyes would light up as he laughed with self-satisfaction in the accomplishment. When it was his turn to hide, he sometimes moved around changing his hiding place several times to work himself closer to home goal. It would take Joseph or Andy to put him out of the game. When we became tired of hide and seek, Larry would sit on the big steps outside our apartment house surrounded by all the boys. He was like the pied piper. The boys would hang on to his every word. The deep discussions were usually on cars or past trips hunting for deer. Girls had to be one of the subjects they talked about too. When that happened, Rosie and I would be chased off. They weren't fooling us. We knew that we didn't fit in to their manly secrets.

The boys weren't the only ones to have secrets. The first time I noticed that Rosie was developing her soft bumps; I had my first girl-talk. "Does it hurt?" I asked Rosie not taking my eyes from her dress front. Rosie sat down on her apartment stoop and self-consciously pulled her dress away from her chest. Now her new developments wouldn't be so obvious.

"Of course not," she answered, "it itches a little, not bad; next month I'll be ready for my first brassier. Mother says I'm a woman now, because I have the curse too," she answered flippantly with a tone that was out of character for my friend.

"The curse?" The words had hardly rolled from my tongue when there was a feeling I shouldn't ask.

"Yeah, hasn't anyone told you about that yet?"

"No."

"That's when you have to wear a cloth between your legs for five or six days."

"A cloth between your legs … why for crying out loud? Rosie if you're telling me a story… "

"I'm your friend, I wouldn't tell you stories. Every woman has it. You will too one day." Then her voice dropped to whisper, "You can't just let the blood run down your legs you know." Not wanting to hear anything further on the subject of blood, it was a relief when the conversation changed.

One evening some weeks later, the whole gang gathered to play a game of hide and seek. Andy was "it." Covering his eyes with his arm he leaned into the side of the building and began counting, "5-10-15-20." Everyone spread out to find a hiding spot. Joseph had disappeared quickly, so had Larry, and when I turned to say something to Rosie, she had disappeared too. It was odd that Rosie would go off without me. Too much time had been spent wondering of my friend's disappearance. Andy was nearing the end of the counting "75-80-85... " I had to find some place fast. There was a place under the stairs in Rosie's apartment building, that wasn't used anymore. Too close to home goal made it a risky choice; it would have to do. Behind me Andy yelled, "99-100. Ready or not here I come." I bolted for the building and made for the long abandoned cubbyhole. Surprisingly, the spot was occupied. Larry was crouched down there with Rosie. The moment I popped into view Rosie started to get up, but Larry grabbed her, cupping his hands over her two newly developed soft bumps and pulled her back down beside him. Rosie was giggling, and at first, it seemed she was only halfheartedly trying to free herself. She stopped giggling and I could see she was struggling to get free. He was stronger than she was. I wanted to pull his hair hard for doing this to my best friend.

"Kali this place is taken," Larry said, waving his hand at me to go away. Then he pulled Rosie even closer to him. "You find someplace else to hide."

Leaving, my Irish temper boiled inside me; who was Larry to think he could get away with something like that. I'll fix him! As I stepped out of the doorway Andy spotted me right away and tagged me out. "There's nobody else in there Andy," I said with a grin. Andy squinted one eye and glanced at the doorway. His steps quickened as he took off for the place under the stairs expecting to find Rosie tucked away. He had no idea he was about to find the biggest game of all. Slowly stalking out his prey, Andy entered the doorway of the building. I watched the opening gradually swallow him as he sneaked inside followed by scrambling sounds. Andy came out fast, Larry close behind. I cheered when he tagged Larry out, but where was Rosie? I reached the doorway in time to see her darting up the last few stairs, and into her apartment. She was upset about something and it didn't take much of a brain to figure it was

Larry's fault. Rosie was gone for the rest of the night, and though she was missed, she was safe at home.

It was never clear if Rosie told her mother about Larry, or if it was a self-imposed rule not to play hide and seek with us again. During the day, nothing changed, but if I wanted to play with her after suppertime, we had to meet in her apartment where we played in her room. Rosie and I never talked about what happened that night, but I couldn't help wondering, with my inexperienced mind, why men were doing things that weren't nice. Not forgetting what Mr. Hollick had done to me, and now Larry and Rosie … why would Larry do that to Rosie when he had a wife of his own?

Larry's wife Regina was a quiet soft-spoken girl. She was several years younger than he was and not versed in the ways of the world. She used Mama as a source of information and advice, and paid many visits to our apartment. Reeg and Larry were trying to have a baby; or at least Reeg was. Without fail, the conversation between her and Mama would end up on the subject of babies; who was a better authority on babies than Mrs. O'Brien? I don't think Larry cared; his interests seemed to be elsewhere. Larry's ritual of going to the Belmont Bar alone on weekend evenings was a sore spot for Reeg. It was an argument that she very seldom won. Larry would come out of the apartment door bounding down the stairs like Jack Armstrong, "The All American Boy," and head briskly down the street. We knew where he was going. When his destination was the Belmont, he wouldn't take time to talk to us. Next, Reeg would come flying out the door after him. Still pulling on a sweater or finishing up the tying of a ribbon in her hair, she would tear along the street to catch up with him. Then the two of them might walk to the bar together, but more often, when she caught up, the scene would have an unhappy ending for Reeg. We couldn't hear what was being said, but there was no question angry words were passing between them. The short argument would end with Reeg returning to the apartment. Her head bowed trying to hide her tears. She returned, like a disappointed little girl.

It was only a short two blocks walk from our apartment to the Belmont; a convenient stop for Dad too. There were times the two men accidentally met there and wound up drinking together. Dad and Larry were never what could be termed "good" friends, but Dad would sit with him for a short time to be cordial. Once, I heard Dad telling Mama how Larry would flirt with women who came into the bar. Of course, this only happened if Reeg wasn't with him. "I don't trust him any farther than I can throw a bull," Dad would bellow. It didn't take Dad long to catch on to our neighbor with the obvious roving eye. Telling Mama about Larry was more than a bit of local gossip. It was meant to be a warning to her; Larry was not to be taken lightly. That big news item was of little interest to Mama; her thoughts were on the likelihood she was pregnant again.

Times were few when we kids didn't tag along with Mama; a trip to the doctor's office though, was definitely out of bounds. The inconvenient absence of Joseph and Andy this time required Dad to baby-sit Richard and me. Relaxing in his recliner in the front room, Dad read one of his electronic books, as Richard napped peacefully in his crib. I was waiting in front of the apartment house for Mama's return when this older kid, Bobby came out of the building.

"Hi Kali," he said tilting his head sideways to see what I was drawing with chalk on the sidewalk; a picture of a house on the hill.

"Hi," I answered. He moved around me and peered over my shoulder for a better look.

"Ya can't draw very good can ya?"

"Nope," I answered.

"Hey, let me show ya a trick, come here, stand up. Come here a minute."

I stood up and faced him. He excitedly rattled on about how he could make me holler by hitting me with two fingers.

"How?"

"I'll show ya."

Grabbing my hand, he extended my arm out turning my wrist upward. Running his two fingers over his tongue, he moistened them. Snap! Down they came on my wrist with such a crack that I was sure it hurt. The joke was all in the slapping sound, you expected it to hurt. It was just a harmless joke, and probably something he picked up from Larry. Bobby laughed at my reaction and though the slap didn't hurt, his tight grip on my wrist did. Moistening his fingers a second time, he readied himself to slap me again. "No you don't!" I shouted. Pulling away from him was not easy. My wrist was tight in his grasp. The struggle to free myself was a short-lived tug of war with Dad's booming voice putting a quick end to it. It sounded like thunder.

"Kali, get up here now!"

Bobby released my arm and scurried into the nearby taxi stand office. I look up at Dad. He was leaning out of one of the front room windows. I certainly didn't need a road map to tell me I was on the most lonesome road in town. That tone of voice raised goose bumps on the back of my neck. I had done something wrong, but what? Maybe Bobby shouldn't have touched my hand. My mind was searched for an answer as I scrambled up the stairs. The long climb gave too much time to think of what was about to happen for doing … I didn't know what. Dad was already waiting in the doorway of the entryway that led to the front room; he was holding the kitchen broom. He had that familiar, fearsome scowl on his face; I knew I was going to get it. Darting past him, crossing through the entry and into the front room, I could feel he was hot on my tail. He grabbed me by the arm with one hand, and with the other pelted my behind with the broom. I danced around trying to avoid the swinging blows; he hit the mark each time. We ended up going round and round in small circles. Dad was yelling something, but my panic kept me from caring what he was saying. When the spanking stopped, tears flooded my face as he pushed me on to the couch. Spanking me with the bristle part of the broom was a little like Bobby's trick. My fear of Dad and expecting it to hurt was the only reasons it seemed to. I was more frightened than hurt. Dad had never spanked me like that before. He hadn't been drinking, and usually wasn't this mean when he was sober. What ever he saw from the window must have looked awful to him. Sitting on the couch, I was aware that my dress and leg's were spattered with something wet. It was so embarrassing. Dad had spanked the pee out of me.

"Go take care of yourself, and go to bed," he said brusquely.

Cleaned and dry, except for a stray tear or two, I climbed into bed and drifted off to sleep. Sometime later, I awoke to a gentle nudge. The room was darker, but I could hear Mama's soft voice. "Kali, come out to supper before it gets cold." Mama motioned to me to follow. Joseph, Andy and Richard were already sitting at the table eating. Supper was almost over, and that told me it probably took Mama most of the meal to convince Dad that I should be allowed to eat. Dad looked disapprovingly at me as I took my usual place at the table. Quickly I dropped my eyes. There was still much anger for him now, and reluctance for me to look at him. Everybody's glances told me that they all knew what happened.

Then Andy broke the strained moment for me. "Hey Joseph, are we gonna try that new gas motor on the model tomorrow?"

"I got a little work to do on it yet. The gas flow still isn't right. We can tune it up tonight. Okay?"

"Yeah!"

That same night we learned there was to be a new addition to our family.

The next day, I stayed close to Mama choosing to play house in the dining room with my doll Patty; our make-believe table was a cardboard box. Kneeling down I poured water into our cups as pretend tea, and cautioned Patty, "Now, don't spill."

"Stay the hell away from that taxi stand. Those people are no good, never will be!" The rise in Dad's voice was hard to ignore. Looking out into the kitchen, I could see Dad at the kitchen table with Mama, finishing lunch. He was holding a hot cup of coffee up to his mouth. As the steam curled up and out of the cup, he was lightly blowing on it to cool it off. Mama's answer to Dad was soft. I couldn't make out what she was saying, but had no trouble hearing Dad.

"All I know is, Edna is in the back room of that place more'n she's at the front desk where she belongs." A fork is thrown onto his plate and quickly pushed to one side. "She gets the kid to answer the phone. She spends more time on the damn mattress than at her desk." A particle of food shoots from his mouth to the table. "She's no good, none of them are." Dad adds, wiping his mouth with the back of his hand.

Dad took another sip from his coffee, wearing that frown that made him look so mean. "SSHHH." Mama hissed. She was aware I was in the next room. Most likely Dad had not forgotten, but assumed I was too young to understand.

Then Dad barked out a direct order, "Just you stay away from there!"

Mama could control herself no longer. "For crying out loud, where would I get money for a taxi? I don't need a taxi for a two block trip to a grocery store!"

"I don't care. Just stay away from there ... and her!" Dad pushes back from the table, lights a new cigar, and gives Mama a kiss good-by. Slamming the door behind him, he takes the tense feeling with him leaving behind a thin trail of cigar smoke cut off by his abrupt exit.

Edna was Bobby's Mother. She never gave us kids a greeting or a smile. When she came out of her apartment, she moved quickly to the taxi stand office. With her rosy red cheeks, and eyes dark from a heavy layer of mascara, she was all dolled up for work. Long after she'd rush by, the scent of strong perfume lingered in the air. The boys giggled when the breeze caught her skirt allowing a quick view of her nylons rolled just below her knees. We never saw Bobby's father; when Larry told us that Bobby had no father I asked if he had died. Larry sarcastically answered, "No, he didn't die." I didn't ask any more questions, though I would have liked to. At lest I understood why Edna worked at the taxi stand. Edna's job there as dispatcher was an easy one. Bobby hung around there all the time, occasionally substituting as dispatcher as well.

Dad felt that being young meant you didn't know what was going on; kids always know more than adults realize. I knew Dad meant Edna was doing bad things in that back room, and though not knowing exactly what, it had to be something shocking. Mama said when Dad saw Bobby pulling on my arm; it looked as though I was being dragged into that den of iniquity. In his own way Dad may have thought he was teaching me to stay out of dangerous situations, and that it would be my fault and no one else's, if I got into trouble. I knew from then on Dad would never have cause to put a hand on me like that again. It's strange how things can be made clear and more complicated at the same time.

CHAPTER 5
When Hungry, Anything Goes

The war was so far away, it was unthinkable that America wouldn't always be a safe haven from the bombs and killing; that was, until the attack on Pearl Harbor. Every kid in Chipwey knew when the blackout drills became routine that the war was moving in on us. When the whistle at the firehouse blew, we'd scurry around and douse every light. Window shades were drawn. Light must not be visible to an enemy plane in the sky. If a home had no shades then blankets were kept close at hand and nailed across the windows. We kept our radio on, but kept it covered to hide its light as well. It was important to keep the radio on. We wouldn't know if this was a real attack or not until the radio told us. Three blasts from the fire whistle was the all-clear signal. We were glad to hear it. Although the blackouts didn't last very long, uncovering the windows was like being released from bondage.

Signs around town spurring us to buy War Bonds and Victory Stamps, made it obvious; the war required everyone's help, it was a big part of our daily struggle. Our family's growing problem of not enough money was complicated further by war shortages. The book of stamps that bought the scarce items was as precious as a wallet full of money. Sugar, butter and meat were among the hardest to get. A stamp from the book entitled each family to their fair share, although having a stamp wasn't guarantee of getting something. If one didn't get to the store fast enough, you could be left standing with a precious stamp in your hand, but no butter. The small supplies the stores received disappeared so fast, often they never made it to the shelves, but were sold directly from shipping cartons. When it was gone, it was gone until the next month, and sometimes longer. Mama would say, "You have to be fast because it won't last." Our local newspaper, *The Chipwey Signal*, or the radio would carry the time and place these precious shipments were to arrive.

When Mama learned that there would be butter or sugar at the grocery Store, she knew there wasn't a moment to lose. Andy was the one who went to the store with her. If anyone could battle the crowd and get the butter, Andy could. When real butter was impossible to get or if we ran out of stamps, Mama bought margarine. Shaped in a block form, the margarine came out of the box pure white. After softening it in a bowl for a time, a packet of "red" coloring was mixed in with a fork. I could never understand how this red stuff could turn something like this yellow, but little by little, the white margarine turned to a golden yellow.

During the years of rationing stamps and small supplies of everything, Andy and I continued our skirmishes around town. Although empty bottles were high on our list, we looked in the garbage bins for anything reusable or edible that grocery stores threw away. Eventually most grocery stores were forced to build pens secured with padlocks to keep the garbage from being scattered far and wide. More concern was given to the several cases of food poisoning in town that pointed to bad choices taken from the pens. That didn't stop Andy. He had a good eye for telling the difference, and what he wasn't sure of, Mama would be. Scaling the pen and dropping down inside was easy for Andy. He'd toss whatever he found over the top of the pen, into my waiting hands. Frustrated from replacing broken padlocks, a grocery store across the street from where we lived, had an unprotected pen. Many times we left the house empty handed and came back with a bag or two of oranges or apples. We'd at least have a couple of mouthfuls to enjoy after cutting away the spoiled portions. The trickiest items to salvage were can goods with missing labels; we called them our "guess what" surprises. Mama would push on the ends of each can. If she found either end had the slightest bulge she'd say, "This one's no good. It's working." The benefits from each trip varied from good to poor. Sometimes we came home with nothing more than the empty bag we left with, not even a can that was "working."

Transient bums that drifted up from the railroad tracks stalked our back alleys around Chipwey seeking sustenance in the same way. Speaking for myself, I never saw a single one of these elusive creatures, but Andy said to stay clear of them.

"Wait for me. Don't go alone" Andy warned.

"Why? I can do it."

"I'm warning ya, don't go alone. If ya meet one of those transies you'll be sorry."

"There's no such thing. Yer just try'na scare me."

"Ya? Let's go to the tracks right now. I'll show ya where they hang out."

"NO!"

"I bet they know you."

"Shut up, Andy."

"If ya never saw one before, how do ya know what they look like to know ya never saw one? I rest my case. Don't go alone." This was to be Andy's latest trick, trying to keep me from reaping the glory of the harvest for myself. Trying to out-think Andy wasn't easy. Well, he wasn't fooling me. Yet, after that, there was a reluctance to strike out on my own. Why take the chance it was true? I couldn't help wondering though; did this mean we were bums too?

One day, when Andy returned home after being out on the rounds by himself, he quietly asked me to go back out with him. He leaned in close to my ear and whispered, "Come on Kali, I want to show you somethin'." It was as though we were striking out on a secret mission, and he didn't want anyone else, not even Mama, to hear him. Trotting along behind, I followed Andy down the stairs and across the street. We headed over a cement wall, and into the back alley of the grocery store. This alley was a shortcut to Main Street when we went on errands for Mama. Here in this familiar musty-smelling alley, we headed to the back wall of the store to a bucket that was only vaguely noticeable. It was full of a solidified mixture of brown and black gunk. During the war, many items such as toys, pots and pans and anything made of rubber, were collected. They were transformed into usable things to help fight the war. Even the housewife was asked to help by saving all grease drippings from cooking. The fat collected in a can and bought by grocery stores for two or three cents a pound, was recycled and used in the making of ammunition. Why has Andy hustled me out of the house to look at a yucky bucket of grease? A stash of empty bottles, yes, but this stuff ... He knew right away that I didn't understand. It was a gold mine, "It's waste fat Kali. Ya know ... we take it to the store, get money ... there's a war on ... 'member?"

"Yes I know."

"Waste fat, a whole bucket of it. Get it?" Bottles were the only things I could relate to, bootlegged waste fat never entered my mind. I didn't grasp the idea that the bucket would be a long lasting harvest. "Kali, waste fat ... three cents a pound ... a whole bucket full."

Finally, "Ooooh! We take the bucket to the store and get three cents a pound. Wow! We'll be rich!" A corner of Andy's mouth curled upward.

"No! Just a *little* at a time. We'll hide it here someplace."

Looking around Andy quickly took in our surroundings. "There," he exclaimed. "We'll hide it over there!" Andy carried the heavy load to the opposite side of the alley. Kneeling down, he wedged the bucket in a crevice between two brick walls. It was a good spot, well out of view from anyone passing through. "Now when Mama needs money for something, just bring an empty can with you." Andy holds up a flat stick for me to see. "And ... use this stick as a spoon to fill it up. Take it to the store like always. The man will weigh it, and give ya the money." I still wasn't sure. "But, sposen he asks where I got it? I don't have your nerves Andy."

"Ya don't need a lot of nerves, he won't ask ya that. Never did before, did he?"

"No."

"He'll think yer mother gave it to ya." Satisfied that our treasure was well hidden, we started for home.

"How'd it get there, Andy? I was here yesterday. I didn't see it."

"I don't know. Maybe … maybe, the driver forgot to pick it up."

Andy didn't care how it got there. He only knew he was the first to find it, and it meant many loaves of bread and boxes of cereal for us. We were to think of it as our bank. When the time came to make a withdrawal, my cautious brother was emphatic about going alone.

"Now remember, don't tell anyone about this, Okay?"

"Okay. But we kin tell Mama, huh?"

"NO! Don't tell anyone. Don't even tell Joseph." This didn't mean Joseph couldn't be trusted with a secret, it meant that I shouldn't make exceptions.

"How come we can't tell Mama? She wouldn't tell anyone."

"Kali listen." Andy stopped and looked me straight in the face his voice was quiet and gentle. "Mama has enough to worry about. You know, worrying about making ends meet. We'll help her to have one less worry if we keep this between us. You don't want Mama getting upset and crying over no money to buy milk for little Richard do you?"

"No. I don't want Mama to cry."

"Good. Then it's a deal?"

"Deal."

Our old bucket remained safe and sound to the day we scooped out the last glob. If Andy had anything to do about it, we were going to persevere through the lean years.

Occasionally we allowed ourselves to spend some of the money on the luxury of a bag of popping corn. Those little hard kernels were cheap; a large bag cost only ten cents, and lasted for what seemed like forever. The aroma of the corn popping in the pan was a treat, but to have a bowl of popcorn to munch as we listened to a story made it special. Butter or margarine was much too precious to use as a topping for popcorn. We were satisfied with just salt. One night as Mama read one of our favorite stories, we were feasting on our hot crunchy popcorn. Shaking too much salt on the corn was taboo because of salt's effect on the intake of water. That night an irresistible desire for salt had gotten out of hand. When Mama became aware a scolding followed. "That's too much salt. You'll be running to the bathroom all night." "Well, she better not wet the bed," Joseph teased. I was insulted.

"I don't wet the bed any more."

True to Mama's warning, I did wake up in the night to answer "the" call. Careful not to awaken Joseph or Andy, I quietly crawled out of bed. Not disturbing them was but a small consideration compared to waking Dad. That was a sin with by far the worst consequence. I had a choice of two ways to get to our bathroom. One way, the best way, was through the outside hallway seeing as how the bathroom entry was out there. That way, I wouldn't have to disturb anyone. The other way was to sneak through Mama's bedroom, and not leave the apartment until it was necessary, just that there was always a chance of waking Dad. I couldn't bring myself to go out in the dark empty hallway alone, so I would have to be extra quiet. Slowly I opened the door that separated our rooms, Dad's snoring was gratifying. It was proof he was asleep. Dropping to my hands and knees, the crawl across the room began. When I reached the door on the far side, I stood up and carefully turned the knob. This was a ticklish maneuver because Dad's side of the bed was but a few steps from the door. The slightest sound could awaken the enemy even though he had his back turned to me. Success was within my grasp. Slipping through into the dining room was a snap. Not letting the door latch would give me an easy return. Because of Dad's hawk-like hearing, my trip back would be done with equal caution. That was nothing to fret about; I could do it again. Returning from the bathroom, I decided that getting this far was so easy, that a side trip could do no harm. Opening the cupboard door, the breadbox inside taunted me. There would be no racket from eating a plain slice of bread. Taking a bite of the bread, the perilous journey back through the dining room began. I didn't know that Ol' hawk ears had heard me moving around and woke Mama.

"Helen something's in the kitchen. Sounds like a dog." Mama lay very still straining to hear, but heard nothing.

"How could a dog get into the house," she whispered?

"It's a dog! I hear toenails scratching on the linoleum. He's coming this way!"

I paused for a moment at the bedroom door to listen. It was quiet. One last obstacle, crossing enemy territory, and I'd be safe. It was clever not latching the door; I merely gave a gentle push I could slip back in. Dropping to my hands and knees, the crawl through Mama's room began with the piece of bread dangling between clenched teeth; a sure cinch … just a little bit farther. Lying quietly, Mama and Dad waited for the bold canine to enter the room. Dad had turned in the bed to face the door, ready to do battle with this four-legged bag of bones. He was patient, and waited for the moment when I was directly across from him. Then he gave out a loud, sharp yell. "Scat!" Allowing for weight, and the absence of a tail wind, no human ever moved as fast as I did. Exiting the room pell-mell, my bread was lost in the rush.

Reaching for the light Dad cried out, "It's heading for the kids room." Dad and Mama raced for the doorway of my room. In the darkness, no one knew what was traveling through the room until the light that spilled through the open door exposed me as the derelict dog.

"What the hell is she doing prowling around this time of night?" Dad looked at Mama as if she had a ready answer. Sitting up in bed, Joseph and Andy were sleepy-eyed not knowing what any of it was about.

"Go back to bed. I'll take care of it." Mama told Dad trying to settle the dust as best she could. Mama tucked the three of us in without saying a word. Passing through the doorway back to her room, Mama stopped to pick something up from the floor. She held the slice of bread up for me to see. Hardly recognizable as a piece of bread anymore, it was as flat as a dollar bill with a bite taken out of one corner. There was a trace of annoyance on her face as she closed the door behind her. Nuzzling down into the blankets, I said a prayer of thanksgiving. First, I didn't get spanked, and second, that small detail of not putting anything on the bread was the best decision I had made in years. It made me shudder to think what would have happened if ol' hawk ears' slipped on my peanut butter sandwich. It took no time for things to calm down in my bedroom. I could hear Dad still grumbling. He was like an old alarm clock running down by degrees; sputter about, " …damn kids … roaming all over the house … all hours of the night." Sure that I hadn't heard the last of my bungled breadbox raid; it was a surprise the next morning to learn the whole thing had already turned into an amusing story. Mama said, "For Dad to find anything funny at 6:30 in the morning is a miracle." Then she said something very puzzling, "By the way, lets check those toenails of yours. I've a hunch they need cutting." I couldn't wait to tell Rosie what had happened. Rosie always needed a good laugh.

I was halfway down the stairs when Reeg breathlessly passed me on her way up. There was an aura of urgency about her. "Is your mom busy?" she said as she rushed past me.

"Naw, just moping the floor." Her impatience stirred my curiosity. I followed her back up the stairs, and reached the hallway as Mama opened the door.

"Hi come on in. Don't mind the wet floor. It takes me so long to mop anymore. But I guess I'm not going to get any faster for a while," Mama joked, as she gently patted her protruding stomach. Reeg entered the apartment and before the door closed behind her, she and Mama were already deep in chatter. I wasn't sure if they knew I had entered and seated myself in the chair by the door.

" …You're all out of breath. Sit down, I'll get us some coffee." Mama said.

"Guess what?" the news couldn't wait. "I'm expecting," Reeg blurted.

Mama, placing two cups on the table, said, "I'm so glad."

I wondered, "Does expecting mean what I think it does?"

Still unaware that I was in the room, they continued talking.

"Have you had morning sickness?"

"Yeah, that's the only bad part, but I'm almost past that now."

"Well, that's good."

"Yea. It's gonna be swell having a baby in the family I can't wait." Reeg persisted in her conversation as Mama poured the coffee, clearly sharing the joy of the moment.

"Just as I thought. Jeepers, we get babies around here all the time and we're never that excited." Not caring to hear more, I headed for Rosie's.

Climbing the stairs to Rosie's apartment, concerned about what we would be doing today. Knocking lightly, I listened, anticipating the sound of her footsteps approaching the door. The door opened just a crack. A chain preventing the door from opening all the way allowed only half of Rosie's face to look out at me. A big smile of recognition changed her uneasy look.

"Hi Kali, come on in."

"Can't you come out?"

"Mother wants me to stay in, but we can play here, Okay?"

"Okay, I'll go get Patty."

"Don't go. Here, take Betsy." Rosie held one of her dolls up for me to see through the small opening then released the chain and opened the door full. I stepped inside. The chain was immediately put back into place. "I was just about to start a birthday party for my baby," she said. I shrugged, and followed Rosie into the apartment as she prattled on about what a great party we could have. She sounded exceptionally glad to see me. "We'll go down to Mrs. Hunt's and get cupcakes, they'll make good birthday cakes." Rosie knew me well. Nothing warmed my heart like a cupcake laden with thick frosting.

"But you said you couldn't go out." Rosie already had the chain released from the door.

"Oh, it'll be all right. I just have to come right back."

As we entered the store, Mrs. Hunt was all smiles. "What can I do for you girls?"

"Hi, I'd like this, and please put it on Mother's bill." Rosie held up a package of two chocolate cupcakes.

"All right Hon," Mrs. Hunt opened a book, and wrote some numbers down as Rosie left the store.

Inside the apartment, again the chain on the door was put back in place. Rosie led the way to her bedroom where she had a table and chairs ready for the party. They were so much better than the cardboard boxes that I had to use. She even had the deluxe set of dishes with forks, spoons and knives. What I coveted most was her doll carriage. Now that was something. A carriage, just like a real mother would have. Quickly we began to prepare for the party. Both of our dolls were given a place at the table. Rosie filled the teapot with milk; real milk not evaporated, and filled the four little cups. We ended up eating the cake meant for our dolls. We lingered there in our made-up world; then Rosie began scolding her doll. "Don't be naughty. Take your nap or I'll have to tell daddy on you."

In all the time I had played with her, that was the first time I had heard Rosie speak of a daddy of any kind. Since she brought it up, I took advantage of the situation.

"Do you have a dad, Rosie?"

"Of course I do!" Rosie suddenly turned quiet. I could tell by her snippy answer that something wasn't right.

Without realizing what a loaded question it was, I pressed her further, "Well, uh … where is he?"

Rosie sat back down in the little chair. With a finger, she began playing with a spill of milk on the table. Spreading the white substance thin, she spoke, not looking at me.

"He doesn't live with us, not for a long time. Mother says he's still my daddy, but not her husband anymore … and you mustn't tell."

"Do you see him … ever?"

"No, not since the day he left us! Kali, you know a person can have more than one father," she snapped back.

I couldn't understand what she was telling me. How can it be? Bobby had no father, and now Rosie had a father but she can't see him, and she was telling me a person could have more than one? Why would you need more than one father? God knows one was enough for me. Feeling uncomfortable with our conversation, I jumped up and started cleaning up the dishes. Rosie wiped the table off. Silently we retreated to our make-believe world; things made a whole lot more sense there. Rosie and I spent the remainder of the day together until her mother returned. It was supper time; time for me to leave.

"See ya tamarra, Rosie ... bye Mrs. Stebbins."

Rosie's mother was pulling groceries from a shopping bag she had brought home with her. Looking up she called after me. "Say hi to your mom for me, Kali. How is she feeling?"

"She's getting slower, but she's fine. See ya." I closed the door and started down when

Rosie called after me. "Kali wait! Here, I want you to have Betsy." We stood on the stairs talking.

"Are you sure Rosie? Gee, real hair and everything?"

"I want you to have her, she'll remind you of the fun we had today."

I thanked Rosie and watched as she waved back to me and reentered her apartment. My mind was so overwhelmed by her generosity that I brushed aside the hidden meaning of what she said, she always had a flair for the dramatic; this was probably just ... well ... just Rosie! I thought of this as only the end of another fun day with Rosie. It was really the last day I would spend with my dear friend. Reaching the foot of the stairs little notice is given to the stack of cardboard boxes piled in the corner of the landing. The kind people use when they're getting ready to move away. Four days later, I stood on the curbing waving good-by to Rosie and her family as they followed a truck loaded with furniture. Rosie's mother had married again. The stranger driving the car was Rosie's new father. My old friend was on her way to a new home. Living up on the hill, her life would be full of new friends and experiences. Standing on the street watching the car move out of sight, I felt lonesome. While Rosie's part of town would be full, my part of town would be emptier.

Now that the Stebbins' were gone, Mama could explain why no one told me before that they planned to move. Divorce was something that was not sociably accepted in Chipwey. Mrs. Stebbins worked at the dress factory, leaving little time to socialize. Since Rosie and I were good friends, Mrs. Stebbins took Mama into her confidence saying it was best not to make her plans known, and start more gossip. Mama said we should be happy for them because they weren't very happy the way they were. Now they would be a complete family again, and I had grown-up a little too, learning how it was possible to have more than one father. Rosie hadn't gone to the moon. She still lived in Chipwey. I saw her almost everyday hurrying along Main Street after school with girls her own age. She always waved and called out to me when we saw each other. Like the caterpillar that blossoms into a beautiful butterfly, Rosie was coming out of her cocoon. She dressed and acted more grown up. It was undeniable. Rosie was ready for the change. Knowing that Rosie was more contented, I was happy for her, who could ever forget the girl with the melancholy personality, and the sandpaper singing voice? She was a good and loyal friend. I hoped she wouldn't mind my envying her moving up on the hill. Maybe someday …

CHAPTER 6
From Toys To Kisses

Mr. and Mrs. Foote ran the only second hand store in Chipwey. The sign above their shop had a picture of a foot with two hands extending from its ankle and read: "Foote's Second Hand." It was exciting being taken to the second hand shop, like a trip back in time. I was filled with feelings of new discoveries by simply breathing in the musty old smells that lingered at the doorway. Let the others travel the world for their new findings. For now, Foot's Second Hand was world enough for me. Here I found a treasure chest that held fragments of past lives. Many things were strange to me and out-dated even before I was born. Every visit to the store included a tour of old things hanging from the ceiling; oily streaked horse collars and halters, oil lamps with smoke stained chimneys, rusty picks and shovels that had felt the grip of many a callused hand. And Mama's favorite, an old spinning wheel dangled from the ceiling. An object of amusement for me was a bicycle that had a huge front wheel and a small back wheel. However, did a person ride it? It was easy to imagine voices in laughter at failed attempts to keep the contraption upright. On the practical side, there was clothing too. Party dresses, no longer in style, waited patiently to see the light of another fancy party; but was more apt to be seen in one of Chipwey's school plays. The shop wasn't all dedicated to the past. Items constantly bought and sold by the Foote's kept the shop in step with current trends.

One day I spotted a snow cutter in the window of Foot's shop. I had longed forever for a winter doll carriage like this, but thought it a frivolous request and thought that I would never own one. The paint on the sides of the cutter had worn thin, and the runners had only traces of the bright red paint that once covered them. Probably some little girl found this delight under her Christmas tree one year, and now by out-growing it, had left the cutter for another girl to enjoy. Through the hot summer months, I never forgot the little cutter, every time we passed the shop, I'd stop for a few seconds to say hello, affectionately running my fingers along the beveled landscape of the handle. The cutter was in a place of honor, on display in the window, until the day it was moved. Now it stood in a back corner almost hidden from view under a weatherworn sled, and an old rug. With the little cutter almost completely buried, it could easily have been missed unless one knew where it was. Then, one day in late fall, the silent shattering of a heart, and the memory of the little cutter was all that remained; it was no longer there. I had loved it and now had to accept a final good-by. Two dollars was more than we could afford I told myself, trying to hide the disappointment. Much more than should be spent on such an extravagant thing, and as Mama pointed out it was something that could only be used in the winter time anyway, but ohhh ….

When Christmas Morning came around that year a wondrous surprise was waiting. Beneath the tree the little cutter and the sled waited, both looking like new again. The sled was for Andy and Joseph. Dad had painted the sled red and yellow, and finished it off with his artful ability with a striping brush. My cutter was painted gray and its runners were restored to a bright red. Years later Mama told me she knew of my love affair with the little cutter. The light in my eyes whenever I saw it was enough to light up the whole town. The cutter had been in the shop for so long Mr. Foote sold it to her for only 50 cents.

One day, I entered the kitchen in time to overhear a conversation between Mama and Dad; the radio shop must go. Rent money for the shop was money lost with little return. Dad still had a drinking problem, but his judgment when he was sober was good. Closing down the repair shop was a hard thing for Dad to do. There was talk of re-opening the shop when things got better, but even so, Mama said this feeling of defeat was hard for him to take. Dad tied to lose the bad feelings by drinking more. Time that Dad normally spent in his own repair shop had shifted between Danahey's Bar and Nick's barbershop. A small room in the rear of barbershop had become a sort of substitute repair shop where Dad continued to make extra money. Only now, Mama would never know how much he made, and possibly never benefit from the money. It was during this down period of Dad's career that he began repairing illegal one-armed bandits. The owner of a cigar store Dad frequented was his contact for these secret repair jobs. We older kids knew which basement in which club on the outskirts of town they were in, and more than likely half of Chipwey knew too, although we never spoke of it out loud. Dad made good money repairing these machines, but Mama suspected that many times Dad exchanged his pay for goods, bar privileges at the club.

Lack of money eventually drew me into the business of helping to keep a roof over our heads. Every month, Eloise Gressler our landlady, paid a visit to each of her tenants and personally collected the rent. It had gotten to where she didn't know if she was going to get her money from us every time. Begging off for another week happened more often than even Mama could take. Frequently, Mama would pretend she wasn't home and I'd cover for her. Eloise would arrive promptly, and expect her money. She was the richest person I knew. It was mind-boggling why such an ugly person was permitted to have so many beautiful things. Dignified and stuffy looking, here was the epitome of the kind of person who could easily intimidate me, unruffled, unwrinkled and not a hair out of place. The earrings she wore were made of what look to me like, diamonds. A ledger book tucked in the bend of her arm was her portable office. Eloise knew what she was about to hear when I was the one who opened the door. The thick glasses she wore made her eyes look like giant headlights as she glared down at me.

"Mama isn't here right now, but she says to tell you she'd have the money next week." What a relief, getting that one sentence out. With a deep sigh of annoyance, Eloise would draw her head back causing her to look down her nose a bit more at me. Pressing her lips tightly and puffing out her cheeks, I was never sure whether she was going to scold me, or come out with a big belch. After hastily scribbling something in the ledger, she'd wheel around, march down the hallway like a storm trooper and descend the stairs. Her haughty attitude was frightening; I couldn't close the door fast enough. My encounter with Eloise was finished off with a silent plea, "Please Dad, have the money next week."

One evening as Dad was entering the apartment house, he met Larry who came bounding out of the building. Ricocheting from each step in his showy athletic style, he nearly knocked Dad over. The two men stopped and exchanged words, and when they parted, Dad had invited Larry and Reeg up to our apartment, a little celebration for the blessed event that was soon to take place for both families. Larry accepted, and later that evening, we all gathered in our front room like old friends. Mama and Reeg were at one end of the couch discussing what two expectant mothers would be … babies. Larry was sitting at the other end of the couch talking to Dad, who was stretched out comfortably in his recliner. Remembering my father's unfavorable remarks about Larry, this gathering was very unusual. Maybe he thought that Larry would instantly be converted into a devoted family man now that he was to become a father. Larry most likely was no threat to Mama now.

Joseph and Andy had gone to an evening movie. Richard had been put to bed for the night, leaving me by myself amidst all that grown-up talk. Andy's collection of comic books had worn my interest thin so I sauntered over to the men's side of the room. Leaning over the arm of the couch I listening to their conversation, but was unable to understand what they were talking about. I found myself staring into the two bright blue eyes that captivated me so. I'm sure Larry felt awkward with Dad sitting there watching his eight-year old daughter carrying on like that. Having Larry right there in our front room was almost as good as having a long lost relative come for a visit. The whole thing filled me with renewed trust in him. It wasn't right flirting like that. Even though I didn't think of it in that light, it didn't take Dad long to recognize it as such. Receiving that icy stare could have the same effect on me as getting a good thrashing. I could feel Dad's eyes on me. Holding his thumb out, and shaking it toward the doorway, he said stiffly, "Hey. Time you went to bed. Goodnight!" After saying goodnight to Larry and Reeg, and giving my parents a kiss, I departed for the bedroom.

In bed, I amused myself by fanning the corner of the blanket at Joseph's models hanging from the ceiling, causing them to swing against the limits of their string leashes. Listening to the muted voices of the four adults in the next room, my ears strained to make out their conversation. Eavesdropping on their secret party was fair payback for making me go to bed so early. Occasionally a voice would rise in laughter followed by a clink of glass as a fresh helping of beer was poured. It was all sort of soothing in a way. The sound of the muffled voices, and the swaying of the models above lulled me into a relaxed trance. Then a door opened and closed. Someone had stepped into the entry hall. I wondered if Larry and Reeg were leaving. Slowly the door to my room pushed open. I expected it to be Mama coming in for a bed check. The figure entered quickly and closed the door silently. It was Larry. "Hi. I just came in to say goodnight to you. You know, you gave Mom and Dad a kiss goodnight but you forgot me." He spoke in a whisper. My response was that embarrassed feeling I got from not knowing how to respond to something. Moving to a sitting position with my knees drawn up to my chest, I nervously play with my toes.

How should I respond to something like this? "He's teasing me. He'll go away." I thought. Larry leaned in toward me and before I could react, he gently kissed me on the mouth. My face felt as though it was on fire with the warmth of a blush, but he still wasn't satisfied.

"Next time I kiss you stick your tongue out," the wicked tempter coaxed. He only succeeded in shocking me with such a repulsive thought.

Cupping my hand over my mouth, I exclaimed, "No, you'll bit it off!"

"Shhhh," Larry hissed, taking a quick look toward the door. "No I won't," he chuckled, amused at my ignorance. Not to be won over that easily, my hand remained over my mouth, as I insistently shook my head no. Larry said nothing then pushed away from the bed. "Now don't tell your Dad, Okay?" I shook my head yes. He left my room and slithered through my parent's room. A few seconds later I heard the kitchen door open and close. He had most likely excused himself to go to the bathroom, and took that opportunity to enter my room.

I had brought this on myself, hanging on to the arm of the couch gazing into Larry's face like a sick cow. "From now on be careful and quiet, be on your guard," I told myself, "like the little people of Ireland who guard their pot of gold from thieves, not with violence but with cunning." Though my fascination for blue eyes wasn't gone, my trust in Larry was. He hadn't changed at all. The day he grabbed Rosie by her young breasts was still a vivid memory, and now this. I wondered what he might do next. He was no longer one of the kids to play games with, He was not a kid at all. Recalling the beating with a broom for something that I didn't understand, I kept the tale of Larry's stolen kiss to myself. It was the only thing to do.

At school, Sister Agnes told us we all had a Guardian Angel to watch over us. I'm sure mine was working overtime. How I wished for someone other than an Angle to tell my secrets to. I couldn't tell Rosie. We had never even talked about what Larry did to her. If Mary were here, and was a little older, I'll bet she would listen and understand.

Mary was just a baby when she left us, I never questioned that she would always live with Mildred. Though we were glad to see Mary every time we visited her, it felt as though we were dropping by to see a cousin instead of a sister. For me, the lonesome feeling was no longer there when we returned home without Mary. When money to take the bus became scarce, our trips to Hartford dwindled, then stopped. Joseph was the only one who continued to make the visits, using his own money for bus fare. We came to depend on our aunt and uncle to bring Mary to us. In the meantime, Mary's Mommy Mildred and Daddy George had become all she could remember as her parents. That "month" that Mildred was supposed to take care of Mary drifted from weeks into months, and then into years. This was too much for Dad to keep his opinion to himself. When he came home evenings with a few drinks under his belt his grumpy mood would brew until it boiled over into a heated argument.

"Have you talked to Mildred yet?"

"Where am I supposed to get money for a long distance call?"

"I don't care where you get it. You better call her before I do."

"I'll call this weekend."

"Sure."

"There won't be any money until Friday. What do you want me to do."

"Just get her back here where she belongs. It's been three damn years."

"It's been two years."

"It's longer than two years. Get her back or I'll go after her myself."

Mama had spoken to Mildred many times about bringing Mary back home, but Mildred always wangled a few more months.

"It's not right to take her away when she has everything she needs here, Mildred would say. "You have so many. You won't even miss her."

"I know you're giving her good care, but she does belong with her family. And Bob is getting madder than a hornet about it." Mama was torn between Dad and Mildred.

Though Helen wasn't willing to give up one of her children, she felt maybe she would be depriving Mary of a better life. This period of indecision earned Mildred more time with Mary. Joseph and Andy had no idea how this dilemma would end and I gave no thought to Mary ever coming home again. The subject would go dormant, but no for long.

Another Christmas had come and gone. It was a winter of one heavy snowfall after another. The storm that kept building all afternoon made the roads and sidewalks impassable. Uncle John and a fellow worker were doing their best to keep the roads clear. The snow fell faster than the big plow could clear it away. As I trudged along on my way home from school, it would have been fun to wind my way along the small paths cut through the snow, if not for the sting of the hail. Struggling to hold on to books, and keep my mouth and nose covered, I was glad to see our building a short distance away. I climbed the stairs, eager to feel the warmth of our kitchen. Little did I know that this feisty day wasn't finished yet, it had a surprise or two up its frosty sleeve for us all.

In the kitchen Richard was busy playing with a chair that had once been his potty chair. Mama removed the little pot from underneath allowing him to use it as a toy chair. I bent down and kissed him, on the head, "Hi Richard, playing cars?" He smiled, and revving up his so called motor continued to push his car across the floor. In the dining room, Mama was rearranging furniture. She was in the process of trying to push ol' elephant-legs flush against the wall. "Oh, good! Honey, give me a hand with this, will you?" Mama looked tired as she straightened up and put both hands on her back. She puffed out a deep breath. "Phew! I always forget how darn heavy this thing is." I tore off my mittens and coat hurrying to help her. Mama was seven months along and it was getting harder for her to be as active as she was used to being. My hands pressed against the table, I braced myself to push the thing with her, but it was no use. There wasn't enough strength between us to start the table sliding.

"Oh, just leave it. Joseph and Andy will be home soon they can do it." Mama sighed.

"What's going on? Why ya moving everything around?"

"You're getting a bed of your own. I wanted it to be here before you got home. I guess the weather is making deliveries hard."

A bed of my own, after three years of sharing with Joseph and Andy, it was too good to be true. Mama had cleared one side of the dining room and had a small dresser with my clothes already in the drawers. There was a big empty space where a bed could fit. It wasn't really a bedroom, but it was mine. All that remained to be done was that elephantine table had to be pushed in place. We were lucky to have a place big enough to push it to.

"When do I get my bed, today?"

"Soon as the man delivers it from the second-hand shop."

Sudden knocks at the door made my heart skip a beat. It was here! My mad dash for the door got me there ahead of Mama. The door swung opened to a man standing with a strange looking mess of frame and springs. "I have a folding bed from Foote's Second Hand for O'Brien … that you?" He rattled off peering down at me over the top of the clipboard. He paused waiting for my answer. A cold draft radiated from his heavy girth as he poked a pencil behind one ear, and rolled a wet, stumpy, un-lit cigar from one side of his mouth to the other. His coat sparkled from the melting snow. " …That you sis?" He asked softly a second time. A broad grin spread over his face.

"Yeah, that's us."

"Could you put it in there, please?" Mama pointed to the dining room. "I wasn't sure you'd be able to deliver it today."

"Fortunately you're not far from the shop. I wouldn't want to be going up on the hill today. Sign on the bottom line there, Mrs.," Mama took the clipboard, as the man headed for the dining room. She signed her name, and handed the clipboard back. "Thank you." The burly figure smiled, waved his hand, and closed the door behind him.

Mama released two levers at each end of the bed and it sprang open, it was beautiful. The mattress wasn't very thick, but it felt just fine as I bounced up and down on it a couple of times. "Lets get some bedding on it right away before I get busy with something else." As she headed for the sheets and pillowcases, Mama's waddle was a sign she was beginning to tire. In afterthought, she called back to me, "Check on Richard, see if he's all right."

Mama had used the term "terrible two's" many times but it seemed to me the three's weren't any better. A seasoned three years old now, Richard played very well by himself; his specialty was to remove all the pots and pans from the bottom cupboard. He could be quite contented for a long time pulling labels off the can goods stored there as well. It took time to retrieve a can from the cupboard because the doors had to be tied closed because of him. Looking into the kitchen, I could see the little ball of energy playing with the wooden potty chair. To Richard it wasn't just a chair but many things; today it was a car.

"He's okie-dokie mama," I called back.

We started to make up the bed when it occurred to me, "How come I'm getting a bed of my own?" Mama sat down and patted the bed for me to sit next to her.

"Dad and I talked about it, and now is as good a time as any to start rearranging things. You know you're getting to be a big girl now, it's time you had your own bed. You need your own place. Richard can sleep in Joseph and Andy's room. The new baby will have to take over the crib. There's something else too. In a couple of weeks, Mary's coming home. She's four now, and so you and Mary can sleep together."

"Why is she coming home? What about Aunt Mildred?"

"Mildred and George have to move out of state. We don't want Mary taken so far away."

"Why? Don't they like Hartford anymore?"

"George is being transferred to Michigan by the company he works for. They'll be there a whole year. That's too far, even Joseph won't be able to visit her." What a surprise! What good news! Mary was coming home at last, at long last! How would I ever stand the wait until she arrived?

A scream from the kitchen shattered the excitement of the Mama's news. A moment ago, it took some effort for Mama to move, but now she moved like the wind. Richard was in trouble. We could see Richard's little bottom jutting up in the air as he bounced the little chair up and down on the floor. He was screaming like a banshee. "How in the name of heaven did you do that? Wait, don't pull, Richard, Mama will do it." The top of his head was wedged in the hole in the chair. Richard was swung up to the table where Mama tried her best to release the chair, but only made things worse. His head slipped completely through the hole and the chair ended up resting on his shoulders. The chair was twisted and turned, but would only lift up as far as his ears. Richard's screams didn't make the situation any easier. Afraid that she would scrape one of his ears off, for they were already turning a beautiful crimson color, Mama decided to wait until Dad came home. Big tears ran down Richard's face. Mama looked as if she were about to cry herself.

"Don't worry honey. Daddy will be along soon. He'll get it off."

"He has to wear that until dark time?" I asked.

"Dad will be home for supper tonight because of the storm."

For the next two hours, Richard waited patiently with that old potty chair riding on his shoulders. He was a sight, with the four legs sticking up in the air moving along with him as he walked. There was a vague resemblance between Richard and a king whose wooden crown was too big for the small head beneath it. We thought Richard was going to wear out his shoes with all the trips back and forth to the stairs to see if Dad was coming yet.

Finally, the door opened and there entered the savior of the day. Dad was home! "How did he get like that?" Dad's smile changed to a wide grin. Richard wasn't crying, but he had a distressful look.

"What if Dad can't get that thing off him?" I thought. "How'll Richard get his shirt off or his nightshirt on?" Oh ye of little faith; know ye not that The Father can fix all things? Gripping the chair with both of his hands, Dad twisted first a tiny bit this way then that. Low and behold, it popped right off. I don't know who was more relieved, Richard or Mama.

A cold blast of air chilled the room as Joseph and Andy burst into the kitchen. They had been lining up jobs to shovel snow. As soon as the storm was over, they would be in business. After we told them what had happened to Richard we talked and laughed about it as smells of supper filled the warm kitchen. As for that potty chair, Richard would have nothing more to do with it.

The wait for Mary's return seemed to take forever. Our sister was coming home after three long years; something should be a little different. We still had our popcorn nights; we still went to church on Sunday, and school during the week. Mama and Dad continued going to the movies on Sunday, adding to the feeling of sameness of our world. One Sunday after dinner, the leftovers were carefully put into the refrigerator. Mama and Dad left for a late afternoon movie putting Joseph and Andy in charge of Richard and me. During the three hours we were alone in the apartment, I noticed Joseph and Andy going into the refrigerator quite often. Each time they closed the door, they walked away chewing something. Curiosity got the best of me, and so I looked inside the refrigerator. Trying to account for everything, I could see dishs of carrots, gravy, and the macaroni salad. Everything looked … oh, oh. They had picked away at the roast until it was dwindled down to half the size. We all knew better than to touch any of the leftovers. Meat was especially hard to get, and it was important that every crumb went into the main dish at mealtime. For some reason Joseph and Andy had an insatiable hunger that only meat could satisfy. I shut the refrigerator door hoping that no one would notice. When Mama and Dad returned from the movies, we knew it was time to eat dinner. Mama began to haul dishes from the refrigerator. When she reached for the dish with the roast, I held my breath. Mama was very good at keeping something from Dad; it was her way to keep the peace. The shock of how much was missing from the dish betrayed her. "What happened to all the meat?" When Mama asked that question, she knew what was likely to follow. Abruptly heading for the stove she hoped Dad hadn't heard. The meat and potatoes mixed together as a hash, there would be no way for Dad to known the meat had been nibbled to death. Now it was too late. Mama had let the beef out of the bag. Busying herself with the pans on the stove, she made a valiant effort to conceal the evidence. Dad shot straight over to the stove to see what she was talking about. Joseph and Andy huddled together like a couple of lovebirds.

Seeing them like that I thought, "Boy what a spot they're in. They know they're going to get it, but good." The expression on their faces should have given them away, or maybe it just seemed that way to me.

Dad's ear shattering voice broke the silence as he glared at the boys. "Did you do that?" Both boys shook their heads no. They were scared; too scared to tell the truth. Who wouldn't be when Dad was looking at you with that thunderstorm scowl that made your hair stand on end? Dad glared at me next, "You ate it didn't you?" I was so frightened my timid denial sealed my doom. "Yes you did. Now you go to bed without anything. You already had your supper. Go on, get out of my sight." Dad delivered a crack to my behind scurrying me into bed. The smack on my backside was nothing compared to the torture of smelling the food cooking, and knowing I was to have none of it. My bedroom was just one room away from the kitchen, and the smells drifted in with no compassion. I didn't plead my case any further; I didn't have the guts to tell Dad he was wrong. Dad had convinced himself I was the guilty party. It was my lot to go to bed, and take the blame. Mama never approved of any of us being deprived of a meal as a punishment, but her protest was overruled by Dad's logic. "She's got to learn to leave things alone!"

Hours later, I awoke to someone shaking my arm. The room was dark, the house was quiet, and the smell of dinner lingered only faintly in the air. Andy was standing by my bed holding out a glass in one hand, and a sandwich in the other. With a spring, I sat up in bed and reached out for the bread. Andy placed his finger across his lips, a signal to remain silent, then he handed me the glass. He wasn't smiling he just stood looking at me for a second, then in a low whisper said, "Get rid of the glass, Pigeon." Andy walked out of my room as quietly as he had entered. He passed through the kitchen and out into the hallway. My discreet brother had gone the long way around so as not to disturb the sleeping lion. My sandwich was heavy with peanut butter; better than beef anytime. The glass had milk in it, and even the evaporated milk tasted good. This was my reward for doing such a brave thing. After devouring my feast, I jammed the glass under a pillow, it wouldn't be seen there. Laying back down my thoughts were on Andy and what a good thing he had done for me. He took a chance passing food to me, but why did he call me Pigeon? I never heard him call me that before. "Pigeon" would remain Andy's own special name for me for years to come. That nickname was never used in a teasing or gloating way, but always with affection, and I took it no other way.

In my private world of things that I kept from Mama, this one would be different. This time two partners would carry the secret with me. United in this silent bond, there was no further discussion of the missing roast incident. It was for us, only the passing of one experience to make room for the next. The day of Mary's arrival was close at hand. The sting of what had happened was swept away, out-done by this joyous reunion.

When the day finally arrived for Mary to come home, it was a hard blow for Aunt Mildred. It was her desire to keep Mary for always, but she had to face it. Mary was, after all, an O'Brien. Nothing could change that. My sister's clothes were carried into the apartment in a huge suitcase. How different from the paper bags that Mary's clothes were packed in the day she left us. Nervously, Mildred rushed back and forth from the suitcase to the closet, to the little dresser in my room, putting Mary's things away. All while she busied herself, she was trying valiantly to hold back the tears. Uncle George stood helplessly, close by. He wasn't as openly saddened at losing his little girl, but it was in his eyes. He was more intent on how his wife was going to survive this heartbreak. "Why, when you have so many, do you have to take her away from me?" Aunt Mildred was still putting up a good fight.

"We never meant for her to be with you for so long. I guess its really all my fault." Mama walked with her arm around Mildred's shoulders. "Just because I have other children it doesn't mean that I can let one go and not miss that one. And what if the job transfer out to be a two year thing?" Mama placed her face along side Mildred's, and as if the words were meant to be a secret pact between them added, "When you come back you can have Mary at Christmas time and summer vacations. You'll have her as much as we will."

Mama hurriedly placed three coffee cups on the table. Mildred, wiped her nose, and tried to regain control as Mama poured the coffee. A freshly baked cake was in the center of the table. Mama lifted a knife to cut into it. "Don't cut any cake for me, Helen." Mildred's voice is quivery. "I couldn't eat anything." Uncle George sips his coffee quietly. Mildred stirred a bit of sugar into her cup, but couldn't drink, aimlessly toying with the spoon. Without warning Mildred jumped up and declared, "Well, I guess we'd better start back, we have a million things to do." Uncle George helped Mildred slip into her coat. He was concerned for her in a way I had never seen before. I watched fascinated by his display of devotion and kindness toward her. He must really love Mildred a lot.

Uncle George, a good looking man with tan complexion and dark wavy hair, looked like some of the leading men I had seen in the movies. Not only was he handsome, he always smelled so good. He and Mildred made a good-looking couple. My aunt and uncle had everything they could want to make life comfortable, even a car. It was a company car, but they had the use of it during the war days when gasoline and tires were hard to get. My aunt had everything but the one thing she wanted most … Mary. What a mockery this was. Mama had kids coming out of her ears; more than she and Dad could feed most times. Mildred and George had everything needed to give a child a good life, but they had none. There was talk at one time of adoption, but Mildred worried that she would get a child that came from the wrong background, adding to her heartache. Mary was made to order. Mildred had no problems accepting her as her own. Mary was family. One last kiss for their little girl, then Mildred and George departed abruptly from the apartment. Mama walked out to the car with them to say good-by. We wouldn't see our aunt and uncle again until the end of the war.

In the apartment Joseph, Andy, Richard and I took Mary into the living room and busied her, looking out the window. It was a distraction so she wouldn't see Mildred and George, the only mother and father she knew, leaving without her. For the first time since Richard was born the five of us were together at home. Mary with the added attention of her brothers and sister was unaware of the change that was taking place. Getting Mary to feel at home with us, and be a full-fledged O'Brien, wasn't going to happen overnight.

CHAPTER 7
Dad Earns A Night In Jail

Mary bellowed on and off for days; when we were ready to go to sleep Mary was wide-awake; she couldn't understand where her Mommy Mildred was. It was a blessing that Joseph was able to console her to some extent, because of his many visits to her in Hartford. Mary found comfort in his being there, Joseph was the only one she would allow to do anything for her for the first week. He had to get her ready for bed at night, and dress her again in the morning. Gradually as the time passed, Mary became at ease in her new environment. She allowed Mama to do more and more for her, then finally the day came when Mary first called her "Mama." Within three months, it was hard to remember Mary not being part of us. Mama and Dad agreed that Mildred's move so far away was the best thing that could have happened. It would be easier for Mary to become an O'Brien again with no visits from Mildred to confuse her,

Mary was the center of attention most of the time, and what a change we all were for her with so much going on and so many people. Up to now Mary's life had been a quiet, well regimented one. Never being allowed to stay dirty, she was the epitome of a little princess. Naps and playtime were on a schedule, and never went to bed without a bath.

She would get only one bath a week with us because the inconvenience created by the big galvanized tub. Besides her pretty clothes, Mary brought an assortment of toys with her. Among the books, games, and dolls, was a little red wagon that I used to take her for rides around the block. It was as close to pushing a baby carriage as I had come. Mary looked forward to those short trips into a world she had never seen so close up before. One morning we were ambled along taking in the activity around us. Shops were opening for business while a light traffic moved up and down Main Street. The smell of fresh popped corn flowed from the Woolworth Store as early shoppers began their day. There was enough activity to entertain Mary as she rode along attracting occasional helloes and smiles from total strangers.

Mary's red wagon was quite a trophy compared to our beat-up possessions; it didn't have a scratch on it. I was so proud of this little piece of perfection; sometimes we would go around the block several times. It was on our last trip around that I noticed a young boy crossing in the middle of Main Street. I knew immediately it was the Goldman kid, Louis Goldman. He and his family lived on the other side of the street above his father's clothing store. Louis was three years older than me, and a bully with a reputation for getting into fights. When Louis reached our side of the street, he stopped and took a casual position by a lamp post. He was dressed to the hilt with his bright blue shirt with fancy gold buttons. I wasn't too disturbed by his presence until I notice of a handful of stones that he tumbled from one hand into the other. I never looked to the left or right, but made believe he wasn't there. Looking unconcerned on the outside, on the inside I was nervous and ready for trouble. Passing Louis proved to be easy, and I thought, "Maybe he's not in the mood for a fight." It wasn't my day for such a break. He let out a laugh, poking fun at the wagon.

"Look at that piece of junk. You think you're so smart." There was no end to his jeers, and he added to them by pinging stones off the wheels of the wagon.

"Hey, watch it." I said.

"What are you gonna do about it?"

I knew he was trying to goad me into an argument. He followed us all the way up Main Street, hopeful that I would try to do something about it. I was determined I wasn't going to; not another word would pass my lips even if it killed me. Still, my anger was growing. We reached Gardner St. corner and although Louis had run out of stones, he continued to sling comments at us about the wagon. The sight of our apartment building gave me a safe feeling. I simply couldn't hold back any longer. "Yer just jealous 'cause you don't own it!" Out of nowhere, a fist slammed into my jaw. Everything went black, for a few seconds. I fell against the glass window of the store behind me. Having never been almost knocked out before it scared me half to death. My outburst of tears sent Louis running back across the street where he lived. All the while Mary watched not understanding, but eventually thought it appropriate for her to cry too. Tearfully we headed for home. Mama met us at the door.

"Kali, what's wrong?"

"That Goldman kid hit me."

"Where?"

"On Main Street."

"No, where did he *hit* you?"

"Right here, and he almost knocked me out."

"That big bully did hit her, Joseph. Look there's a big red mark on her face." Joseph, who had been sitting at the kitchen table, jumped to his feet. "I'll take care of him. Where is he now?"

"He ran home." I whined.

"Come on. We're gonna find him!"

Joseph grabbed me by the hand as he darted for the door. My tears weren't dry yet and we were on our way to get revenge. He never spoke another word, but Joseph's vigorous stride kept my feet moving like trip hammers. The older boys knew Louis, but they generally ignored him because his size made a confrontation seem unfair. This was unbelievable. People generally tried to avoid this blockhead, but here we were trying to find him. By the time we reached the building where Louis lived, my hand was red inside of Joseph's tight grip. In the hallway where he lived, Louis sat on the stairs with another boy. Joseph moved from the street into the doorway, popping into view with the sprung of a jack-in-the-box. Louis looked up not realize at first who was glaring at him with a not too-happy look on his face. When he did realize it, his eyes grew big and a sagging jaw revealed a red piece of candy in his mouth. Joseph walked silently closer to Louis. My brother was overwhelming no doubt, being older and taller. The second boy bolted out the door, passing the giant as fast as he could, and high-tailed it down the street. Louis tried to scramble to his feet, but there was no room for him to stand up with Joseph looming over him. Joseph grabbed him by the shirtfront. Golden buttons flew in every direction pinging off the wall and floor like mini machine gun bullets.

"Is this the kid that hit you?" Joseph asked. He had drawn Louis up close to him, face to face.

"Yes," I answered.

With a hand full of shirt, Joseph swung Louis toward me. Louis, helpless as a marionette following the pull of its strings, gasped as the piece of candy unexpectedly slid down his throat.

"Hit him, go on. Punch him in the face just like he did you." Joseph's anger was frightening, and Louis was swung even closer to me. I expected Joseph to do the punching, not me.

"No," was all I could squeak out. Then Joseph, his fist aimed at Louis's face, lowered his voice to a most unsettling softness.

"You want to know how it feels to be a punching bag for someone bigger than you? If I ever hear that you've touched my sisters or anyone else in town again, I'll punch your nose clear to the back of your head. Only next time I won't come alone."

"I'm gonna tell my father what you did to my shirt."

"Good. I'd love to talk to him. How 'bout right now?"

"Okay … Okay," was all Louis could muster up. With a push, Joseph sent Louis sprawling against the stairs. A position that he rapidly recovered from, and ran up, taking steps two by two with his button-less shirt flapping like wings.

Joseph turned to me and grinned, "He won't bother you again. He won't stop running even after he runs out of stairs."

When Joseph and I returned to the apartment, we told Mama how scared Louis was when he saw Joseph; that alone was satisfaction enough. I was so proud, and Joseph was right. From then on, not only did Louis behave, he wouldn't even walk on the same side of the street as me.

"Next time I see his mother I'm gonna tell her about this and don't think I won't!" Mama wasn't that easily satisfied. "You go back out there … walk around the block all you want," she told me. Mama reminded me of a mother bear protecting her cubs whenever any of us had a problem. She could turn from the soft gentle spoken soul she was to a mass of protective energy. It mattered not who the offender was. No one escaped her fury. Not that she got violent; it was all in the way she acted, and what she said.

Sometime after that scuffle with Louis, Mama did prove how serious she was about protecting her brood. It happened on a Saturday night after Dad had been downtown all day. Because he worked only a half-day on Saturday, it was usual for Dad to spend the remainder of the day there. It was a short walk from the bicycle factory to Danahey's Bar, but Dad wouldn't go to the bar right away. He'd stop at the barbershop first. Sitting contentedly in the big chair, tucked away in a corner, he would read Nick's copy of the "Chipwey Signal" from beginning to end. Dad had everything he needed down there … if he got hungry there was the little meat market across the street, if he got thirsty, there was always Danahey's right next door. We were in bed fast asleep, when Dad finally came home that night. Coming into to a quiet house didn't mean he had to be quiet. His talk was loud, and as if a prelude to sleep, he had to start an argument with Mama. Depending on how much he had to drink, and how fast sleep would overtake him. The arguments could be anything from a small rumble to a full-blown earthquake; no one knew until it was over how bad it would be.

For some reason on this particular night, he was both very drunk and very argumentative; perhaps he had lost a bet on the fights or the horse races. Being the bad looser he was, his temper would reflect the anger he felt. Whatever the reason, a loud confrontation followed from the minute he entered the bedroom. Mama tried to hush him, but that only seemed to annoy him more. Mary and I were awakened by his loud voice, so were Joseph and Andy, and probably a couple of people in nearby apartments. Joseph and Andy waited the argument out, not saying a word, but ready to intervene if things turned rough. Dad had never hit Mama before, but there was always a first time. The sound of a lamp falling to the floor alerted both boys. Andy was first to respond. Sitting up in bed he called out, "Mama, are you aw right?"

Before Mama could answer him, Dad had jumped out of bed, and made his way to my brother's bedroom. Dad threw the door open shouting, "Keep your damn mouth shut," following it up with a swinging blow to Andy's face. Andy had spent his twelve years proving he was tough enough to handle anything, but that hard wallop brought tears to his eyes, and blood running from his nose. Joseph had jumped out of bed and was ready for whatever had to be done. Mama was close behind Dad and seeing what he had done, became blinding mad.

"Look what you did to that boy, get out of here and go to bed where you belong." Mama yelled at him.

"Kids should mind their own business."

"Shut up you big coward… "

Dad slunk back to bed concerned only with sleep.

Mama wasn't thinking about going to sleep, she was fit to be tied. She would see that he didn't take his anger out on the children again. After applying a wet washcloth to Andy's throbbing nose, she quietly dressed and slipped from the apartment disappearing down the two flights of stairs. With Mama's absence, an eerie silence filled the apartment. Mary drifted back to sleep, but I remained awake, afraid to move. Joseph and Andy waited and watched from a front room window for Mama's return. A short time later a car drove up in front of the building; a police car. Much to their surprise, Mama emerged from the back seat, and two policemen from the front; together the three walked into the building.

The two boys stayed in the darkened room and listened to what was going on.

"Come on Bob. Come on get up … get dressed."

His response was a low-pitched mumble as the two policemen helped him from the bed. Giving no resistance, Dad dressed and was escorted out of the apartment, down the stairs, and into the patrol car. Joseph and Andy watched from their front row seats at the window, and couldn't believe what they saw. They watched as the car drove to the corner, heading in the direction of the police station. There would be no more hitting or arguing this night; Mama Bear had seen to that.

Mama's good common sense served her well. The most important thing to her in life was her family, the same family that Dad seemed to be able to emotionally distance from. Still, Mama was trapped by a firm conviction that she couldn't get along without him. Even when, what he gave was never enough, Mama thought it was better than she could do by herself. I know too, that something called love molded Mama's forgiving nature.

The morning after Dad was arrested he was to be taken to the county seat in the town of Morgan, where he would appear before a judge. Mama did it up right the night before. Not only did she have him arrested for the night, but swore out a complaint against him. Dad would have to answer to a judge now. Before starting out for the twelve-mile trip to Morgan, Dad had asked for a change of clothes, and a talk with his wife. They agreed, and around nine o'clock Dad was escorted home by two officers. Mama asked Joseph and Andy to take the rest of us into the front room to remove us from the grown-up talk. We marched single file in the direction of the front room with me last in line. I walked looking back over my shoulder, and became a little straggled from the ranks. There was a strange air of excitement seeing two fully uniformed policemen standing in our kitchen with our very disheveled father. I had never known anyone who had been in jail before, and it was hard to believe there was someone in the world that could tell our father what to do.

"Kali, go along now." Mama was impatient and motioned with her hand to keep walking. I scurried through the doorway, but stood behind the door listening.

Dad took Mama into the dining room where they talked. The two policemen watched from the kitchen. Dad pleaded with Mama to drop the charges. His biggest defense was that he would lose his job at the factory, and all the seniority he had built up over the past fifteen years would be destroyed. Then there was the matter of Mama being in a family way, it just wouldn't do anyone any good with him sitting in jail. Mama had a big decision to make. She was insecure and scared enough to think Dad made sense. He was a pathetic looking thing, unshaven and dressed in rumpled clothes. He obviously moved Mama with his lost little boy look. She made him promise never to touch any of us kids again, because the next time she wouldn't drop the charges. Peeking a look through the crack in the door, I saw our terror of a father close to tears as he embraced Mama. To see Dad in tears was an uncomfortable experience. Mama demanded that he stop drinking. This gave her hope that maybe he had received a good scare this time; perhaps he would stop. She didn't realize that it couldn't be accomplished as easily as that, none of us did … Mama was the only one to believe he would change, but the pattern would continue.

After Dad bathed and changed into a set of clean clothes, Mama made his breakfast. He was quiet and acted withdrawn, very different for Dad. He retreated to the solace of the front room, turned on the radio to polka music, and settled into his chair to read.

It was Sunday, Joseph and Andy were out together, Mary and I had been outside playing but there was a strange attraction pulling me back into the apartment. Mama was in the kitchen making a salad for Sunday dinner.

"Where's Mary?" Mama asked as I entered the room.

"Bathroom. Where's Dad?"

"He's in the front room, why?"

"Can I go in and see him?"

"Sure you can, but don't say anything about being in jail."

"Okay," I answer on the run.

Heading for the front room, I couldn't help wondering if he would look different or something, he used to be a good looking man when he was clean shaven. Crossing in front of him to get to the other side of his chair my eyes were glued on his face. He was made uneasy by my steady stare. He adjusted himself in the chair, and fidgeted with the paper trying to fold it. Finally he spoke. "Hi." I walked closer to him, and smiled.

Dad looked puzzled, waiting for me to say something, and what came out would have been better off forgotten. "Were you really in jail?" The words were hardly out of my mouth when I knew. What a blunder, and Mama had warned me too. Dad looked up from his paper with a blank look on his face. Boy, I really knew how to hurt a guy. I walked out of the room faster than I had entered. When would I learn to keep my big mouth shut? Traveling like sixty, I made my way out to Mama and told her what I had said. She puffed a sigh of exasperation.

"What did he say?"

"Nothin', he looked at me funny."

"It's all right, take Mary, go back out and play."

"Are they gonna take him away again when it's dark out?"

"No! Now run along and watch out for Mary."

Ah, but there was still something more. "Did they make him eat bread and water?"

"NO! Will you go outside and play, and please forget about last night? PLEASE!"

Dad was so good for several weeks after that. He came home earlier, and wasn't drunk once. He didn't stop drinking, but he was quieter, and easier to talk to; life was peaceful. Five weeks later Dad came home drunk again for the first time. It had been some time since Dad brought ice cream home with him, an obvious peace offering. A measure of control still seemed to exist.

April, the month of warming weather, was Joseph's birthday month. On the fourth, he would turn fourteen. Seven days after that Jimmy was born bringing our total to six. The crib in Mama's room was occupied again. Three months later Reeg had her baby, and it was a boy just as Larry wanted. Larry began working night shifts at his job to earn more money, and this took him out of our lives in a more permanent way. Our summer games dwindled without him, and Joseph and Andy didn't find it very challenging playing only with smaller kids.

For Andy and me the hunting trips up and down back alleys went on as usual that summer, but as winter closed in on us, slim pickings got even slimmer. In the winter, harvesting anything of value was difficult because of the snow. We found that oranges and apples lying overnight beneath a cold blanket of snow didn't survive with much flavor at all, and empty bottles were as scarce as T-bone steaks. Still, all was not lost; if one avenue of resource were closed, we would find another. This particular winter my two older brothers decided it was time I had a hand in earning some money of my own. Except for an occasional movie, I was never welcome when the boys went out together; so being included when they shoveled snow, made me feel quite grown up. Every Friday the three of us would watch and hope for a fresh snowfall, and when it did come, we would be up early Saturday morning to get the best places to shovel. Joseph and Andy had several regular customers, mostly older people who found it difficult to do the job. The first time I went snow shoveling was on a Saturday morning after a heavy snowfall. With shovels slung over their shoulders, my brothers led the way as we headed out. Tromping through the heavy snow, grown up or not, I had a suspicion that this might not be fun; although it was going to take me to my favorite place up on the hill. Unwilling to carry my shovel as my brothers did, I took the easy way and dragged it behind. We slogged through the fresh snow down Main Street, up past the Rialto Theater, and into the park. The benches that usually lined the paths there had been stored weeks ago, exposing the park as a wide-open stretch of ground. The round cement pond that filled the summer with refreshing sounds of bubbling water lay mute. Buried beneath the cover of winter its outline gave only a vague hint as to its being. The bandstand stood at the far end of the park, draped in winter's white coat. The outdoor sounds were muffled in the earth's fullness of the snow. I could hardly hear the sound of my shovel trailing behind me over the white surface.

We crossed the street from the park, and headed for our first stop, a dark, menacing-looking structure. It loomed three stories upward and stood in ghostly contrast against the white snow. Something about this house made me feel uneasy. It was a house of at least a hundred windows, some were tall and skinny, others wide with arched cornices. The windows on the upper floors with shades half drawn, looked like eyes with lids half closed. There was no mistaking it. Those windows were the eyes of the house giving me the once over! An enormous porch stretched across the front of the house and wrapped around to the side, I wondered where it led. The bare trees that surrounded the front grounds seemed to claw with bony fingers upward at the gray winter sky. What a setting for this scary pile of bricks!

"W-we don't want to go here, do we?" I chattered, chilled by the cold. My remark got instant reply from Andy.

"You bet your life we do. This is one of our best customers. Look at all the paths to the back yard, and look at all that sidewalk. Come on Pigeon keep up. It's not gonna look good if you can't keep up."

Joseph had already climbed the steps and was ringing the front door bell. I was beginning to be sorry that I had come along on this venture. I hung back refusing to climb the giant stairs of the scary porch. A few moments after Joseph rang the bell, the door opened. The conversation was brief; I wasn't able to see who they were talking to. When the conversation was finished, the two boys bounded down the porch steps. "Dig in Pigeon. We got lots of shoveling to do." Andy beamed as though he had found a dollar bill in the snow.

"You take the side path over there. You should be able to handle that," Joseph pointed to a depression in the snow that concealed a walkway. Unsure of the task, my shovel made a pitiful attempt at first. Oddly enough, the longer I shoveled the easier it became. The longer I worked the warmer I got. The melting snow on my warm gloved hands sent little whiffs of steam in the air. Snow shoveling was a whole new delight.

An hour later, we had shoveled everything. When Joseph was satisfied that we had done a good job he headed for a side door. "The man told us to come to this door when we finished," he reminded Andy.

This time I wanted to see who lived here. Standing very close to Joseph as he reached for the doorbell, I was prepared to see a grumpy old man. He surely will have small squinty eyes, and deep wrinkles in his face. A worn old blanket will be draped over his shoulders to keep his frail body warm. I'll bet he won't have a warm house either, probably too stingy to pay for heat. Finally, he'll be leaning on a gnarled wooden cane, most likely a branch cut from that ghastly old tree in the front yard. Well … he'd better pay us for our hard work. The door opened, the face that greeted the three of us was a smiling happy one, almost elfin-like. "Come in children you must be frozen." The little man stood back allowing the three of us to enter. The part of the house we were in was a large pantry where he had three cups of cocoa shelf.

"And … and what's this? Peanut butter cookies!"

"Drink the cocoa it will help to warm you, have all the cookies you want, I'll get your money." The small figure moved across the room with no effort at all. He passed through a swinging door and the absence of a cane was very noticeable.

We gulped the cocoa down. Joseph and Andy munched on their cookies, but I chose to stash mine in a pocket. Presently the man returned and handed Joseph four dollars. It was a veritable fortune to my eyes. Joseph took the money, "Thanks Mr. Young."

For once, we had folding money for our efforts and not just a handful of coins. Now I understood why Joseph and Andy picked this kind of work; it paid well. Gushing with excitement over our good fortune, I began babbling away about the money. It was Andy, the realist, who brought me back to earth, "We're not finished yet Pigeon. We may get a couple more small jobs up the street. Come on. Shake a leg." Grabbing my shovel, I swung it over my shoulder. Quite proud of myself, I had a spring in my step following my brothers as their long strides carried them steps ahead of me. Pausing for a second, I took one last look at the house that had frightened me so. The ominous look was gone. Huh! What could have made the change?

I notice Andy brushing snow from a low sign that jutted out of the snow bank. The sign read: Home of the VFW. The boys continued talking as they walked along, but I wanted to know what this meant. I interrupted their conversation.

"Hey, what's VFW mean Joseph?"

"It means Veterans of Foreign Wars."

"What do they do there?"

"Why, are you thinking about joining?" Andy teased.

"It's like a club for people who have fought a war in another country," Joseph explained.

"Like the solders in the war now?"

"Yea."

"Veterans are nice, aren't they? Think you and Andy will ever be a solder?"

"Maybe … someday."

Joseph looked down and smiled at me. His short breaths puffed spurts of white steam in the cold winter air.

"Company Harch!" Andy held his shovel like a rifle and barked out the command. Joseph reacted by holding his shovel like a rifle too. "Hut 2-3-4, hut 2-3-4." The boys stood straight and tall then stepped lively as they pretended to be soldiers marching. I trailed behind mimicking them.

The rest of the morning was spent on our snow shoveling jobs. We earned five dollars and thirty-five cents for our mornings work. Mama would be given some of the money to help buy food. It was good to be heading home at last. The spark had waned from our step as we trudged home tired, and hungry. My cookies had given out long ago. The only thing that kept me going was the thought of spending the afternoon in a warm movie theater, my reward for helping. The newsreel at the movies was my only way of understanding what war was really like. I couldn't imagine how anyone could stand the noise of the bombs and shooting.

Eight months later peace would finally silence the guns and bombs once and for all.

At school, special trips were made to the church to say the rosary for peace. Mama stayed close to the radio throughout her day, and said her prayers as she waited patiently for good news. August 14, 1945 at 7 PM the good news came. The man on the radio announced very emotionally, that Japan had signed an unconditional surrender. The war with Japan was finished. The word spread like wildfire around Chipwey, sending an outpouring of people into the streets like nothing I had seen before. Running to the corner of Main Street, my brothers and I watched an unforgettable celebration exploding before our eyes.

People were leaning out of windows up and down the flag-lined street throwing shredded paper and hats out to the road below. Many picked up the hats and threw them up into the air again. Some were throwing handfuls of nickels, dimes and pennies into the street for the sake of having nothing else to throw. Others threw confetti and rolls of toilet paper from the windows. They cheered as the cylinders of paper unraveled, trailing their quivering long tails in their earthly flight. The jubilant crowd had completely taken over Main Street making car travel impossible. Stranger embraced stranger and many kissed in celebration sharing the long awaited moment of joy. Young men shaking bottles of beer and soda sprayed them into the air like small fountains. Someone shoved a bottle of soda into my hand and said, "Here kid … celebrate!" Not having the knack for doing it, I shook the bottle and ended up with a sticky wet face. I laughed. My brothers laughed. The whole world was sweet and bubbly.

The whistle at the firehouse was sounding a frantic voice but this time not to warn of a fire or a blackout. It was saying that peace was tight in our hands. There could never be another war as cruel as this one was. It was time to celebrate not the time to wonder of another war, and so we danced in the streets and sang "God Bless America" until we were hoarse. All the churches around Chipwey rang their bells in thanksgiving for all the prayers that were answered. It was midnight before the crowds finally started to break up. For a little town that usually put the cat out at nine o'clock, that wasn't bad. In the morning, we were up earlier than usual. The excitement of the night before was still hanging in the air. Even the birds sounded more cheerful. Sleep was the last thing we wanted now. Andy was on his way out the door as I ran to catch up with him.

"Where are you going?"

"Main Street."

"Why?"

"Treasure hunt."

"At 6:30? Can I go?"

"I guess."

Main Street was deserted in this early hour, not like the night before when it had all the activity of an anthill. Walking down the middle of the road, Andy occasionally kicked the mass of paper and debris to one side or the other hunting for the treasure that all this stuff could be hiding. He knew it was important to get to the street before the street sweeper did. If anyone was going to get the coins that lay there, he was. This time the money wouldn't be pooled and divided, Andy said. Whatever we found we could keep, that was the rule for today. Our find wasn't overwhelming, but what we found made us feel fortunate.

Then we heard a familiar rumble, Uncle John was coming down the street driving the huge sweeper. Soon, this thing with the ravenous appetite would gobble everything up. "Did you find anything?" John hollered above the noise. Andy did a "thumbs-up." John shook his head and winked.

The next two days were declared holidays, and on August 15, a parade marched down Main Street and into the park where some city officials made speeches from the bandstand.

An unforgettable moment that day was the last entry in the parade. A convertible drove very slowly down Main Street; it was unlike any car around Chipwey. Mama told me it was a foreign car. Standing on tiptoe, I did my best to see around the taller adults that stood in front of me. The top of the convertible was turned back revealing the occupants inside.

The driver was dressed in military uniform and in the back seat; I could only see the tops of three heads of the figures riding there. When they rode by, the crowd went wild. It was easy to tell. These men were not very popular.

"Who are they, Mama?"

"They're not real men they're dummies." Mama looked at me for a second then laughed. "I mean they aren't real people, and yes they were dummies. They're replicas of the men who kept the war going all these years."

"What are they gonna to do with 'em? Can we follow too?"

"Come on."

For Mama, cutting a path through the crowd, with Jimmy in the stroller was easy. I held on tightly to Richard's hand, as the whole crowd seemed to move like a giant wave, carrying us along in the direction of the slowly moving car. It came to a halt in front of City Hall. The crowd was silent as, one by one, the dummies were taken from the car, and a rope slipped around their necks. A sign dangling around the neck of each dummy had a name written on it, Hitler, Mussolini, and ToJo. Not until the last one was hoisted into place on makeshift scaffold, did the crowd let up an ear splitting roar. I thought this a rather gruesome thing to do until Mama told me; "They're hanging them in effigy; the people's way of letting off steam for all the suffering they caused. Families will be reunited now, but it's going to be hard for those whose loved ones didn't survive the war." They hung there like that the whole day, swinging with each push of a breeze.

It was over, but the healing was just beginning. For us luckier people whose country had not been torn apart by the war, we would concentrate on smaller losses. The end of this wearisome struggle had brought some immediate changes in our everyday life. The rationing of canned goods and gasoline were lifted immediately. It would take two more months before meat and butter would be in the stores in good supply. Our precious two scoops of sugar for our milk had to wait even longer. It wasn't until January of '46 that the rationing of sugar, like the war itself, took its place in history. For my family there was still one war left to fight. The struggle to survive each day would continue.

CHAPTER 8
Mama Reveals Her Secret Hoard

The fire escape outside the front room window was a favorite retreat for Joseph and Andy on humid August nights. The infrequent drafts of air outside were warm, but life was more livable out there than inside the stuffy apartment. One evening Mama and I leaned out the window talking with them as they lounged on blankets spread over the uncomfortable iron bars. We exchanged thoughts about everything from stars to a stray cat that prowled the street below. The main topic seemed to linger longest around Eloise, our illustrious Landlady who did not approve of anyone sitting out on the fire escape. She worried that the bolts holding the fire escape to the building would loosen, or that one of us would fall to the street below. On nights like this, it was too tempting.

"Boy if ol' Eloise could see us now," Andy quipped, "She'd have a heart attack."

"I wonder how she keeps cool. Could be she's floatin' around in a big pool right now," says Joseph.

"Nope. A moat around her house loaded with crocodiles is her speed." We giggle at Andy's sarcasm.

"Eloise has all anyone could want, a beautiful home, a yard full of flowers and trees," Mama interjected. We were surprised that Mama knew anything about Eloise's backyard.

Andy was quick to question. "When were you at Eloise's house?" "Not me, Daddy. A few years ago, he fixed a radio for her. They let him in by the back door."

"Huh. Back door." Joseph mumbles. "That figures."

Mama continues. "Daddy said her back yard was beautiful. No swimming pool, but there was a gazebo and a glider swing. We don't have to worry about Eloise."

"Was Grandma's house bigger?" Andy asks.

"Our house was a good size, not a mansion like Eloise's."

"But you lived by the woods. Eloise doesn't. That's better than an old ga-zeee-bo," With an air of anger Andy punches up the pillow behind his head.

"It must be nice to live close to the woods, n'go exploring, n'hiking, n' swing on Tarzan monkey vines," Joseph adds.

A peculiar vine that grew in the woods was said to have once hosted a wild grape. For some unexplained reason the grapes disappeared leaving only the vines to carry on any trace of their existence. The vines took several years to grow up the trunk of a tree, and after withering, hung from tree branches like thick ropes just begging to be swung on. Pretending to be Tarzan of the jungle and having his own monkey vines was appealing to Andy. "Yeahhh." He sighed.

Mama toyed with the plain silver band on her finger. Thoughts were off in a different direction from monkey vines. She spoke softly and slowly. "In the woods there's a spot I called Moss Rock. It was a secret place to be alone and solve problems. Sitting there, I could lose my worries just listening to the winds as it swept through the trees. It was the sound of rustling skirts at a dance." A compassionate, soft breeze curled around us as though it was thanking Mama for those good memories. Mama lifted her face to feel the gentle touch from her old friend.

"Nuts to the rustling skirts," Andy snapped. "What else did you do? Were there any monkey vines there, or apple trees?"

"Only crab apples, but lots of berry bushes, and wild flowers. I picked violets and lilies of the valley every spring." Mama paused, closed her eyes and drew a deep breath; "I've never smelled a perfume that good. I used to pick little bouquets and take them to my mother and … oh … I almost forgot … the diamonds." Mama struck a bare nerve in Andy. His leap to get closer to her was a careless move.

"Ouch! Andy, watch it." Joseph said drawing his legs up.

"Sorry," Andy didn't even look back to survey the damage. "Diamonds? How could you forget that? Where do you find them? Are they worth anything?"

"Not much."

"Where do you look for them? How do you find them?"

"I found them mostly around that big mossy rock I used to sit on. After a rain the diamonds came to the surface around its base."

"How do you get 'em. With a shovel?"

"The best way is after a rain. When the topsoil gets washed away, they'll break the surface. All you need are hands to brush the dirt away. After a winter thaw is a real good time to look for them."

"Did you ever try to sell them?" Andy asked settling back on his haunches.

"A jeweler told me they were a type of crystal, and it wasn't likely that you would find a flawless one. If you did, it could be made into a ring. A whole bunch was only worth a couple dollars."

"Can you still find them there"

"I don't know … it's been a long time. I would imagine so."

It boggled our minds to think we grew diamonds right here in Chipwey. We agreed, valuable or not, it was incredible to be able to pick diamonds out of the ground like violets. Feeling sorry that Mama's diamonds weren't real, I put my arm around her and snuggled close, "That wasn't fair, they weren't real." Mama hugged me back. "Don't feel sorry for me," she said, brushing stray hairs from my forehead, "I have all the precious diamonds I could want, right here."

"I never saw any diamonds. Where are they?"

"She means US ya lunk head." Andy throws me an agitated look.

We talked on a bit more about the diamonds, and the woods, until we heard the cat on the street below give out a howl. "Git outa here." Dad grumbled, as he swung a foot out causing the frightened cat to scoot under a parked car. That was the signal; everything was over, it would soon be bedtime. Joseph and Andy would spend the night on the fire escape. That night I fell asleep dreaming of a tree-covered wood that grew flowers for Mama, and diamonds enough for all our fingers and toes.

It was almost as though Eloise had overheard our un-flattering remarks that night, and was retaliating by raising our rent. It was the second time this happened in our five years on Gardner Street. Dad said it was time to look for another place. Dad found a place for us all right. The apartment was around the corner and only a half a block down the street from where we lived. There would be less rent to pay and it did have one more bedroom for our growing family. When Mama saw the apartment, she was disappointed. The price paid for getting one more bedroom was smaller rooms; size wasn't the only drawback. The apartment was dirty, the walls were yellow with age, and the floors … nothing covered the stained, scared wooden planks. A black electrical wire hanging from the ceiling in the middle of the kitchen had a light bulb screwed into its socket. That was the kitchen light. From the moment I laid eyes on it, it was a hateful sight. I had passed by this building many times in my travels around the block. It was strange to know this was to be our next home. My beautiful bay window was to be left behind for this plain flat-faced building on Albany Street. I felt any chance to live up on the hill was slipping further from our grasp.

Our "new" apartment was one of four in the building, and again we were on the third floor. We still had two flights of stairs to climb, but these were narrow and dimly lit. Quite a difference from the wide stairs and spacious hallways we had on Gardner Street. The first room that would need a going over was the kitchen. Wallpaper was in order here. "Something cheery, and for heavens sake clean looking," Mama said.

Andy and I watched the kids the first day, as Mama and Joseph started out with several rolls of wallpaper to begin their work. The papering took all day, and by late afternoon, they were tired and pushing to finish the job. The last strip had been pasted. Joseph steadied himself on the pasting table ready to stick it to the wall. "Be careful, Joseph. That table has an awful wobble." Mama stood back to watch Joseph match up the wallpaper. His strained arms slapped the paper against the wall.

"Does that look … ?"

"Oh! Joseph… " The table tipped sideways carrying Joseph and everything with it. " …The table. Look at the table!" After all, the table was a rented piece of equipment that Mama didn't want to have to pay for it.

"Oh fine, worry about the table, never mind me," Joseph sat in the middle of the spilled paste. They laughed as they pulled the pasty strip of paper from Joseph's hair. Mama and Joseph were still laughing when they returned home. Despite the minor accident, the kitchen was a credit to their hard work. We must have looked like a small army on maneuvers as we traveled back and forth from Gardner Street to Albany Street carrying paint cans, newspapers, brushes, and rollers. Every one of us who could handle a brush or roller had to help. The faster the job was finished the faster we would see moving day.

Upon entering, a long narrow hallway ran from one end of the apartment to the other. To the right of the door, I could see the newly papered kitchen where two long windows graced the far wall. Between the windows was the only space in the room where our faithful old stove could fit. Laying my armload of papers and rags down, I was drawn to look out one of the windows. It gave a magnificent wide view of a large courtyard. Each building that bordered all four sides had businesses on the street level floors. To the left of us was a noisy auto repair shop emitting the smell of car oil and gas. To the right of us was a tall brick wall, a warehouse for beer. Although the center of the courtyard was roomy enough, it was covered with crushed rock, not a blade of grass in sight. An alleyway served as gateway from the street to the courtyard.

"Look Pigeon, that's the back of the Woolworth Store, and over there, that's the back of Newberry's." Andy was giving me a king's tour of our new backyard. Certainly if anyone knew the back alleys of Chipwey, Andy did. There was an aura of excitement in Andy's words. Imagine, playing in the backyard of the five and dime stores, almost an honor. Then pointing to the extreme left of the window, Andy brought attention to another business. There it stood, the back of the Belmont Bar and Grill. "Look at all of those empty bottles stacked out there. Have you ever seen so many?" Andy whispered. "Think of all those deposits." The sight of those empties alone, were enough to make this move worthwhile.

Looking over our vast empire, I notice that there was a landing outside the window. It was the porch roof of the apartment below. It was apparent that we would have to stand out on the roof to hang laundry. The clothesline was strung from alongside the kitchen window to the brick wall of the beer warehouse, a precarious place to hang clothes. There was no railing around the roof, and anyone wandering too close to the edge could easily fall three stories down. We'd have to keep a watchful eye on the small kids. Continuing my tour, I saw the dining room that Mama spoke of. She was doubtful that our dining room table, ol' elephant-legs, would fit there. There was no way we could all gather around the table at one time in the small kitchen; big or small, this dining room would have to do.

Two bedrooms opened to that tunnel-like hall, but Mary and I wouldn't share in this convenience. The only way to our bedroom was through our parent's room. A touch of the past from our old apartment made worse by the absence of a door between the rooms. A cloth drape would be hung for as much privacy as it would allow. I'm sure Mama recognized all of these shortcomings. The fresh paint gave a smell of newness to each room, and with the new kitchen linoleum shinning back at us; we were pleased with the results of our labor. Maybe this wouldn't be so bad after all. Our faithful old stove was the first thing moved into the apartment and was placed between the two kitchen windows. As Mama suspected, when ol' elephant-legs was moved into the dining room, its massiveness nearly devoured the whole room. With the six chairs placed around it, there was no more than three feet of space on any side.

Sometime after moving into the apartment, we learned that we were destined to share our living space with roaches. In the beginning, we never suspected a thing, thanks to the strong smell of the fresh paint; as the odor grew weaker, they slowly began their invasion. We had never lived with bugs, and these must be the worst of the lot. They were into everything. After a few inquiries with some of our neighbors, Mama found that they were the plague of all four apartments. We loathed these dirty beggars. In the darkness of the cupboard, they crawled over dishes, cups and bowls, anything that lay in their path. It became automatic for us to wipe every dish off before eating from it. At night, Mama covered the caps of the salt and pepper shakers with wax paper and held them in place with rubber bands to keep out the contamination.

We came to know the full meaning of the words, "scattering like roaches." We hated that time most, coming into the apartment at night and turning the light on. Reaching out in the dark until we felt the string that hung from the dangling light bulb, then giving it a tug, was a dread none of us ever overcame. Roaches crawling up the electrical wire, or clinging to the ceiling, would drop to the floor when light flooded the room. A quick step to the side with an arm slung over the head was one way to avoid the enemy from dropping down on us. Mama sprayed when they became intolerable, but this was done with much discretion. She was afraid the smaller children would get into the stuff and poison themselves. If one of the other tenants sprayed and failed to warn the rest of us, there would be an exodus by the hundreds into the other three apartments. Once there were so many, they even took refuge inside the clock on the kitchen wall.

The bathroom measured only six feet wide and five feet deep, just enough room for a toilet, no sink. It was a chilling experience going into that little room, especially at night. It took only once to feel something crawling across your bare foot, so when we sat on the toilet, we rested our feet on the backs of our heels or drew them up from the floor completely. The kitchen was the main attraction for the roaches. The only sink in the apartment was in the kitchen. Everything from dish washing to teeth brushing was done there. Hiding under the sink was a favorite hangout. If a dirty frying pan was left in the dishwater to soak, it was an open invitation; they'd use the water like a swimming hole. Day after day Mama continued to do battle with them. Unable to endure the struggle any longer, she went to the landlord for a solution. He was a short man with a perpetual smile, who gave the impression of being easy to deal with. Mama's light-handed conversation was met with unyielding resistance. Forced to use stronger language, which for Mama meant words like darn, stinking, and skinflint, she insisted it was his responsibility to exterminate.

"Each tenant has to take care of that, Mrs. O'Brien."

"You're renting infested apartments. That's unhealthy."

"I'm not wasting money on people whose bad housekeeping habits keep bringing the bugs back. Read your lease."

"I didn't agree to anything like that."

"Bob did. See." A thin finger pointed to Dad's scrawl on the lease. "My building is better than most. Some have rats."

Mama had fought a good fight, but lost. She was furious, grumbling all the way home about his attitude. We were hardly inside the door when Mama began telling Joseph and Andy of her encounter with "Simon Legree," as she took to calling him. "Can you imagine him saying a thing like that?"

Andy was peeling a potato as he listened to Mama's story. It was customary to sprinkle salt on a raw potato then eaten like an apple. With one eye on Mama and one on the saltshaker, Andy began to shake the salt on the potato. Suddenly, he grimaced. The shaker had the squashed remains of a roach stuck to its bottom. "Even though we have to share our food with roaches, I guess we should be thankful. At least we don't have any rats hogging the food too," Andy said. Holding the shaker up for a better look at the victim hanging there by a thread, he added, "Can you imagine a rat hanging there like that?"

The four of us broke out in laughter. The anger of the moment was gone; there never were any rats, the roaches did remain a curse for our entire time served on Albany Street. There was no choice but to adjust we all had to learn to do battle with the bugs. We'd crush, stamp, beat, and pulverize any that dared to show face in the open. One thing for sure, there wasn't much food for them to find. When there was something to eat, every morsel was devoured by us. I'll bet ours were the skinniest roaches in all of Chipwey.

The changes that invaded our lives on Albany Street were far from pleasant. Every time a modern well-equipped kitchen was shown in a movie, I wondered what it would be like cooking in a kitchen like that. I was certain, Mama and I would never know. We were doomed to our inadequate surroundings and daily fights with these panhandling pests.

Starving roaches weren't the only headache that Mama was confronted with. Jimmy, almost three years old, was able to play outside with us. Mama had two more knees to patch up from spills on the gravel in the courtyard. Interest in our new surroundings, with all the new places to explore, waned as they became more familiar. The only source of excitement that never lost its spark was the back of the Belmont Bar. It was so simple to lift one of the bottles from a case, and take it to a store for the deposit. The bottles were never monitored very closely; until we came along it wasn't necessary. It took little effort to walk by, snatch a bottle from a case, and continue walking without missing a step. We never took more than was needed, and many times throughout the summer this was the only way to raise money for a loaf of bread and a can of potted meat for sandwiches. Andy and I never thought twice about taking advantage of this source of revenue. We had relied on it so often the owner of the bar was a nervous wreck watching over his bottles.

We had been in the apartment a little more than a year when Johnny joined our group. Johnny was born on October 31, and was the first infant that Mama let me bath and dress. I was twelve years old and knew how to handle a baby. When I was allowed to take him for an outing in his carriage by myself, a milestone had been passed in my growing up. Johnny resembled Andy when he was a baby; both had the dark hair that was as straight as a string. The glint in his eye must have taken Mama back to Andy's earlier days. We were now five boys and two girls.

Aunt Mildred and Uncle George had returned from Ohio the year before, and bought a new home in rural Hartford. Mama honored her promise; Mary was allowed to spend all of her vacations with them. At Mildred's, she would have a bedroom all to herself, leaving me with a room to myself for the summer.

Things continued to move forward, settling into a pattern. A routine that would help Mama keep track of her day's happenings with comforting predictability. Routine may have been a source of security for Mama, but for Andy it was monotonous and boring. We should have known that one day Andy would become restless, and repelled by everything around him. Andy and his new friend Eddie would hatch up a four-day adventure that would put some spark in their lives, but anxious days in the lives of their families. Mama was the first to notice that something was wrong. Andy wouldn't miss a meal without letting Mama know. We hadn't seen him since he left for school that morning. By six o'clock, I could tell Mama was getting bad feelings as she questioned me.

"Did you see him at school today?"

"No, I don't always. Sometimes he's already gone."

"Did you see Joseph there today?"

"Yeah."

Mama's intuition was serving her well. She could feel it in her bones that something was amiss. The first thing she did was call on Mrs. Malone; Eddie's mother thinking the boys could be together.

"Oh they're together all right. Helen, I'm so sorry, but Charlie gave 'em his 'ol junk of a car to tinker with, to keep 'em out of trouble…. We just never guessed what they would do"

"They're in a car?" Mama wailed.

"They got it running; the car is gone. That doesn't leave much to the imagination does it?"

When Dad heard the news, he persuaded Mama to be patient a while longer. He was certain the boys wouldn't get far and would come crawling home after the car broke down. We were still getting ready for school the next morning when Mrs. Malone came to the door. She looked tired, and nervously twisted and yanked on a handkerchief she held.

"Helen, have you heard from Andy?"

"No, I'm worried sick. Has Eddie... ?"

"No, I'm not waitin' any longer. I'm on my way to the police station." Mama didn't hesitate a second, but hurriedly pulled a comb through her hair. I was to remain with the smaller kids. The two women headed for the police station. After the police were notified we waited, thinking something magical was going to happen. We thought we would at least hear some news before the day was over, but night fall brought nothing but tension from another stressful day.

I tried to imagine what it would be like to run away like that. Being out in the world alone would terrify me. Andy had to be so brave to set out on his own. What if I was never to see Andy again? It was scary. By the third day, even Dad was showing some concern, but he continued to believe that all would end well. The boys would be found. The police had notified the authorities in the small towns east and west of Chipwey. It was logical that the boys would take one or the other of these routs. The roads in both directions were good roads and the way was dotted with many small towns. The police were bound to spot them sooner or later. Two boys, fifteen years old, wouldn't be hard to miss sitting along side the road in a broken down junk of a car.

On the fourth day we finally got word, Eddie and Andy had been found after spending the night parked by the side of the road. They had nursed that old clunker along the whole four days until it finally broke down beyond their means to repair. Tired and hungry they appeared relieved that help had come. It was a mystery to everyone how they kept the car going that long. They had gotten more than sixty miles from home. Another couple of hours they would have been in Buffalo. Because we had no car, Dad rode with Mr. Malone to pick the boys up. It was a good thing the police found them when they did. The last of the seventeen dollars and eighty-eight cents they saved for the trip gave out the day before. Andy would tell us later, "I'll bet we walked half the distance. We spent more time outside pushin' than inside drivin'."

Andy never did say why he ran away from home. I was told that it was for the adventure of it all. Something told me there was more to it than that. If he were happy at home, why would he leave? Andy was escaping; escaping from his home life. Dad's drinking, the constant arguments and our poor living conditions combined with his struggles at school had become intolerable for him. Joseph and Andy were aware of Dad's bullying ways with Mama long before I was. Mama was supposed to be there to service Dad when his needs arose. These were the reasons that would move my brother's lives in the direction they would eventually take. One day, they would both escape what they felt they were powerless to change. For now Andy's failed attempt would be chalked up to a new learning experience.

Over his school years, Andy continued to be a poor student. Each year he did worse than the last. Joseph seemed to do well in school, and Mary enjoyed her day with beads, crayons and pencils. As a young girl, she always emitted self-confidence. She even made friends with the nun that taught her. Whatever Mary did, or whomever she played with, she looked and acted as though she belonged doing just what she was doing. I had become ill at ease with others, and this made a classroom full of students an uncomfortable place for me. For Andy and me, school was a punishment rather than a place of learning and growing. Hating school so much, I would use any excuse to stay home. Skipping school wasn't my speed; my method would be different from Andy's. After everyone returned to school, I would busy myself sweeping the floor or washing the breakfast and lunch dishes. A light scolding from Mama was the usual result when she found out I had dilly-dallied until it was too late. She needed my help, and soon I became Mama's right hand man. She had grown so dependent on me, and nothing could have made me happier.

My life there with her was safe and secured from the unpredictable outside.

Andy's method was simply not to show up. He was notorious for skipping, so the nuns reported it to Mama each time he was absent. Being reprimanded only kept him under control for a while, and then he would start in again. At one point, he was getting someone to write excuses for him. That trick worked until the nun had gotten suspicious of the handwriting. I was the courier of a sealed note sent home to Mama that would blow the whistle on Andy. Poor Mama she had to stay on her toes when dealing with him, for he was continuing to move in a world of his own making. Mama never knew half of what he was doing when he was out of her sight, and for sanity's sake that was probably best for her.

Joseph and Andy began to grow in opposite directions during that year. They still went to the movies together occasionally, but different interests were flowering, and they had different friends. Joseph had become part of a small group from school. They were well-bred boys living up on the hill. He and his friends were on St. Michael's basketball team, and this common interest made for solid friendships among the three boys. One of the boys was a happy-go-lucky sort. His plump girth seemed to go with the constant smile he wore. He was tagged Bosco, because of his fondness for his favorite chocolate drink. The second boy was a good mechanic. It would be commonplace to see his feet sticking out from under the car or his rear end hanging out over a fender as he leaned headlong into the motor. His clothes were full of grease and oil all the time. Joseph and Bosco called him Crud. They were careful not to rib him too much, Crud supplied the transportation for the trio. Joseph looked so much like an Irishman it didn't take much imagination to figure out a nickname for him. He became known as "Dutch" to almost everyone, but Mama. Crud and Bosco were the only friends Joseph ever brought into the apartment, and that was to introduce them to Mama.

Andy's friends were boys like himself. They had no direction and came from the poorer part of Chipwey. The only reason we ever met Eddie, was his family was Catholic too, and he didn't live far from us. Corkey was another friend of Andy's that we never met, and only had fleeting glimpses of him when the boys met in front of our apartment. Mama didn't approve of all of Andy's companions, so he purposely kept them unknown to her. She couldn't disapprove of what she had no knowledge of. Andy and his friends had one thing in common, no love for school at all. Andy remained quiet and detached from the family for a while after his running away. He went back to school and did what he was told with a silent resentment for authority. Then one day, he asked me to go on one of our scavenging trips again. I was glad. No one could be certain for how long, but for now the old Andy was back.

CHAPTER 9
Shopping At Our Local Dump

Our cramped living space in the Albany Street apartment made life uncomfortable during the summer. "August is hotter than Dutch love," Mama would say. Although Expandable screens in the front room windows were a flimsy solution, they did serve two purposes. They kept the breeze coming in, the kids from falling out. We tried everything to get more air in the apartment, but anything we did never seemed to be enough. After sunset, sitting on the big step in front of our building gave us some relief. Occasionally a neighbor joined Mama to chat for a while, a pleasant note to her escape. It never occurred to Andy and me to let the heat of this summer month interfere with our trips to the back alleys and the dump. When Andy snapped his fingers, we were off. That wide view of the courtyard from our kitchen window made it easy for us to spot the truck when it came to collect trash from Woolworth's. We could depend on Andy to be there to keep an eye out for the numerous boxes of throw away stuff. One of Mama's favorite sayings, that one man's trash is another man's treasure, proved so true. Andy could always spot some treasure worth recovering. There was just one snag in his plan. The store had a strict rule. No one could claim any of the treasure until it had been thrown away at the local dump. The trash, now a few steps away from home, would be headed for a dump two miles away, how frustrating.

"Pigeon, get the wagon," That's all Andy had to say, and within seconds, the wheels were in motion. In the rear of our building was a shed that had once been used as a shelter for horses and buggies. Each apartment was given a stall to use for storage or coal bins. Our old beat up wagon was kept there. It was my job to run back, get the wagon, and catch up with Andy before he got too far ahead of me. So many times, we raced along our well-traveled path to the dump. It was best to get there at the same time, or shortly after the truck arrived. We weren't the only ones aware of the good pickins' in this first come first get kind of a place. Other people knew and so did the rats. If the treasure was something we could eat, it was even more important. The race with the rats was on. The rush to catch up with my long-legged brother made the excitement of the hunt as the carrot dangled in front of the donkey's nose. There was no way of knowing just how profitable this, or any trip would be. The thought of unknown discoveries was invigorating.

I scurried along trying to catch up. Andy's driving energy could easily give him a half block lead on me. He was serious about getting there first as he plowed along the street by the railroad tracks, crossing the middle of a main highway, and up a steep rocky hillside. Finally, reaching the top of the rocky ledge, we'd pass through a patch of blueberry bushes. It seemed an odd place for them. They took root and thrived on the train soot that gathered in the openings of the rocky surface. Once we passed the berry bushes, the hardest part was over. It was an arduous path getting to the dump. I was huffing and puffing but never considered how our rusty companion was surviving this trip. Our faithful wagon, bumping and banging, trailed behind me like the tail on a kite. Today our trip was made in good time. The truck was leaving as we entered. It was a disgusting, smelly place to have to forge for treasure, but the excitement of the hunt outdid any objection to being there. A column of smoke drifted slightly to the east from the far side of the dump where something was burning its last breath. The mingled odor of smoke, garbage, and burning rubber, was hard to take when it first hit my nostrils.

"Phew."

"Oh, you always say that." With a smirk, Andy looked over his shoulder at me and pinched his nose.

Because the treasure we looked for was last to be loaded on, it would naturally wind up at the bottom when it slid from the bed of the truck. The edge of the dump was on a downgrade. It would take a heap of digging to uncover it. There was always a scattering of green sawdust throughout the pile of debris. It wasn't just sawdust, but a special floor sweeping mixture. It had oil in it that left the Woolworth's floors smelling and looking clean. That was all well and good for the floors. I wasn't fond of the smell it left on my hands, and Andy wasn't fond of my complaints. "Quit bellyaching. It's not gonna kill ya." Andy would say, "Soon as we hit the green stuff, we've hit pay dirt. Now cum on Pigeon, help me."

It didn't take Andy long to find what he was looking for. "Bingo," he yelled as he maneuvered a long box from underneath a pile of debris. Carrying it to the wagon, he set the slightly battered coffer down. Was he going to be pleased? "This is it, what I was looking for. Let's seeee... " His voice trailed off. Anxious hands tugged at the lid. The box popped open. Andy sprang back; thrust his hand to his forehead with a smacking blow. Words came out with a gush. "Jackpot. Get a load of this Pigeon. Look!"

If that box had contained Medusa's head, with lunging snakes and all, and we had instantly been turned to stone for gazing upon it, the two of us couldn't have become more immobilized. We stared in disbelief at the box filled to the brim with cookies. Still packed in neat little rows, except for a few broken ones on the top layer, were more cookies than I had eaten up to this ripe old age of twelve. They weren't peanut butter cookies, but the next best thing. The tops of each cookie had peanut halves stuck all over them.

"How many do you think there are?" I asked.

.e box says thirty dozen ... never been opened so ... thirty
.n!"

"Didn't sell many, huh? Maybe they don't taste good."

Andy gave me his one of his squinty, one-eye looks. "Okay." We
sampled a cookie, then another. The box received our final blessing.
Together, we hit the pile of trash with renewed spirit, and couldn't
believe it when Andy pulled out another long box. This box wasn't full,
but there were enough Spanish peanuts in it to satisfy our whole family;
maybe a little stale, but not bad. It would seem that the Peanut God had
chosen this day to smile on us. That box was loaded on the wagon too.
We dug into the pile again, scattering trash in all directions. Then a
shifting of the debris around me made my heart jump. Was that a rat
closing in on our territory, creeping beneath the cover of paper and
boxes? My head spun around as I tried to spot "it," before it spotted me.

"Andy: sumum's down there."

"Oh just kick at it. It'll go away."

"It could be a big one."

"Baloney. It's just the pile slidin'."

As I scanned the junk for the phantom rat, a deep, red colored box
caught my eye; the lid still tightly in place. I picked it up, still clean and
crisp, the box was pleasingly smooth. Giving it a gentle shake, there was a
muffled sound; something soft was inside. To prolong the moment of
surprise the lid was lifted slowly. Instantly the subject of rats is forgotten.
"Look Andy. Look!" I scrambled over the trash to show Andy my find.
"Look Andy, Ribbons!"

He barely glanced at them. "Uh-huh."

Some ribbons were attached to hair combs. Others were straight
lengths of ribbon. They were satiny and soft to the touch, some solid
colors and some plaid. Occasionally Mama bought me one ribbon to tie
on my short pigtails, but never had I owned so many. Here were enough
ribbons to wear a different one every day for a week. I carried them to
the wagon and set them snugly in a corner. Andy continued to search
through the unexplored jumble of boxes and paper, occasionally pushing
back the wad of hair from his forehead. He was rewarded with several

spools of thread, a package of needles with one or two needles missing, a drinking glass with no cracks, and a colorful silk scarf with one frayed corner. Mama could use those. It would seem that we had found all that was to be found. I couldn't wait to get home to show Mama how well we had done, but leaving this profitable spot wouldn't be done in haste. Andy would make certain he had probed every box before he called a halt to the search. I sat on a nearby rock munching a cookie, keeping a look out for rats and a close eye on my ribbons. At last, the searching ended.

Normally, Andy would have lingered a while more in this cemetery for castoffs. He considered it a good sport to practice his aim on the rats with his trusty slingshot. Our find today was exceptionally good so we started for home right away. The trip back would take longer walking the sidewalks, now that the job was done. Andy grabbed for the handle of the wagon, "I'll take first pull."

When Andy and I arrived home, Mama was surprised with what we had found. She agreed that I'd be a total knockout in my beautiful bows. The next day, the biggest and most colorful bow was chosen for my hair. It was so good having something new to wear to school. The other girls had new things all the time. Now it was my turn to have something new. There was a stark contrast between the bright bow in my hair and the faded color of my dress. I didn't care. I flaunted it with an arrogance never felt before. This was poor timing for such feelings. Sister Francis was the nun who taught my class that year, and she had a reputation for being very strict. At the onset of a new school year if another student was to ask which nun would be teaching you and the answer was, "Sister Francis," it created all kinds of sympathetic comments. Although they meant well, their remarks left some of us feeling like condemned prisoners passing through the doors that first day. Sister Francis was an older nun who had more face wrinkles than a prune. She was should an inch or two taller than her tallest student. What she lacked she made up with a feisty nature. When Sister was upset she had a way of looking like the wicked witch in "Snow White alone would fluster me so much I could never recover

On this particular day, Sister was sitting at her desk listening to each student recite the times table she called out. She never took her eyes from the individual to be sure there would be no prompting from a fellow student. Whenever I was called upon to recite, something peculiar would happen to my brain. Gaps the size of bottomless pits would crop up like dotted lines in my memory. This time was no different. My throat suddenly went dry. My tongue became thick as a marshmallow. I stammered, fumbled badly failing to continue. Sister jumped up from her desk, and came charging toward me like an enraged lion. The huge rosary that hung from a cord belt around her waist rattled as the wooden beads slammed together. "Did you study?" She was so close to me now I could easily count all the little trenches in her face.

I squeezed out a week, "Yes." It didn't matter if it were true or not, if a lie was my defense, I would use it. She was only angered more.

"Why don't you know them if you studied?"

"I don't know."

"Well, you will know when you finish writing them twenty-five times!"

Slowly she walked away from me, and then suddenly looked back. "I ought to snatch that bow right out of your hair." She added, her hand making a grabbing gesture in the air. I pulled the bow from my hair drawing little attention to my action. A burning sensation spread over my face. Chastised, I would never wear my bows to school again. Mama was right when she said, that Pride goes before a fall. I had fallen, no doubt about that. Anyway, bows are a little babyish, I told myself. Mary could wear them better than me.

This would be Mary's third summer with Mildred and George. I missed her when she left for those three long months, but it did mean one less mouth to feed. Mary and I weren't very close yet. I was twelve she was only seven, still a baby to me. Besides, with helping Mama, my time was fairly confined. If I did get to go outside it was certain there'd a "little one" on my hip to carry around. Mary would leave no void in summer. As Mary grew older, she began to realize there was a mom with us that didn't exist with Mildred. All the attention, at the beginning of her visits to Hartford was new and very desirable. Vacation time would not be over yet, but the fun of being the center of attention would be. Mildred kept close track of her throughout the day. Mary was the storybook princess locked in a tower with no doors and only one window. At home, she could blend into the crowd. Be less noticeable.

The biggest breach of etiquette at home was dropping a fork on the plate. The shrill clank of metal hitting glass must have been an abomination to Dad's ears. His piercing glare was enough to make the offender well aware of their wrongdoing. When Dad wasn't around, it was normal for us to lick every crumb and speck of juice from our plates. Nothing was lost to a stuffy display of good manners in the O'Brien household. Not true at Mildred's; table manners were very rigid there. Because my aunt and uncle entertained and visited with friends often, it was important that manners showed as though they was first nature. Proper etiquette was driven home constantly; Mary was quick to remember how to be a little lady with each visit.

The one time that Mary's two different lives did collide during dinner, was quite a shock to poor Aunt Mildred. Mary loved to eat from the special set of dishes at Mildred's. Each plate was a different color, and deciding who would get which color made setting the table fun. This evening, Mary put the sunburst yellow plate at her place. During the meal, the two adults were giving Mary little notice until she impulsively raised her dinner plate and, with much gusto, began to lick it off. Mildred was appalled at the sight of Mary's dark brown eyes peeking over the rim of her sunburst yellow plate. George was amused and giggled at Mary's backslide. A stream of astonishment was hurled at Mary: "Why Mary, have you forgotten everything we've taught you; you never did that before, do you do that at home?" Mary still appearing over the top of the plate, sheepishly grinned and nodded, yes. Mary was careful never again to do such a thing in Mildred's presence. Aunt Mildred meant well, but she didn't seem to understand what it meant not to have the things in life that came easily to her. Mildred only knew she was going to have Mary the way she wanted her. The way she would have raised her own daughter. Oh no! Mary wouldn't be allowed to act like that wild bunch of O'Brien kids.

The nuns kept a tight watch on our manners throughout our school day. At home, Mama did her best to keep up with our behavior. She was a stickler for us saying "thank you" when someone said something nice to us or gave us something. Mama didn't sit down and eat with us the numerous times we ate supper without Dad. She ate … when we finished. Mama was more concerned that we had enough to eat, not how we were eating it.

For Mary to be brought up with rules galore seven months out of the year, it's not hard to realize how complex the transition was from home to the reserved life at Mildred's. Over the next four years Mary would become more aware that being home, as bad as it was, had advantages. My little sister loved the Roy Rogers and Gene Autry movies; there were plenty of horses to see. If anyone thought Mary were interested only in the story of the movie then they would be very much mistaken. She studied how the halter and saddle were put on a horse, and how one should correctly mount and dismount. After the movie, Mary would talk on and on about details that she noticed this time about her favorite subject. She couldn't wait for the day when Mildred would take her horseback riding for the first time. This was what she yearned for most at the age of seven. It was that old confidence of hers, not being afraid of anything, that envious trademark I saw repeated many times, as we were growing up.

One Christmas, Mary told Mildred and George she wanted Santa to bring her a toy gun and holster set. Then she graduated from one gun, to two guns, a memorable year. She also got a hat and vest to go with her dual holsters. Mary ran around the courtyard and streets to her heart's content playing cowboys; she was no doubt reliving the last movie she saw. Decked out in her cowboy outfit, she'd ride her imaginary horse with style. One day Mary and her whimsical steed would share a first experience that involved Father Kelley.

Father was the Pastor of Saint Michaels Church. A tall husky built man, he loped along with a smooth gate missing nothing within a block of where he was. He would never miss one of St. Michael's students. He'd call out a hello to them followed by the individual's name. Despite this outgoing friendly manner, it would be unwise to think of Father as a pushover. He could make your blood run cold if ever you had to stand before him in a reprimand. Mary raced up the street unaware that he was walking toward her. With both hands clasped behind his back, Father moved briskly for a man of his late years. Walking along with his typical wide strides, the gap between him and Mary closed rapidly. Mary decked out in her western rig hopped along mimicking the bumpy gate of a horse. As she galloped up to him he smiled, entertained by her complete concentration at play.

"Good morning," Father sang out. He stopped and watched her as she passed him by.

"Mornin' sheriff, I … I mean Father!"

"Oh, it's the sheriff, am I?"

Mary giggled and the two of them laughed at her slip of the tongue. Upon request, Mary handed him one of her pistols. Playfully squinting an eye, Father aimed the toy into the air. The trigger was pulled a few times … click, click. When they parted, Mary flew up the stairs, imaginary horse and all, to tell Mama what had happened. We talked often about Mary's encounter with the Good Sheriff Father Kelley, and couldn't help being surprised at how he left his guard down. Giving the impression that he was as straight-laced as a shoe, he proved how easily it is to be pulled into the charm of a child's world.

Only at special times can the gates to those wonderful worlds inside be opened. Those worlds of your own making that take you any place you want to go. All that is required is that you be young at heart, willing to explore as deep as your imagination will allow, and most of all that your spirit be permitted to enter.

There is excitement every summer when Mary prepares to leave with Mildred, but she always seems glad to return home. The strict upbringing at Mildred's and the lax ways at home has probably been a good balance for her. Mary will be able to walk with a degree of confidence, a gift from Mildred and George, and her ability to be young at heart, defiantly from being an O'Brien. For us, it was a good thing to be both imaginative and young at heart in order to get through the tough times still to come.

CHAPTER 10
Operation Belmont Bar

$\mathcal{F}$reedom from school for three months was all we would have to look forward to during summer vacation; that would change after the summer of 1947. Dad decided it was time to buy a car. It was a surprise to all of us, even Mama. Although not new, the '39 Ford sedan was dependable enough to give a few hours escape from city life. Every Sunday, starting in August until Labor Day, Dad took us on a sixty-five mile trip to Barter Lake. After Mass, the kitchen churned with energy as we prepared for our trip. We'd rush around packing food into several shopping bags and a bushel basket. Everything was carefully loaded into the trunk of the car along with a jug of Mama's lemonade, and the baby's stroller.

There was no doubt, when we had a picnic like this, there would be no leftovers. A few crumbs at the bottom of the potato chip bag would be the last tangible evidence that there had ever been food in the basket at all. Mama's budget would suffer dearly from the cost of the picnic food and gas. We were like children stealing roast beef out of the refrigerator. Today we would eat drink and be merry, even though tomorrow we were destined to go hungry. Though our practical mother may have been aware that we would have to pay for it the next week, she knew we needed to do something as a family. Anyway, when things got too tough, there were always the bottles behind the Belmont Bar....

With everything snug in the trunk of the car and five of us piled in the back seat, all was ready. After traveling for an hour, Dad would stop at a bar in Seneca, one of the small towns we had to pass through. Seneca wasn't half as big as Chipwey, but the town supported three bars on the road passing through. We dreaded the sight of that little town, Mama would try to persuade Dad to wait.

"Can't you wait for a drink until we get to the lake? We're not far away."

"I'll only be a minute."

"You say that every time, but we wind up waiting out here for an hour."

"Who the hell's doin' the driving here? I'll be right back."

Mama knew once Dad walked into that tavern, we were prisoners in the car. It was hot and crowded sitting in the back seat, and as time dragged on, Mama had her hands full with cranky Johnny on her lap. Frayed and hot herself, Mama would go into the bar and try to pry Dad out. He was never ready to come out, so he'd give her a couple of bottles of soda pop and a bag of potato chips to distribute among us. This was intended to lure us into believing we were having a good time. When the scant offering disappeared, we, the angry masses in the back seat would become hostile again scrapping with each other, making life miserable for Mama. Just when she thought she couldn't take it any longer Dad would emerge from the bar wearing a big smile. Tearing the cellophane from a new White Owl cigar, he'd climb into the car, strike a match, and draw a couple of deep puffs to insure a well-stoked fire. Only now would he ready to start the car; we were on our way again.

The grumbling and groaning from the back seat, and the bawling from the front seat would diminish very quickly, as the landscape change from small town to countryside. Several times, we'd see open-bedded trucks loaded with bails of new hay. The hay, still green with moisture, was a special kind of hay. Mama's words were almost melodic.

"New hay. Make a wish, don't look back."

"Whada ya mean, 'don't look back'?" Richard asked.

"New hay. Wish on green hay, never look at it again or your wish won't come true." It was the hardest thing to do, not looking back.

The growing number of pine trees lining the road told us just how close we were. The fragrance of pine, carried on the soft breeze, seemed not only guided the car, but also seemed to nudge us along. We'd crane our necks to see as far ahead as we could. It was a sort of contest to be the first one to get a glimpse of the lake. Then someone would shout, "I see it. There it is." Under the guise of a small blue spot, it glistened in the summer sunshine, winking back at us as it darted in and out of view between the pines. The shimmering spot grew bigger until we were riding along side the shore, the smell of water, and fish mingling in the air. Summer camps, nestled in the surrounding woods, proudly displayed their own private docks. Boats stood moored at each one waiting the next trip out. When in full view, the lake laid a wide path that gradually diminished as it stretched for miles. We O'Brien's wouldn't need it all; for today, a small corner would do. Life would be sweeter for the next few hours; we had arrived at Barter Lake. The car slowed down as we drove through the busy section of the midway. Music from the merry-go-round cast an immediate spell over the car. All grew quiet, too busy looking at the sights to talk. Delectable smells of French fries, Mexican hots, and popcorn dominated the area, completing the promises of Barter Lake. Rides of different varieties gave the park a carnival-like atmosphere. The first to come into view was the gigantic Ferris wheel. We would all have had a ride on the wheel, but before we did anything, we knew Dad would want to eat first.

After we managed to consume the better part of our picnic lunch, Mama would insist we wait at least one hour after eating to avoid cramps. It could have been a long hour if it were not for the happy activities that surrounded us. Joseph and Andy would run off to experience the fun of the midway by themselves. I'd stay with Mama and Dad to explore the penny arcade and its many games. With so much to see, the time flew by, and before we knew it, we were heading for the water. The beach was a smooth sandy strip. A welcome mat spread at the water's doorstep. The gradual depth of this good-natured lake made it ideal for small kids to paddle around. We could walk out quite a way before it became too deep for us. Mama and Dad sat on a blanket spread over the warm sand with little Johnny between them. Acting as lifeguards, they kept a close eye on us as we ran and splashed in the water. Joseph and Andy went out farther to reach the deeper water. They would swim a ways out to a float where they spent much of their time diving.

While Mama did all the watching, and we did all the splashing, Dad did all the drinking. He never remained with Mama for long on the beach. Minutes after they got settled on the blanket, he would take off to the other side of the midway, where there were several bars. He wouldn't get away, however, without a warning.

"I'll be right back, Mom." He'd say.

"Where are you going?"

"Just across the street for a few minutes."

"Take it easy on the drinking. You have to drive us home yet."

"Oh horseshit. You just worry about yourself."

Instinctively we headed for something to eat when the swimming was over. When Dad returned from the bar, he found us at the picnic table snacking on the remaining potato chips and cookies. The big smile on his face told us he was in a good mood. Dad's world was still treating him well, making our world all right too.

Joseph and Andy were preparing to go off again by themselves when Dad called them back. He suggested that they go with us to the midway to play a game or two. Dad liked the games of chance and would try to beat the odds at all of them. Sometimes he would even win. I knew this was a special place for him. Here, he gracefully accepted losing. "You know the games are all rigged." He'd say. Mostly, Dad seemed to be drawn to the horseracing game, and so we spent much of our time there. We O'Briens were good for the man's business as we gathered close to watch Dad, Joseph and Andy play. We made a small crowd all by ourselves. Our squeals of joy at the start and end of every race seemed to attract others on the midway. Before we knew it, people were crowding in to play the game too. The man in charge of the horseracing booth stood to the left of the game board. The board was a replica of a racetrack with a starting gate and mechanical horses of different colors that moved along assigned tracks. An electric cord with a ball-like device was attached to the game board. A button was pushed in the center of the ball to start the race. The shrill sound of the starting bell announced to everyone up and down the midway that a race was beginning. When the starting gate swung up, the horses moved forward. Lights winked and blinked all around the outside of the booth until the race ended. Shelves on both sides of the booth were full of prizes for the winners; huge stuffed dogs, bears, cats, pocketknives, and pink-feathered Kewpie dolls. On the top shelf were four very noticeable prizes that stood out like a gold tooth. They were statues of a golden palomino horse standing next to a clock. It was almost too much to wish that Dad would win one of them. "If Dad wins, tell him to pick one of those horse clocks." I whispered to Mama.

She glanced up at them. "He's gotta come in first to do that."

The man yelled out, "All bets are in. All bets are in. Horses are at the starting gate!" Holding the ball contraption up for all to see, he announced loudly, "They're off!" The button was pressed, the bell screamed out and the horses began to move with a jerking motion toward the finish line. This was not to be Dad's race either. His horse came in third.

"Pick a horse, Kali." Dad slapped a quarter down placing his last bet.

"Me?"

"Go ahead, any color you want."

I chose the green one hoping the Irish color would be lucky.

Then something else unexpected happened; the man handed the ball down to me. "Lets' have this young lady push the button this time," he said. I hesitated, not sure I'd heard right.

"Go ahead Kali," Dad said, "push it!"

The little black button gave way under my finger. Immediately lights flashed, the bell rang, and the starting gate swung up. "They're off," the man yelled. The horses began to move forward, jerking and inching their way with first this one in the lead then that one. For a while, I thought the yellow horse would win but at the last-second, our green horse sprinted ahead and crossed the finish line. I couldn't believe it! The screams of surprise from Mama, and the kids were deafening. "You won! You won!" Mama shouted. The man drew one of the horse clocks from the top shelf and handed it to Dad.

"Here, it was your race. This belongs to you," Dad said. Holding it tightly in my arms, I walked away as proudly as could be.

Behind us in the booth the man was yelling, "There she goes a big winner! Try your luck! The horses are ready for another exciting race. Place your bets folks. Place your bets!" People crowded in quickly filling in the empty space we left behind.

Walking alongside Dad, I asked, "Wasn't that somethin'? I pushed the button and won. But … didn't that look kinda funny to everybody?"

"Wha'da you care? You only pushed the button not the horse. Just remember Kido, things aren't always what they seem to be." Our golden prize was snuggled a little tighter in my arms.

Our day at the beach was nearly over, and it was time to think about our trip home. First, Dad had to head out to the bar across the way for one last drink. Mama's words of warning made no difference. It was a long half-hour to wait; when Dad returned there was a sway to his step that wasn't there before. Mama was angry when she saw him making his way toward us, so unsure of his steps. Telling her that he could drive twice the distance, he snarled back, "Get in the car and let me worry about the goddamn driving." Both Joseph and Andy, thanks to friends who owned cars, knew how to drive, but Dad said no to that suggestion. Quietly we piled in the car, knowing that the next two hours would be anything but pleasant.

That ride home was enough to unnerve a tightrope walker. Dad started out okay, but less than an hour on the road he got sleepy, leaving Mama to be his eyes as he continued. She yelled at him when he grew increasingly drowsy. "Bob, watch out. You're running off the road!" Slowing down to the point of almost stopping, Mama yelled again. "Bob you're going too slow. Pull over and take a few minutes to rest."

"Oh … horseshit, I don't need to rest we're almost home." Though his words were sluggish, Dad tried to sound as if he knew what he was doing. Blinking his eyes a few times he recover. A mile or so down the road we had a new problem. Instead of too slow, he was going too fast around a curve. The car jerked back and forth, as Dad struggled to keep it under control. Mama grabbed the steering wheel to help steady the car. Then everything calmed down again. On a straight road, everything seemed all right. Then our old Ford slowly strayed over the white line in the middle of the road. Another car, coming straight at us, was blasting its horn. None of us dared to breathe. Mama cried out, "Bob!" A quick jerk of the steering wheel, and we were back on our own side.

Our guardian angels must have been in the car with us. I have no other explanation how we survived these trips without an accident. Turning down Albany Street and seeing the old apartment house was a welcome sight. It was good to get home in one piece. Even our dreary apartment felt good, roaches and all.

Hauling the empty picnic basket and all the baby's gear upstairs was our job. Dad wouldn't even move from the front seat. At last wide-awake, he was ready to go downtown to his favorite hang out. First thing, the golden horse had to be put in a place of honor. We choose the big table in the front room. Joseph set the right time and plugged it in. Even little Johnny applauded with us as the second hand began to sweep around the face of the clock. It looked twice as beautiful at home, than it did at the beach. There was no doubt that it was truly a thing of beauty; a fantastic prize to win.

Joseph and Andy didn't go to the beach with us anymore after that summer. They were getting older, and going anywhere with your whole family was not for grown boys. The only excitement left for them was the ride home, and nobody needed that kind of excitement. Joseph was looking for a job so he could buy his own car. Andy wasn't quite ready for a commitment of that kind, but he had his own way of keeping contented.

One day, Andy and his friend Eddy decided to hike up to the treacherous cliff above the railroad tracks. Over the objections of motherly guidance, they had done it many times before in their travels for adventure; this time they stumbled across something that would be to them the find of the century, the shell of a deserted airplane. Andy's curiosity about flight still ran high. Finding that old thing must have seemed like a stroke of sheer luck. The motor and propeller had been removed, but aside from its weathered condition, the body was intact. One wing, torn because of its rough landing, hung so low it touched ground. There was no way of knowing how long it had withered there in such disgrace, but from its faded color, apparently a long time. How could anyone leave a thing of beauty such as this to the mercy of the elements to grow weaker with each passing day? Its renovation would surpass the success they had with Eddie's old car. There was no reason why they couldn't put this in working order too.

The would-be aviators spend weeks going up to the hill. Anyone else would have looked at it as a hopeless cause, but not the youthful energy that moved excitedly about it. It was a unique way for the boys to occupy their time. They weren't getting into trouble, at least not yet. This labor of love kept them occupied for what was left of the summer. Repairing the numerous breaks in the skin of the plane was a tedious job, and setting the broken wing was in itself no small project. No one knew where they were spending their time each day, and that was just fine by the boys. They didn't need an overly concerned parent to squash their plans for this, their best achievement of all. Eddy's brother Paul was forever trying to get in on the things his big brother did. The mere thought of a tag-along ten years old was an impossible notion. Besides, as Eddy put it, Paul ran off at the mouth like an auctioneer. It would have been nothing short of a miracle for him to keep a secret. When the boys started making their trips to the plane, Paul was turned back a couple of times with sharp warnings.

"Get lost Paul. Go play with your tinker toys."

"Come on Eddy. Why can't I go with you guys just once? I won't talk or nothin'."

"Stay here! I ain't watching out for no baby."

Andy and Eddy went about their business everyday feeling that their secret was well guarded. No one could possibly know where they were going when they started out in a different direction each day. Supplies needed for repairs were secretly stored at the house of a friend. The boys worked hard searching every corner of Chipwey for the materials to do the repairs. One item in particular came from our own kitchen. Andy singled out the oilcloth table covering from our kitchen table as good material to repair the skin of the plane. While the cloth backing gave strength to the glue, the slick coating on the outside was a perfect water repellent. Andy had cut off strips of the material that hung down from the edges of table, counting on it being some time before Mama noticed anything missing. Then one day … "What happened to the tablecloth?" Mama's questioning eyes searched our faces for an answer. The once sufficient cover now hung down only an inch from the edge of the table. I had no explanation, nor did Mary, Richard or Jimmy. No one could explain to Mama how an oilcloth table cover could possibly shrink.

Although Andy and Eddy thought they had everything figured out, they hadn't counted on Paul getting back at them. What a good joke, to shadow the older boys, and their not suspecting a thing. Paul must have done a good job because Andy and Eddy never suspected they were being followed. It was exciting to keep from being spotted that first time because Andy and Eddy looked behind them often, as they'd hurry along. He knew he had to stay quite a ways behind, and when to duck in here and there at the right moment. After he found out where they were going, all he had to do was be aware when the boys were on their way up to the hill. Paul could wait until they were far enough ahead, and follow at his leisure. Just like the two older boys, Paul would share his secret with no one.

In the fall, every spare minute the boy's had after school was spent fixing the plane. Paul was there each day too, stretched out on his belly watching from behind a matted tangle of berry bushes. A coffee can with a candy bar and some graham crackers were stashed under the cover of the bushes, just in case he got hungry during his long vigils. Paul watched the progress of the hopeful repairmen as they set about sealing up holes, and restoring the torn wing. By mid fall the repairs were as complete as their inexperienced hands could get them. One day when Paul took his familiar place behind the berry bushes, he felt something about the scene below was different; of course, the airplane had been moved. The plane had been moved closer to the edge of the cliff. From the top of the cliff, it was a plunging drop to the railroad tracks some fifty feet below. Paul studied the scene before him for a few seconds, and watched as each boy took his turn sitting in the cockpit. They were really going to do it. They were going to fly that thing to the ground below. At first Paul wanted to shout out, "You guys must be nuts," but he knew they wouldn't listen to him. He was just a little kid. The best way was to tell his mother. She would stop this crazy thing. Quietly Paul slipped out of his hiding place and made his way down the hill toward home. Would he make it home and back again before they… ? Running even faster Paul pushed on, wondering which one of the boys would fly the plane off the cliff. The plane only had room for the pilot.

After Paul told his mother what was happening up on the hill, Mrs. Condon came directly to Mama. "Helen, they're at it again. We'd better get ourselves up to the cliff, before they kill themselves!" Spurred on by fear, they panicked at the thought of not getting there on time; the two women took off in a flurry with Paul leading the way. For once, I was glad to be left behind to watch the kids. I couldn't bare it if one of the boys had already flown off the cliff.

Andy and Eddy were surprised to see both of their mothers making their way toward them, stumbling over rocks and tangles of berry bushes. "What are you doing up here? Don't you dare!" They hollered frantically waving their arms. Mama was so upset she didn't realize until she got home that her arms and legs were scratched from the thorny bushes. She didn't care, what was important was she had Andy safely in tow. Mama said she was going to tell the fire department about the plane. They would dismantle it. She was very upset at this latest close call with Andy, and for the first time didn't seem to hide her anger, but Andy had an answer for everything.

"Oh for crying out loud, we weren't going to fly it down. That was stupid Paul's idea. We might have pushed it off. Just to see if it would glide."

Mama didn't seem to be completely convinced. She knew Andy. The temptation to fly that thing could have gotten the best of him.

"My heart was in my mouth when I saw Andy sitting in that dilapidated thing. It was pulled right to the edge of the cliff," she later told me. Then with a grin she added, "Besides being a wreck, it was the strangest looking airplane I ever saw."

"How?"

"With patches of strawberry design oilcloth pasted all over its body, it looked like it had a bad case of measles."

Dad got only sketchy details of the airplane incident. He was told him just enough to let him know something had happened. Mama Bear was still protecting her cubs.

It was depressing for Andy, after all that work and planning, never to know if the plane could have flown. And in a final blow to be destroyed.

Andy always reminded me of a cat. When the bottom of his dreams fell out, he managed to land on his feet. Was it as easy as he made it appear? I have no doubt that Andy strained under the weight of failure many times. But he cleverly hid behind this undaunted image that he wanted the world to see. He was a pro at burying each hurt out of sight.

Sunday night continued to be movie night for Mama and Dad. After the airplane incident a few hours of escape were in order. It also gave her a break from the drudge of the apartment and constant care and attention that we kids demanded. For three hours Joseph, Andy and I would be left at home to watch the little ones while Mama and Dad were gone.

When we were there alone, with no adult around to tell us what to do, we could choose the radio programs we wanted to listen to. We knew, however, that a good radio program could only be enhanced by a big bowl of popcorn, and it was a cheap fill for empty spaces in our stomachs. There wasn't two cents to rub together among the three of us, so Andy and I had the money detail. While we were gone, Joseph watched over things at home.

Because our need was immediate, there was no time to go hunting for empty bottles; no time to find someone to run an errand for. Andy and I would have to go no farther than our back yard to embark on, "Operation Belmont Bar."

The cases of full bottles were protected by storing them in the back room of the bar, and that kept it amply crowded in there. The only place left for the bar owner to keep his empties was outside the building on both sides of the back door. When deliveries were made to the bar the truck drove up the alley to the back door and exchange full bottles for empty ones. Missing bottles were charged to the bar. And if cases were missing too, that was a double expense.

It had become a game of wits between the owner and us. Try as he may he couldn't seem to catch us in the act. It was like a cold war. The man knew he was losing deposits at a regularity that was positively frightening. We could tell by the way he watched us when we were in the courtyard that we were prime suspects. The man made numerous trips during the day to check on those bottles. His suspicions that we were a good part of the problem were at an all time high. Could there be others? He couldn't be sure. So, his hired help was instructed to keep tabs on those empties.

When I took bottles, they were brought back before there was a chance they'd be missed. It was fast and easy taking them from the back door, and running around to the front door to return them for deposits. The only empties that vanished forever were the bottles that Andy and his friends took. They'd snatch the bottles, case and all, and high tail it up the street with the case swinging between them. They knew better than to take the bottles back to the Belmont. Andy would take them somewhere else, anywhere else.

Because Dad frequented the bar often, taking the bottles back was a perfectly normal thing to do. If the bartender should ever question where they came from, a good answer was, "They're my father's." It was such an easy solution to our money problem. Though I prided myself that no more was taken than necessary, it no longer justified the deed, and the challenge that made it fun had faded. My derrring-do blood had thinned out. This would be the last time, I vowed.

Andy and I left the apartment and walked the short distance to the alley. The evening was still young, but the sky was already velvety black. The stars were up there, but tonight; they seemed less radiant and more distant; probably because there was no moon. When I mentioned this to Andy his comment was, "Good!" Andy didn't miss the moon at all. He knew the dark night was in our favor. The only light around us was at the road's edge to the left of the alley. Between the street and the bar the alley was comparatively darker, though not impossible to see once one's eyes became accustomed to it. The dingy shaft of light that streamed across the upper portion of the alley came from the back door of the bar. That was all the light there was. Its meager glow gradually gave way to a very dark courtyard. Everything was right; there was no reason for failing to accomplish our objective.

Before we entered the alley, Andy briefed me about tonight's maneuvers. Besides keeping in close, one other instruction was mentioned several times, "No talking." Andy started inching his way ahead of me. His body pressed against the brick wall. It was painfully slow going, but step-by-step we began to close the distance between the Belmont and ourselves. My kneecaps quivered with fright.

I stayed so close to him one time, that both of us were walking with his right foot. He stopped short angered by my clumsiness, and jerked his foot out from under mine. Muffling a giggle in the palm of my hand wasn't good enough. A short snappy, "Shhh," from Andy sobered me up in a hurry.

We were a little more than half way to the end of the alley when Andy suddenly threw his arm across the front of me, stopping me in my tracks. Raising a finger to his mouth, Andy motioned me to be still. I not only heard my heart beating, but the blood rushing up to my head; it made a strange sound like a waterfall. I could feel both of my kneecaps quivering. Everything sounded so loud. A simple swallow was bound to give us away. What did Andy hear that I didn't? Motioning toward the street he flattened himself closer still, to the brick wall. Then I heard it; a low whistled rendition of, "You Are My Sunshine." There was someone out there. Footsteps and whistling were coming our way.

Our situation had to be faced. We were trapped between the Belmont Bar, and this unknown someone who was still coming our way. What if he should walk into the alleyway? When the dark figure crossed the dimly lit opening of the alley, the silhouette of the hat he wore told us he was a Cop on his door check rounds. As he passed by, still whistling the happy melody, we held our position plastered up against that old brick wall. He stopped not too far from the ally, turned the doorknob of the office to garage and jiggled it a few times. Satisfied it was secure, he moved on. The rattling of the doors, clicking of footsteps, and music steadily faded up the street. Andy didn't move a fraction of an inch until we couldn't hear them any more. Then he began sliding along the brick wall again. I followed.

During the day it took a few seconds to walk from one end of the alley to the other. But tonight, in the dark, it was as though it had grown a block long. When at last we reached its end, we paused giving Andy a chance to survey the terrain. Stacked on both sides of the back door, the cases appeared as giant dominoes neatly piled one on top of the other. We were closer to the enemy now. The door was a screen door and noise could be heard though it as if there was no door at all. Andy was right. Silence was of the utmost importance. Giving me a signal to stay put Andy crept toward the screen door. He had to scout out the area, and make sure no one was in the back room.

Sounds of the men laughing and talking, the clink of glasses and hiss of popping bottle caps filtered through the screen door as Andy moved forward with all the skill of a commando. For a moment his head and shoulders were bathed in the dingy light as he leaned forward, peering in the screen door. I turned my face away. He was so exposed in the light; but Andy said many times, "You have to take chances sometimes to make things come out right." I was relieved when he returned, and took up his position along side of me. "It's all clear, but we have to move fast," he whispered.

Andy had chosen a safe stack of cases close to the wall of the building. Our chances were better in a darkened corner, should someone suddenly stepped out of the back door. With Andy on one side and me on the other, we gingerly lifted off one case after another until we got to the bottom case. Andy pulled four bottles out and handed them to me. I took them to the alley, and returned to Andy. Slowly, silently, we re-stacked the wooden cases back the way we found them. Not only did Andy pick a bottom case, but the label was the same that Dad bought. Andy sure was clever.

Returning to the alley, we collected the four bottles and hurried toward the street. Halfway down the alley, we heard a noise behind us, the familiar sound of the Belmont's screen door ... then the thud of bottles being dropped into a case. Moving in unison, we squeezed closer to the brick wall. All was still for a few seconds. I knew until the door banged for a second time we mustn't move. Were we in trouble? Andy gave me a big grin. I knew then that we were still all right. The bartender was only doing his job of looking over the cases to make sure every thing was accounted for. Unless he had x-ray vision like Superman, the four empty holes in that bottom case wouldn't be discovered yet. Then finally we heard the second bang of the door.

"Phew, that was close! We could've been caught," I felt calmed with each step away from the alley.

"Naw, we had lots of time. They'll never find those bottles missing until the truck comes in a couple days."

"How da you know when the truck comes?"

"I just know; that's all."

Rounding the corner we continued up the street, neither of us saying a word. My thoughts were on the next step ... taking the bottles into the bar. Soon we would have our coveted popcorn. I could smell it popping already.

Andy broke the silence. "You'll have to take the bottles in alone, Pigeon."

"Me? Alone?"

"Well, I can't go in there. You know he won't give me the money. One look at me and he'll say the bottles aren't his, or something. It's better if you take 'em in. I'll wait right here … out of sight."

I hesitated and glared back at Andy. With an air of controlled impatience, Andy's voice softened. "He'll take one look at you and never question where you got 'em. He'll think they're Dad's. Go on Pige. It'll be OK. I promise ya."

Slowly I walked to the doorway of the bar. The door was already propped open because of the warm night, making my entrance easy. My mind was working a mile a minute, "All I have to do is walk in, and go right up to the bartender and hand him the bottles. Yeah … *sure* … that's all."

Inside the doorway, I stopped to glance back at Andy. Doing his best to stay out of sight, he motioned me to keep going. Resigned to the task, I began picking my way across the obscure room. Several tables and chairs filled the center of the room. A couple of men sat at one of them. I headed for the far end of the room clutching the bottles tightly. "I can't drop one now," I thought. "This must be done with a smooth step up, over to, and out!" I hate walking by the table where the men are sitting. Each man looks at me as I pass.

Approaching the bar, a couple of men sitting there turned to see who this pathetic creature was who had invaded their domain. With no other woman in the place, I felt like a mouse in a room full of cats.

"What can I do for you, Hon," the bartender asked with a broad smile. Nervously, I held out one of the bottles for him to take. His smile suddenly trickled away to a blank stare. For a second he studied the arm full of green glass I was holding. "I know you. You're O'Brien's girl. You're bringing back bottles, eh; I suppose that they're your dad's?"

"How lucky can I get? This guy is carrying on the whole conversation by himself, even answering the questions." All I had to do was nod yes. He took the bottles from me. "Wait here a second." His tone wasn't a friendly one. He took the four bottles and started for the back room.

"For the love of Ned, give the kid her money." The ear shattering voice of the big bellied man sitting at the bar made me jump. A second man chimed in. "Give her the lousy money Gil. Its Bob's kid." Undaunted, Gil grumbled something low about losing his job, as he headed straight for the back door.

"He's gone out to check the cases," I thought. "Holy cow, he didn't believe me at all. That Andy, I'll murdalize him if I ever get out of here. Maybe I should just run out now and… " Before I could think another thought, Gil returned. Without a word, he walked to the register and pushed the key that made the drawer pop open. He pulled the right amount of change from the little compartments, and with the big smile back on his face, winked at me. "Here you are, Hon," he said dropping two dimes into my open hand. "Thank you." My voice was thin. I doubt he even heard me.

Not wasting a second, I turn and walk briskly across the room. Nearing the open door, my eyes were attracted to an object that seemed to be holding the door open. It was hard to believe what I saw; an iron doorstop in the shape of a cat. There it sat, looking back at me with little slits for eyes. It grinned like the cat that caught the mouse. I hastened my step losing no time passing through that wicked portal to the safety of the street, and the waiting Andy.

Already on the run, I dropped the money into Andy's hand. With a grin he said, "See? I told ya."

Our next stop was the little grocery store on the street by the railroad tracks. The store was run by a little Polish woman, and was open late on Sunday nights. She was good to us and very generous when she portioned out things that had to be weighed, things like our popping corn. We never knew her by name, only as the little lady with the chicken on the window. That ancient picture of a chicken sitting on a nest of eggs was as much a part of the window as the glass. We were comforted by it's dull, faded image greeting us when we climbed the steps to her store. It was like a welcoming friend adding to our security in a small way.

Operation Belmont Bar had been a success. We were returning home exhilarated, and satisfied. Our spoils well in hand, tonight we would have our popcorn. Mission accomplished.

Richard, now approaching the age of six, found his own way of earning spending money by observing the goings on around this street we called home. When the Methodist Church across the street from our building had doings such as weddings, and more often funerals, Richard was sure to take notice. Several days after the service the custodian would throw wilted flowers on a rubbish heap in an alley behind the church.

Richard knew what kind of ceremony had been performed days before, but it didn't matter to him if it was the happy or sad one. The important thing was that the flowers ended up on the rubbish pile. After combining the freshest looking flowers into small bouquets, he'd canvass the apartment houses on our block selling them to housewives for two or three cents a bouquet.

"You sold people funeral flowers?" I was shocked it seemed disrespectful somehow.

"Uh-huh," he answered with a grin.

"Funeral Flowers? That's sacrilegious." My voice rose a pitch higher in disbelief.

"They don't look like fooneral flowers. A flower's a flower," he said. I really couldn't argue with logic like that. It was an honest way of earning money, which was more than I could say for Andy and me.

We were all growing up so fast. It wasn't too long ago that Richard was doing dumb things like getting his head stuck in potty chairs, and tearing labels off cans. Now he was a little businessman.

Being young, and in a hurry to be older, you don't realize that the years your wishing away are making the grown-ups in your world older too. It never occurred to me that I was being reckless with their years as well. My parents had looked the same to me forever except for an added pound here and there, and a few gray hairs. Time had also taken a toll on our only living grandmother, who had become ill and was finally hospitalized. She was 68 years old when she died in late spring of '48 from pneumonia. Dad, Mama, Joseph and Andy attended the funeral. I stayed at home to watch my little brothers.

Our years on Albany Street had grown increasingly hard for us. Things we once took for granted had ceased to exist, fading from memory like snow disappearing under a warm spring sun. Mama's evening stories would never be a thing of joy for my brothers and sister as they had been for Joseph, Andy, and me. There were too many of us to occupy her time now, and she couldn't wait to get the smaller ones to bed at night let alone read to them.

The awful ritual of taking a daily dose of cod liver oil was in the past too. There was no money for such a luxury, and though we stayed healthy for a time, one day our luck ran out. We were in quarantined for over a month, because of scarlet fever. It affected Jimmy, Richard and me at the same time. It was a challenge for Mama to keep the healthy ones separated from the sick ones.

We couldn't afford to have a doctor from private practice. A nurse employed by the city paid us regular visits to check on our condition until our recovery was complete.

The following winter whooping cough took its turn keeping us from school for six weeks. We weren't allowed to join the main stream of activity until that quarantine was lifted. For two years in a row, we had all missed a month of school. I would never recover from this setback. Though the nuns kept passing me from one grade to another in the past, the time of failure was coming.

The day Andy turned sixteen he couldn't wait to get his working papers. It was his first step into the grown-up world. A job as "carry-out" boy at the Farmers Field Market was a beginning. In early fall when Harvest time came around, Andy moved from Farmers Market to the farmer's field.

When harvest time began for the farmers of Chipwey, Andy got a job as a hired hand on one of the biggest farms in the area. Every year, Mr. Glover hired ten strong, able-bodied young men to help with the extra work that harvest time created.

Mr. Glover offered room and board to any of the boys who didn't have a car to get back and forth. Andy had no car and would stay on the farm for the full three months. He drove the tractor, cleaned fields of the remnants of crops already harvested, and hauled and tossed and raked. As usual this was another adventure that Andy couldn't wait to start. We missed him during those months, and although the hours were long accompanied by a blister or two, he thrived on the hard work.

Andy's first permanent job was a pinsetter at the Chipwey bowling allies. He was earning about thirty cents for each game. His friend and sidekick Eddie worked there too, so the boys would meet and walk to work together.

According to Andy, nothing irritated a bowler more than to have to wait for a slow pinsetter. The faster a boy could clear the pins and set them in place, the more valued he was. A pinsetter that hustled got good tips. To Andy, it was a job with many good paydays.

Andy and Eddie made most of their money in the fall when the bowling leagues started. This kept them busy the whole winter long. Their services were often requested. He and Eddie made as much as two or three dollars in one night in tips alone. What a relief to both mothers. The boys had found a safe and legal way of working off all their excess energy.

Late one afternoon, as Andy put the finishing touches on for work, I watched as he stood in front of the kitchen sink. He meticulously combed every hair in place, giving special care to the wave in front, and then began patting after-shave on his face. I couldn't help teasing.

"Now that you know how to work the after shave, when do you think you'll have to shave?" He turned slowly and stared at me. We stood looking at each other straight in the eye, both of us trying to keep from laughing. "Mama, make Pigeon leave me alone," he yelled.

"Pigeon leave Andy alone." Mama was on the other side of the room ironing a shirt for Joseph. As usual, she was doing two jobs at once, keeping an eye on the stove where a pan of frying potatoes and hamburger patties snapped and sizzled. Joseph would be coming in soon to get ready for work too.

"Well, I never saw such primping in my life, as bad as a girl," My last remark moved Andy to swing the towel from around his neck and snap it at my legs. I dodged it by the skin of my teeth. Mocking him I hollered out in an exaggerated man's voice, "Mama, tell Andy to leave me alone!"

"You know you're not so smart. I at least have a job and that's more than I can say for SOME people." Andy was trying to get the last word in, but he should have known better.

"I have a job, helping Mama. Dad pays me a quarter a week."

"But I get real money." Andy moved his thumb and forefinger together, and gave me a smirky smile.

"Well, at least I bettered myself. You just don't seem to be able to get out of the alleys, do you?" For a moment, I wasn't sure I had gone too far, but his glare turned into a crafty look. "The pickin's are good in these alleys," he added smugly waving a couple of one dollar bills in front of my face.

Mama, listening to our goings-on, didn't turn to look but continued to tend the food on the stove, and with a laugh in her voice said, "Honest to heavens, you two. Pigeon … I mean Kali will you finish that shirt for Joseph, we're gonna lose the potatoes if I don't watch them." I took up the iron to finish the job.

My constant duties at home, and Andy with his new life; we and I had come to a fork in the road; but that was how it should be. All was going well. Andy's circle of friends was growing and he was discovering a different kind of social life. It was certain we wouldn't have to worry about popcorn money again, a fact that most assuredly would have delighted the owner of the Belmont Bar.

When I found out where Joseph had gotten a job I was green with envy. For almost two years he had been working odd jobs around town, now he had gotten a steady job at the Rialto Theater. He started out working only five days a week, and as the other boys quit, Joseph was soon in the position of being the longest employee there. He enjoyed working at the theater, and his trustworthy nature came through for him. Joseph was made head usher. The promise of becoming assistant Manager was in the wind. Joseph was working every night but one. Mr. Kauffman had come to rely on him to do the different jobs that kept the theater going. He knew whatever needed to be done Joseph would pitch in and do it. Many times Joseph stood on the tall ladder and changed the marquee when a new movie came in. He also had to be sure that the odd shaped metal cans that housed the reels of films, were ready and waiting at the door for a courier. There were times when Joseph himself had to carry the film to the train depot for transportation to the next town. When the woman in the ticket booth went home at night, Joseph filled in there too. It wasn't long before Mr. Kauffman was depending on Joseph as he would a son.

I had a problem calling this kind of a job work; nothing but movies every day.

"It's not all fun. I can't stand around watching movies every day. I have to walk up and down the aisles all the time, especially when there are little kids like you in the theater."

"I'm not a little kid," I said resentfully. "You do get to glance at the screen a little, don't you?" If he didn't say yes, I would have crumbled to dust. It just had to be the job that I imagined it to be.

"Yeah sometimes, especially at night during the week when there aren't many people in the theater. I can stand in the back of the lobby and watch a little. Mr. Kauffman never minds me doing that."

Joseph, so different from Andy, had a quiet easy going personality. He gave the air of being very reserved when he wanted to. Joseph was intelligent and very serious about his responsibilities. Not to say that Andy wasn't some of those things too, but somehow in a different way. Maybe it was that Joseph acted more grown up sooner than Andy, and had a serious side that happy-go-lucky Andy didn't.

I had become quite good at ironing the white shirts that Joseph had to wear to the theater. I was so proud of him in his usher's uniform. The gray jacket and pants, with the maroon striping here and there made him quite handsome. Dressed in his soldier like uniform, he often caught the eye of one giggling girl or another.

When Mr. Kauffman found he was short-handed because one of the ushers had gotten sick, Joseph would be asked to work a double shift. It seemed he was always short of help on weekends, the busiest time for the Rialto. Joseph would slip home long enough to ask Mama to send him a sandwich and coffee at suppertime. I always looked forward to running this errand. I'd get to see the inside of my wonderful place of storytelling, if only for a few minutes. I felt so special walking up to the two big doors, pushing them open, and walking in without paying. Joseph would be inside the door watching for me. As many times as I had run that errand, he never let me stay to see the movie free. Though I was disappointed each time he told me it was time to go, I understood when he reminded me that this was his job, and he had an obligation to Mr. Kauffman.

If nothing else, I had learned one thing from the environment we lived in; accept without question, things that can't be changed … for the time being.

CHAPTER 11
My Trip To Cloud-Cuckoo-Land

*A*s girls attending a Catholic school, we were expected to keep our hands busy and minds clean. When the day came when each girl in my class was no longer a child but a woman, the license to talk about grown up things was a bonus. To gather information on boys and sex was paramount regardless. It was no secret that the girls at Chipwey Public School were quite advanced along these lines. Nevertheless, that didn't mean because we went to St. Michael's we were angels, but cloaked in this veil of innocence imposed by our upbringing, maybe worse.

As we gathered at school waiting for the doors to open for afternoon session, the conversation was laced with giggles and squeals from any juicy tidbits. I never joined those raunchy gabfests, how could they find anything amusing in it? Deep inside, I felt they were making fun of my family because a new O'Brien was being born about every other year. Our Catholic Faith encourages big families, so weren't we doing what was expected of us? Turning away in disgust, I told myself these jerks didn't know much about anything. Although I didn't know anything either, I didn't want to learn the facts of life on the street like they were. I would learn then in the right place, at home, it just wouldn't be in the right way.

Joseph and Andy had both become very busy with their jobs. Andy, who always had to have a place to run off to, had a good reason to leave the house every night. These jobs gave both boys a built-in excuse for coming home after everyone was fast asleep. There was less contact with Dad this way. Trouble was, the demanding schedule began to take a toll on Joseph's schoolwork. For Andy, who wasn't doing well in school anyway, the late hours were certainly no help.

Dad's coming in at a late hour after a night out with his cronies suited us just fine. The atmosphere was so strained when he came home after drinking; we never knew what mood he would be in. During summer vacations from school, Mama allowed us to stay up past our nine o'clock curfew, and listen to programs we'd normally miss. When we began staying up later, Dad started coming home later, perhaps to avoid the crowd. By then the house would be dark and quiet, everyone would be in bed. Mama wouldn't be asleep for long after Dad made his entrance into the bedroom. He'd sit on the edge of the bed huffing and puffing as he dropped first one shoe and then the other with two dull thuds. Then he'd slip from his clothes. After removing them, his trousers were thrown across the cedar chest at the foot of the bed. The unmistakable sound of the ring of keys and coins in his pocket would shatter the quiet like a fire alarm. There was no question; Dad was going to bed. I was awakened every night by this noisy ritual. Dad knew that my two brothers had not come home from work yet, and may have felt the rest of us would sleep through anything. Mama and Dad's bed was flanked by cribs where Johnny and Jimmy slept. Still, no thought was given to the racket he was making.

I had reached an age of awareness of what was about to happen; I couldn't understand why Mama stood for this thoughtless behavior. He had become increasingly demanding of her, bullying her to get his own way. As usual by the time Dad had finally settled himself into bed I would be fully awake; I could hear Mama talking to him in stage-like whispers. She always seemed to be agitated with him, scolding him to be quiet. Typically, his answers were loud, punctuated with a swear word, as he shrugged off all objections. This was when I hated the thin drape that hung between our two rooms. Sounds that filtered through were very disturbing; Mama breathing a deep sigh, and the confounded bed creaking in a monotonous rhythm. There was the impression that Dad sometimes fell asleep or something, because Mama would be coaxing him on, "Will you *come* on!" I felt she was being made to do something she didn't want to, like Rosie was the day I saw Larry take advantage of her. Why should Dad be able to force his will on Mama? She wasn't a little girl; she was our mother, a grown-up. No one was supposed to make grown-ups do anything they didn't want to. Trying to think this out only made me angrier. If I could only have become temporarily deaf, it would solve my problem. To block out the sounds, I'd cover both ears with my hands or stuff my head under a pillow and pull it down tightly, releasing it on and off to hear if the ritual was over yet. Some nights it seemed to take forever. Dad's heavy breathing as he moved in the bed would eventually come to an abrupt end. More creaking of the bed as he settled himself down, and Mama's quick exit from the bedroom, then her return. There would be no conversation after that, only Dad's labored snoring. These amorous nights, so disagreeable for Mama, had worn my nerves raw. I had once seen a war movie where a prisoner was tied to a chair and tortured by the constant dripping of water on his head. By now, I knew something of what that must have been like.

One night I found a way to escape. I imagined that I actually left my body through the top of my head; it was a wonderful escape. I floated gently like a graceful mist, carried out of my bed, out of my room, out of the window toward the sky. Each time I performed this magic it became easier, and lasted longer. At first, surrounded by a plain gray sky I discovered things could be added or take away. The desire was to be alone surrounded by the soothing gray color. This was the right color for my world; soft, comforting. Concentrating real hard, there was a feeling of cool air brushing my face. The air refreshed me, drying the perspiration from my forehead. Gliding in smooth flight, I was free from the torment of earth. It was like being cradled in cotton. There were no birds, no stars or moons, just silence. There wasn't the slightest hint of earth below at all, only me drifting through the gray foggy mist, free, free, free. Was this what it was like to be in Cloud-cuckoo-land? When the irrepressible desire struck, and my outstretched hand left my ears to feel the damp cool clouds, all would disappear. There were times when I returned to silence and found that the enemy had been avoided. Other times, the rhythmic sound of the creaky bed was still there. I never seemed to be able to retreat a second time to my Cloud-cuckoo-land. Once I returned to my room of torture, I wasn't permitted passage out until next time. My only recourse then was to bury my head beneath a pillow again. To confront Mama with such an embarrassing subject was out of the question. It was my father's business; it didn't concern me. By now it had become easy for me to put distasteful things out of my mind during the day, but like a child fearing the darkness, there was a dread in my last thoughts before sleep.

One night, I had reached the end of my rope. There would be no more contending, no more coping as the nerve wrenching procedure dragged on in the next room. I sought the asylum of my pillow. Despite my efforts, the nerve wrenching sounds continued on and on when there should have been no sound at all. Tonight the Cloud wouldn't be my temporary escape. Something inside said, "You'll runaway no more." I set up in bed and yelled at the top of my voice, "Mama, will you hit him in the head with something?" Immediately my hand slapped across my mouth. "Did I say that?" My yell must have been like throwing a pitcher of ice water on Mama. She left the bed, ran into the front room and dropped down on the couch; I had made her cry.

Dad was not to be put off, and began barking out orders to her. "Helen, get back here. Get back ta bed!"

"Will you shut up I'm not getting back anywhere!" Mama's voice was shaky. Her yell had a determined tone I never heard before.

Laying myself back down in the bed, I was scared to death of the anger that may have been unleashed in Dad. What would be next? Maybe he'd come in here and beat me. I was wrong; dad scrambled out of bed and tried to drag her back to the bedroom. Mama was crying louder now.

Then there was a scuffling sound, a struggle. The couch pushed against the wall, its short legs banging against the floor. Then she let out a painful scream. All went quiet except for sobbing. I knew Mama was hurt. It took Mama's scream of anguish to turn Dad around and head him back to bed. Pulling the corner of the drape back the tiniest bit, I could see Jimmy sitting up in his crib. "Lay down. Go to sleep," Dad snapped. Jimmy quickly lay back down. The sheet wrapped about Dad's waist trailed behind him. He climbed back into bed still grumbling, "No snot-nosed thirteen year old kid's gonna tell me what to do!" Dad was asleep in no time. The rooms were starting to smell of his alcohol breath. I didn't care. He was going to sleep. Thank God!

Mama spent the rest of the night in the front room rolled up in the corner of the couch. I wanted to go to her, but not with such furry so close by. If I were to awaken him, it would start everything all over. So I stayed put, waiting for sleep to carry me out of this chaotic mess. Soon everything, even Mama's sobs, grew quiet. After a time of regretting what had happened, and wondering why I hadn't kept my big mouth shut, sleep finally did come. When I awoke the next morning, the stillness was unnerving; I wondered where Mama would be. The bedroom was empty except for Jimmy and Johnny who were still sleeping peacefully in their cribs. Cautiously, I approached the doorway and peeked into the front room. The couch was empty too. Stepping into the hallway, I could see Mama in the kitchen, drinking coffee as she read a newspaper. The radio on top of the refrigerator played softly. Mama looked up as I entered the kitchen. She looked awful. I have seen these red swollen eyes before; crying was not a stranger to Mama. This time her eyelids were so swollen that her eyelashes nearly disappeared in the puffiness.

"Are you up already?" Mama said softly. I nodded yes, and sat at the table with a cup of coffee. I busied myself with the small task of adding the milk and sugar to cover how stunned I was at her swollen face. This being Saturday, Dad would work only a half-day. He was already on his way to the factory. Thank God for small favors. After what had happened the night before, I wasn't sure how to act in front of him. I knew it was bound to be uncomfortable, but for now, I'd put that worry in my pocket for another day.

Mama's attempt to fold the newspaper drew a winced from her. She grabbed her elbow.

"Yer elbow hurt?"

"Yeah." Mama answered in a gravely voice as she rubbed her elbow.

"What did you do to it?" I felt at ease. We had finally broken the tense silence that had hung between us.

"I guess I must have banged it or something." Mama rises and busies herself cleaning Dad's dishes from the table. Her attempt to dodge further discussion tells me I asked one question to many. "How stupid can you get, Kali?" I thought, "How could you ask such a dumb question?" Conversation was awkward again, but neither was there escape in the silence. I drank the coffee to keep my big mouth shut.

During the daytime, I was able to bury the bad feelings about having to face Dad that night. With the long shadows of twilight came a growing uneasiness, and thoughts of how I might handle the problem. Maybe he'd come home after we were all in bed. No. With my luck, he'll probably come home early. Well, I won't look at him at all. Maybe I *will* look at him ... stare real hard and make *him* feel uneasy, after all, he was the bad guy not me. That was a bold plan, but beneath it laid a sniveling coward.

I had just finished washing dishes for Mama when zero hour came. I sat submissively in a chair in front of the cupboard. It was as far away from the table as I could get in our small kitchen. "I'll pretend to be so engrossed in the radio program I won't look his way." Not the most strategist plan, but it would have to do. Dad came in the room as usual and placed his brown paper bag on the table. Mama continued wiping the dishes I had just washed for her. No one spoke. He headed right toward me. I braced myself. "Here it comes," I thought. His huge hand reached out. He was so close I felt the sleeve of his shirt skimming across the hair on the back of my head. He opened the cupboard door behind me and withdrew his tall, thin beer glass. He returned to the table and filled the glass with the yellow, foamy liquid, sat down and began nibbling on the sharp cheese and salami he brought with him. It was incredible. You would have thought nothing had ever happened the night before. I was put off by the whole subject and couldn't explain to Joseph and Andy what had happened, but I did see Richard quietly talking to them that morning. The yelling must have awakened Richard; although a seven-year-old child couldn't be expected to understand, he heard enough for my older brothers to figure it out. For a long time afterwards, we were all reminded of what happened that summer night. To this day, when Mama uses her arm in a certain way and is caught off guard, there's a little cry of pain.

Dad continued to come home early evenings after that. He brought home ice cream for us which we enjoyed as we listened to the radio. When we were fully involved with what was supposed to be our distraction, Mama and Dad would disappear. The first time this happened I looked up in time to see Dad herding Mama into the hallway. Mama was looking back at me as though she was asking for help. Perhaps I read her wrong, but that was the impression. There was confusion and anger that I hadn't helped Mama more. This relationship that grown-ups shared was too complicated for me.

By now, picking up the pieces and continuing with our lives was a matter of course for the O'Brien family. It was July, school had been out for a month, and Mary was with Aunt Mildred for the summer. For the rest of school vacation Mama and I would have to deal with trying to keep the shoes on the smaller kids. The danger of getting cut by broken glass in the courtyard was always there. All summer long we had scabs the size of crab apples on our knees from falling on crushed rock in our backyard. Between the scabs and cuts, Mama gave up trying to fight the shoe problem, and continued patching up the bruises. Every Wednesday evening, after Mama and I scrubbed our little group as clean as we could, we packed them off to the park for a two-hour band concert. By the time the band was into their third number, a good size crowd had gathered close to the bandstand. There were never enough park benches to go around, so many people sat on blankets spread on the grass. We didn't have a blanket that was presentable enough to be seen in public. "Anyway," Mama said, "sitting on the grass is cooler."

Without our concerts, we would have been left with a Wednesday evening like all the other evenings, empty. Concerts were almost as exciting as going to a movie. This special night was not only for an evening of pleasant music. It was a place for meeting and greeting people. Friends who hadn't seen each for weeks were sure to meet at the Band Concert. It wasn't necessary for Aunt Hanna to be in the park to enjoy the music. Her house sat high on the hill. The music would rise into the warm summer night, and spread up the hillside surrounding each home as it rose upward. Aunt Hanna would come down from the hill and occasionally attend, but our cousins Carol and John Jr. were always there with friends. Mama chose a patch of ground at the edge of the crowd that allowed the smaller kids to run in an open area of the park. Surrounded by their scattered shoes and socks, Mama and I could enjoy the music with little worry. Someone Mama knew would eventually stroll by, allowing her to have a grown-up chat.

Like a ballplayer running from one base to another, Andy would zip by, say "hi," then he was gone. He and his friends would be taking a tour of the park acting out a age-old custom called girl watching. The concert was a good place for young people to meet, and possibly end up at The Chocolate Bar, a soda fountain where teens gathered.

Our Great Aunt Katie was a regular at the concerts, too. Since her husband, Uncle Bill, had died, she went many places with her circle of friends. Everyone was so concerned three years ago when she went through surgery to have a cancerous breast removed. A year later, the disease destroyed the other breast. This terrible ordeal left her thin and frail, but it didn't slow her down. She kept active and even worked as a cook for the priests at St. Michael's Parish. I always marveled at the number of hairpins that secured the knot of gray hair to the back of her head. They created a non-stop job, pushing them back into place as they worked their way out of the gridlock. It wasn't unusual, in her daily travels, to leave a trail of pins behind. She was a tough Irishman with more life and inner strength than many healthy people I saw every day.

Mama and I visited Aunt Katie often to run an errand or wash dishes for her. Aunt Katie loved her home-baked cookies, but since her surgery, there were no muscles in her arms to help her mix the heavy batter. Mama did it for her. Made from her old Irish recipe, our reward would be some of the best molasses cookies we ever had the pleasure to eat.

Aunt Katie and Grandma Desmond were sisters; they came to America together forty years ago. Aunt Katie, now the surviving sister, kept her Irish heritage obvious through the trace of Irish Brogue that lingered in her speech. Her calm nature could convince me things weren't as bad as I thought. The probability of life getting better was always there. When I was down, she would give me gentle pep talks; one such talk I've never forgotten.

"Aw, don't be so worried about your problems," she said. "Trying to change what can't be changed is such a waste of time. Something good will come along and replace the disappointment." Then she added, "When I was a little girl my mother would tell me, 'put that worry in your pocket for another day.'"

My dress had no pockets to put my worry in. "What if I have no pocket?"

"Then put it in your sock."

There were many times I had no socks. What to do then?

"Put it in your shoe."

Lifting my right foot to examine the bottom of my shoe, we could see a wee round hole in the center. My left shoe was no better, showing round circles of wear. "What if they have holes?"

"Put it in there anyway. The worry will fall out and you'll be well rid of it," she answered, with the quick wit of a Leprechaun.

When St. Patrick's Day rolled around, an old friend from Ireland would send Aunt Katie a memento; a card with a relic of a saint, a bit of moss that can live without water or even a real shamrock. My favorite was a sliver of stone taken from a rock at Blarney Castle in County Cork Ireland. In kissing the stone, a person can be blessed with the gift of blarney. It's hard to resist the possessor of this smooth talk, but the stone is very selective, and not just anyone who kisses the stone is granted this fine gift. I kissed the magical stone a couple of times, just to be sure.

One afternoon, I climbed the stairs to Aunt Katie's second story apartment, expecting nothing more than our usual visit. School was out for the day, but before returning home, I would sometimes drop by to see if I could run an errand to run for her. If she didn't need me, the two of us would have a chat over a cup of hot tea. I must confess the thought of one of her molasses cookies motivated my visits. I would wait for her familiar, thin, high-pitched voice to holler out, "Come on in the door's open." Her front door opens into her dining room. The furniture from bygone days is old but well cared for. A large dining room table, with four high backed chairs tucked in neatly, is covered with a lace tablecloth. A bowl of slightly puckered apples is in the center next to a box of mouth-watering chocolates. The walls of the dining room were dressed with just a few scant pictures. Individual portraits of Aunt Katie and Uncle Bill were adorned with heavy, wooden, oval shaped frames. The glass in them bowed out like a bubble. The pictures were of how they looked years ago when they were first married. The picture of Aunt Katie is a forever reminder of what a beautiful girl she was. These two pictures hung in the same spot, year after year, for as long as I could remember. I was always drawn to them because of the unique way the glass curved outward. Passing by them each time they seemed to beckon me to run my fingers over the bloated glass.

On the other side of the room was a oil burning stove that heated her three rooms in winter time, and near by, her old rocker draped with an Afghan she had made. At this time of the day, still wearing the kitchen apron she wore all day while cooking for the priests, she'd be resting in that old rocker listening to the radio. Stella Dallas and Lorenzo Jones were two soap operas she would never miss. Today my timing was bad. She was glued to the radio, in the middle of one of her programs. I drew up a chair next to her and listened too. Within a few minutes, I found it necessary to make use of Aunt Katie's bathroom, but the doorknob was a problem. It felt loose, and kept turning in a complete circle. Oh well, this would just have to wait. I wouldn't interrupt her program … not even for this.

"That old knob has been giving me trouble on and off," Aunt Katie said heading for the bathroom, pushing a loose pin back into her knot of hair. She gave the doorknob a few of her special twists and the door popped open. "Don't try to shut the drippy faucet off, that has to be fixed too. Mr. Crowley has some repairing to do for me." As we continued our visit, I was telling her of some of the things that happened in school. Always being a good listener, she'd cling to every word. On this particular day, I was relating how silly some of the girls at school had acted over a new boy. She then began telling me of an experience she had while still living in Ireland.

A young man named Packey, had become quite smitten with her, and did his best to win her acceptance. Having lived no more than fifteen summers, she had no desire to be courted by him or anyone else, so she tried to discourage him. Stubbornness being an Irish trait, Packey's persistence was a credit to his heritage. Finally, the young Katie had enough, and was forced to come right out and tell him she was not interested. Would he kindly stop bothering her? Crushed by her rejection, his last comment was, "Katie, if you change your mind, I'll be 'round. I'd smuther me muther far ya!"

"Boy, that guy should have kissed the blarney stone, huh Aunt Katie?" My remark made her giggle. Despite the good laugh we had over the story, the retelling of it affected her in a special way. For the moment, could it have made her feel young again? She made me feel as if I were visiting a giggly girl friend as she leaned forward in the rocker, her head tilted as that of a shy young girl.

While there, I usually visited the many potted plants she had on the back porch. The glass-enclosed porch was like a green house, and modestly she credited that with her luck. I knew better; those plants loved her. "What's this one, Aunt Katie, is it new?" It was a tall heavy leafed plant.

"That's a plant that was a birthday gift, it's called Mother-in-law tongue."

"Mother-in-law tongue? What a funny name for a plant!" I said.

"See how the leaf comes to a very sharp point? It's like the sharp tongue of a Mother-in-law." The grin on her face and one hand up to her mouth tells me that there is a joke in her answer.

Walking to one of the porch windows, I pushed it open. As it swung out, I leaned forward to see into the backyard. A mixed variety of flowers were growing in a profusion of color that just dazzled the old flower lover in me. For a moment, I envisioned the little garden Mama and I had when we lived up on the hill. "How beautiful the flowers are! Can you pick them, Aunt Katie?"

"Yes." Joining me at the window, she listens as I try to identify each variety. Among the roses and peonies, one flower stood out over them all. Standing tall as sentries along the back of the fence were hollyhocks with blooms so big and colorful they would have challenged a blind man to ignore them.

"They have short stems, can't make a bouquet, huh?"

"Did I ever show you how to make princess dolls?"

"Dolls … make dolls out of hollyhocks?"

"Come on we'll go down. Take care on these stairs. Hold the railing." Sliding her hand along the railing, Aunt Katie begins cautiously down the steep flight of stairs. On the way down, my curiosity grows. Crossing the lawn to the flowers, I can already smell the fragrance of the pink peonies. Their huge heads are swaying back and forth in a gentle breeze that makes the fragrance airborne. I bend down to them for a closer smell as we pass by.

Aunt Katie reaches out for a fully opened hollyhock. "What color do you like best? Red?"

"Yeah, I love Red."

She pinches off a fully opened bloom and an unopened bud. Standing on tiptoe to see what she is doing, some green leaves are pulled away from the round unopened bud, and joined to the fully opened flower. Standing in the palm of her outstretched hand is a flower doll, a miniature princess. "How did you do that? Show me!"

"Lets do a pink one this time. We don't want to take too many from the same stalk. First, pinch off an unopened bud. This will be the head of the princess." Handing it to me, she watches closely until I have followed all her instructions.

It was the cleverest thing I had ever done or seen. The fully opened blossom turned upside down became a dress with its skirt flaring out on all sides. The small round unopened bud was the head of the doll.

"Can I take some home with me to show Mama?"

"Yes, but you'll have to hurry or they'll wilt,"

"I'll run. I won't let them wilt, 'til I show Mama."

The discontent I had when this visit began was already forgotten as I started out for home. Tucked in one arm is the box containing my flower dolls; in my other arm, schoolbooks and a bag of four slightly shriveled up apples.

Early one summer evening Mama and I made a quick trip to Aunt Katie's. The reason for the visit was to pick up some food left over from the priests' evening meal. These donations had a way of coming our way when they were most needed. Aunt Katie had sent word to us about the food. It wasn't often Mama went anywhere without pushing a stroller loaded with a kid or two, but this evening our small charges were not with us. It was Joseph's night off work and he would watch them until we got back. We embraced our freedom like two schoolgirls out for a night of fun. The walk wasn't a long one and much too soon, Aunt Katie's house came into view. Climbing the stairs to her apartment and knocking, we waited for the familiar voice to invite us in, but there was no response. Mama opened the door and leaned in. "Aunt Katie, are you here?" There was no reply. Entering, Mama walked through the apartment calling out again, still no answer. Mama walked to the closed bathroom door and called again, but to no avail. She stood with her ear pressed against the door. "Kali, listen. That's water running in there,"

"Yeah I hear it, but Aunt Katie has a bad faucet. Remember?"

Mama pressed her ear to the door again then turned the doorknob. The knob continued to turn in circles devilishly guarding its secret. Mama began rotating it more frantically now, and pushing on the door hoping it would somehow pop open. "No. That water is running too fast. Glory-be to God, maybe she's unconscious on the floor, or maybe she's fallen in the bath tub." Mama didn't even look at me as she spoke. She just kept frantically tearing at the uncooperative doorknob.

"What'll we do Mama?" Her panic was spreading to me. I could envision poor Aunt Katie lying in there on the floor. We were meant to come here tonight to save her.

"Call the fire station! Tell them we think she's locked in the bathroom and may be sick." At the sound of her own words, Mama's voice trembled.

"Number, please." The operator said.

"We need the fire station, hurry." The next voice I heard was the calm voice of a man.

"OK, now slow down, and give me the address. They'll be right there, honey, stay calm."

"They're on the way," I called out as I hung the phone up.

Mama continued to fight the stubborn doorknob, and not for a moment did she stop trying to open the door. I ran down to the front porch and waited for help to arrive. Mrs. Reardon, a next door neighbor, wandered on to her porch and sat in a chair fanning herself with a folded newspaper. When she spied me, she called out, "Hi Kali. Visiting Katie are you?" Quickly I told her the story. "Why Katie isn't home. She went to church twenty minutes ago," she said. A feeling of relief welled up inside me, then a feeling of dread; the sound of the fire truck was fast approaching from down the block with its fire bell clanging away. There was no time to tell Mama that our aunt wasn't lying in a heap behind the bathroom door, but kneeling down inside the church door. The truck noisily screeched to a stop in front of the house. Two firemen, partially decked out in fire-fighting clothes, jumped from the truck before it had fully come to a stop and clamored upstairs. Holy cow! One of 'em has an ax. I stayed on the porch. If anyone was going to do any chopping, I didn't want to be around to see it. The firemen removed the doorknob and pushed the door open. The bathroom was empty. They were very understanding and could see that Mama had true concern. Handing Mama the doorknob they departed, with a word of advice for Aunt Katie to get her doorknob fixed. I could hear the giggles as they jumped on to the truck and pulled away.

Mama was going to find out for herself. We'd go to church, and see if Aunt Katie was there. We hurried downstairs and stepped out to the front porch. Mama didn't expect to see people, all the way down the block, were standing outside their homes looking our way. Several small groups of men standing in the middle of the road were muttering to each other. Feeling like fools, we darted from the porch. Mrs. Reardon called out after us, "Helen, she's at church." We crossed the street quickly and headed for St. Michael's. Pulling the heavy church door open we could see the silhouette of a lone, small figure seated in a front pew. Aunt Katie was there safe and sound. We were grateful Aunt Katie was alive and well, but for us, the sting of embarrassment was still there. Through her Irish sense humor Aunt Katie maintained it was hilarious, and assured us the whole time she was in good hands. The next day an apologetic landlord fixed the leaky faucet and broken doorknob. When Mama and I finally set aside our punctured pride, we had to admit it couldn't have been a better joke on us if it had been planed. Still, it took some time for us to live it down. Joseph and Andy continued to razz us about it without mercy.

Life was changing again. Richard and Mary were next in line to take over scouting back alleys. Joseph and Andy are contributing a portion of their pay to Mama, giving her a couple of extra dollars; that was a good change. Every time a new O'Brien was brought into the world, our delicate balance was tilted once again.

CHAPTER 12
A Fling For Free Frieda

We never knew much about what went on in Dad's life on lower Main Street until one night when he came home from an evening at Danahey's Bar in an unusually giddy mood. From the expected brown bag that he carried, he pulled a package of pig's knuckles, and a pickled egg instead of the usual hard salami, and next, the quart of beer. Everything was set on the table. The brown bag was crushed into a ball and thrown toward the garbage bin. He missed, but ignored it. Dad was in a playful mood, giggling like a schoolboy over a prank that turned out well.

Seated at the table, the scrumptious knuckles, egg, and foamy glass of beer were spread out before him. Dad began talking about someone who had come into the bar; someone he called "Free Frieda." I overheard Dad telling Mama once, Frieda wasn't just a lady of the night, but any time she could get "it." Like all kids curious about the adult world, we were all ears. Little furrows popped up between Mama's eyes. Her disapproving frown told us maybe we were about to hear something that we shouldn't. Talking about Frieda had that effect on her without fail. Mama wouldn't take her eyes from Dad until she was sure the story wasn't going too far. "Bob not around the kids," was a warning that was ignored.

Frieda had wandered into Danahey's that night looking for a sympathetic ear. Choosing to sit by Dad was her downfall. Dad, who was seated at the bar talking to his friend Louie, wasn't interested in her problems. "She plopped down on the stool right next to me ... sure was in a loud, bitchy mood. Even after Louie and me bought her a beer, she didn't shut her big mouth ... kept talking and talking about people walking all over her." Dad paused for another giggle, "Must be sumthin' new ... never heard that one before." A big bite was taken out of the pickled egg, a couple swallows of beer washed it down and the story continued.

"Every once in a while she would give me a nudge with her elbow, pretty soon she was leaning against me not just nudging. I warned her, I told her, 'quit;' ...didn't listen, so I shoved her with my elbow. All ya could see was arms, legs and skirts flyin' all over the place." Naughty giggles filled the kitchen again from Dad's recall of Frieda's hard connection with the floor.

"Don't be telling those stories around the kids." Mama tried to camouflage her amusement with another scowl. Dad didn't hear a thing anyway. He was too busy reliving the picture of Free Frieda flying through the air.

At one time or another, Dad belonged to several clubs around Chipwey. They all had family parties at Christmastime. I envied Joseph's and Andy's freedom from family outings. Their jobs were their passport. But Dad's membership in the club paid off well when he traipsed in with the six of us kids close behind, chomping at the bit for a holiday party.

One club that Dad joined was an all-male German club where singing as a group was part of their routine. Dad wasn't a member for long, but I like to refer to that time as his musical years. Coming home after a club meeting, with sounds of the heavenly choir still pulsating in his breast, he'd start singing at the top of his voice. Not able to guess which song we would be blessed with, it eventually boiled down to two of his favorites, "Melancholy Baby" or "A Shanty in Old Shanty Town." We

knew when Dad was singing he was in a good mood. He never noticed
the grins that he drew from us. Dad posed quite a comical picture. His
pants hung so low that his potbelly, protruding over his belt, was more
conspicuous than ever. It might be thought that something heavy in his
pockets was inching them down his hips as he wobbled back and forth.
His only concern was that he was ready for another drink. Immediately
he would look for the special glass that was his alone, and God-help all
of us if he didn't find it. It was very thin and delicate with no curves or
fancy decorations. Mama was forever trying to keep us from using it.
Despite her efforts to put it out of reach, someone would snatch it from
the cupboard as if by some Svengali command. Times when the glass
met with a disastrous end, Dad would become enraged.

"I've only one damn glass and ya can't keep the kid's hands off it.
Kid's are running the house."

"Here, this one isn't bad. Use it until I get you another one." Mama,
trying to pacify, would hand him one of the thinnest jelly glasses she
could find.

"I'm not drinking out of a lousy jelly glass. Who broke it?"

"I did. I dropped a cup on it in the dishpan so don't go blaming the
kids. If I had a few dollars in my pocket once in a while, I could buy you
more than one glass at a time."

"Sure, buy a whole dozen so they can bust 'em all. And what the hell,
I gave ya thirty-five dollars Friday."

"Thirty-five dollars last Friday! Where do you think it all went? How
far do you think thirty-five dollars goes?" Mama's cynical remark was
infuriating. Dad's voice would turn up in volume, and the argument
would continue until Mama refused to argue anymore. With no one to
spar with, Dad would wind down. At some point in the argument he
would painfully concede, and pour the long awaited drink into the thin
jelly glass with pink bunnies on it.

Dad's special way of filling a glass was to tip it to one side. What kept
the liquid from spilling out? The foamy white head would ride up to the
very rim of the glass. It was timed out to the split second. Dad would

right the glass without losing one tiny droplet. One night the thin, sleek glass waited for him all in one piece. He began to pour and his hand grew increasingly unsteady as his sway moved him back and forth. The accuracy of that shaky hand amazed us. We couldn't help expecting this to be the time it would overflow. Somehow, he always seemed to be able to zero in on the target, up-righting the glass at the last moment. "Now that has to come from a lot of practice," I thought. All while this unstable pouring was going on, he would be singing out in his nasal tone.

Telling him that he had enough, and not to drink would result in a full-blown argument. Mama had come to know what to say, and when to say nothing at all. She had learned to handle him reasonably well, but you never knew what would set him off. Sometimes he would just doze off sitting at the table. It didn't have to be for very long, but if Mama woke him to tell him to go to bed, he could be transformed from the once jolly singer into a roaring lion. So Mama learned to let the sleeping lion alone until he awoke by himself, and even then there were no guarantees he wouldn't wake up ready for a fight.

One night as he belted out, "A Shanty in old Shanty Town," I took care to listen to the words he sang. In exceptionally good voice this evening, he sang the song all the way through with no stops. The more sentimental a song was, the more feeling he'd put in it. That night for some reason, I was drawn to examine his face closely. His dark brown hair appeared to be a washed-out color because of the ever-crowding white hair. The day's growth of a beard was also speckled with gray and made his face appear fuller than normal. I was touched most of all by the haunted look of his eyes. A look I wouldn't soon forget; he had somehow become a pathetic vision. My giggling dissolved away as he sang on, his eyes transfixed on the glass of beer. Not that he was taking any special note of the glass, more as if he were in a private world of his own; his Cloud-cuckoo-land. He began to sing the song a second time. "It's only a Shanty… " The words slurred out. His eyes glisten with moisture. I didn't realize it then, but that song could have been written with him in mind. The words were moving him to tears. The song tells of a little shanty sitting by the railroad tracks; exactly how Dad lived when he was a little boy. It goes on to say that memories of the past are taunting, pulling him back. The words carry a message of regrets and sadness for things that used to be. Dad was completely lost in his Cloud. Unaware that anyone was taking notice, he allowed himself to be deeply moved by the song. The last line telling of the silvered-hair mother keeping vigil for someone's return caused his voice to break with emotion.

One night some weeks later, as Mary and I slept, whispering in the next room woke me. "Oh no," I thought ... but no, this sound was someone crying. That someone was Dad. Quietly I listened to the conversation that easily passed through the cloth door.

"All this time she's been living alone. I should have gone to see her ... I couldn't." Dad gave in to the tears.

"Don't blame yourself. You were a young kid when those things happened. You were hurt. It doesn't matter anymore." Mama's voice was soft, comforting.

Who were they talking about? What could possibly cause Dad to cry? It was beyond my guessing. I parted the curtain between our bedrooms and peeked through. Mama and Dad were in bed, and in the faint light of the room, I could see Dad lying in bed with his arm covering his eyes. Mama was sitting up propped against the headboard. Dad said something about it being almost twenty years since he last saw someone as he wiped his eyes with a handkerchief that Mama handed him. Allowing the curtain to slip from my fingers, I lay back down. I would have to wait until morning to talk to Mama. I couldn't figure this one out.

The next morning the conversation overheard in the darkness was forgotten with the brilliance of a new day. Traveling through Mama's room, I was suddenly brought up short. The sight of her bed was enough to bring back thoughts of Dad, and what was heard the night before. My light-hearted mood gave way to a feeling of apprehension. In the kitchen, Mama stood at the ironing board moistening clothes with the sprinkling bottle. The crackling sound coming from the iron told me she was preparing to use it.

"You ironing already?"

"I have some things to iron out for Daddy. His suit will need pressing too."

"Where's he going?"

"Daddy's mother died yesterday. We'll have to go to the wake and then there'll be the funeral. You'll have to watch the kids for us until it's over."

"But, I didn't know Dad had a mother. I mean, I thought she was … already dead."

"Oh no, she's been living up on Furnace Street all this time. She made a bad decision long ago. After Daddy's father was killed, she allowed men to come to their home all the time. Daddy never forgave her for that kind of life." Mama didn't look up at me. It's not easy to speak of such things. I was surprised that Mama was talking to me about such a grown-up subject at all. She quickly said what she had to; probably hoping I wouldn't ask any questions.

"Not long after we were married Daddy took me to meet her. It was the smallest house I'd ever seen. It was hard for him to go back there. He never went back again after that." Mama lowered herself on to a chair. She was folding a pillowcase in her lap, and stroked it repeatedly as if to rub the wrinkles out with her hand. Lost in thought, her words came slower.

"The man she married after Daddy left her has been dead for some time now. She's been living up there for years, growing old all alone."

"No wonder Dad was crying," I blurted.

"You heard him last night." Slightly embarrassed I nodded my answer.

"Well, he's feeling bad. She was his mother. And it's bringing back a lot of hurt feelings."

"Does that mean … all this time we had two grandmothers?"

Mama's pensive mood was replaced by silence. Abruptly, she rose from the chair, and spread a dampened shirt flat on the board. The steam hissed as the hot iron slid over the moist cloth. "Yes, you had two grandmothers." Strange that we, her own grandchildren, were not aware she was alive … until she was dead. It was too late for anything else but sadness. It made sense why I felt the strange way I did the night he sang that song. Instead of feeling scared of him, I was feeling sorry for him.

Dad had to attend to the details of the funeral, so Mama and I went alone. It wasn't the first time I'd been to a wake, but the closer we got, the more unsettled I felt. We climbed the stairs, stopped in the entryway and were greeted by a man dressed in a black suit. I was still holding on tightly to Mama's arm. In a few seconds, I'd see for the first time, a relative who was a stranger to all of us. Meeting someone new wasn't a problem, but with them lying there in a coffin, was. I snuggled even closer to Mama. The man led us to a room at the end of a short hallway. Chairs were lined up on both sides of the room where a coffin and kneeling bench stood at the far end. The voices of two lone figures sitting there echoed in the emptiness. "They're her neighbors." Mama whispered to me. We exchanged smiles as we passed them by. Large baskets of flowers standing at each end of the coffin filled the room with a lovely fragrance. One basket had a white ribbon across the front of it with the word "Mother" printed in gold. For once, I wasn't consumed by the flowers, but by the form that lay before me. Not sure what I would see, the worst was expected. She must have been an awful person to be kept from us all these years. Mama told me that girls who live a loose life end up looking old and tough before their time. Grandma O'Brien was in her late sixties, and had to look awful by now.

Mama and I approach the kneeling bench. My eyes were cast downward. Nothing could make me look at the still figure before me. Kneeling side by side, we made the sign of the cross preparing to say prayers. For me prayers didn't come; tangled in feelings of dread, I couldn't look at the woman in the coffin much less remember the words to a prayer. "Andy will never let me live it down if he finds out I was afraid to look at grandma," I thought. "You have to look. You have to."

I raised my eyes, studying the puckered satin lining on the coffin's enormous lid, then lowered my eyes gradually until they rested on a light gray dress with a pattern of tiny blue flowers. Still, pale hands, with a plain band of silver on one finger, were clasped around a crucifix; my eyes went a bit further, stopping on a decorative pin at the throat of the dress. Now, just a little more, and there she was; a slightly plump lady, and not very tall. It was hard for me to tell if Dad resembled her, but her face was a gentle one, lined with the wrinkles of her sixty-some odd years. She wasn't frightening; she looked peaceful. Her snow-white hair was fixed just as she would have wanted it; somehow, I just knew that. She looked … she looked like a grandmother. I don't recall saying any prayers, but softly whispered, "Hello Grandma."

Later that night Mama went to the wake again with Dad, Joseph and Andy. I watched the kids at home making sure they got to bed on time. Mama and Dad were the only ones to go to the funeral.

For days after the funeral, Dad continued to come home for dinner. We sat together around the table for the last meal of the day as we used to. This was a big change. He was still drinking, but it wasn't the same. Dad turned again to his books for escape, something he hadn't done since we moved to Albany Street. We didn't speak about any of this between ourselves; instead, we accepted it as though this was how things really were. Except for Grandma's death, it was a good way to end the summer of '48. These peaceful weeks were her gift to us; through her death, she had given our family this pleasant time. Unfortunately, in a gradual decline, the magic spell would end.

Early, one fall morning Mama and I prepared to take a trip. I had been hounding her to show me where Grandma O'Brien was buried; finally, she gave in, agreeing to take me to the cemetery. Dad had the knack of popping in the door at the right moment; he could sense when Mama planned on going someplace without him. He would unexpectedly come home for lunch, right on schedule … his schedule. Dad normally bought his lunch downtown or carried something with him. Still, there he'd be walking in the door, and it always took him twice as long to finish. He would lollygag at the table with not a care in the world. There was always a chance that one of the kids would bound in the door and ask when we were going to go to … wherever. Maybe that little slip of the tongue was what he waited for. If he did find out, that was one sure way to get an argument off and running.

"What the hell are ya going there for?"

"Just to get out of this place for a while, that's all."

"Well, when are ya coming home?"

"We'll be back for supper. It's just for a visit."

"In time for supper? You'll never make it back in time for supper, so don't tell me that."

"For crying out loud it's only a couple blocks away. We're not going to the moon. You don't come home for supper anyway, what do you care."

Dad's voice would get louder as he tried to yell Mama down. "It's all the way to the other side of town. Don't shit me. I know where it is. It's gonna take ya a lot longer than ya think to get back here. Jumpin'-jingeling…"

Mama cut him off before he got to the curse word, "Don't be swearing around the kids."

"Then don't get me all riled up. I know what I'm talking about."

"Get you riled up?" Mama's words dripped with sarcasm, but we all knew what this meant; kiss the trip good-by. Mama would buckle under to end the quarrel.

Lately we found a way that let Dad believe we sat home from morning till night. By leaving early in the morning, Dad would never know that Mama had escaped from her cage at all. A nerve-racking way to live, but it was worth it to do something different for a few hours. At the beginning of the day speed was the key, get out of the house before Dad came home.

It was my job to get Jimmy and Johnny dressed, while Mama made her bed and tidied up her bedroom. Dad hated to see their bed unmade when he came home. If, for some reason, it didn't get made, he would be sure to inquire, why not. His agitation over the incident was always puzzling. Mary and Richard waited outside for us. They would make a game of today's trip, as they did with everything. Mary would probably bring her imaginary horse.

"It's going to be at least a forty-five minute walk to get there, so be ready for a long hike," Mama warned. "I have fifteen cents. First, we'll stop at the flower shop on the corner. Maybe we can buy a few daisies."

"Oh, that'll be good." It was seldom that we had a reason to go to a florist. This was a surprise I didn't expect. Spurred on by the thought of visiting the flower shop, I combed the last head of hair, and warned the boys to stay clean. I felt a little guilty, being excited about the flower shop. I knew I shouldn't feel this way, going to a cemetery and all. The mere thought of going into that shop made me move faster as I readied myself.

The six of us hurried along, Mama pushing Johnny in the stroller. Hardly a word was spoken because we were entering the most dangerous territory of all, Main Street. There was a constant feeling we would run into Dad there. Finally, there it was, the Forget-Me-Not Florists. Mama wheeled the stroller inside the shop. A little bell above the door rang out a delicate jingle. Mary, and Richard rushed over to a refrigerator case. Pressing their faces against the glass, they gushed over the display of flowers inside, breaking the silence of the small shop.

Mama disapproved, "Shhhh! Don't be so noisy."

"Yea," I added, "Dad might hear you." My remark earned a giggle from my very proper mother.

The lean figure of a man with graying hair emerged from a room at the rear of the store. The room was his workshop; a mysterious place where he performed magic on the flowers. He approached us, wiping a pair of spectacles on a corner of the green apron he wore. Words printed on the front read, "The Secret to her Heart--Send Flowers." Replacing the spectacles to his face, he leaned over the counter, curious about the head of curly hair barely visible over the counter top.

"Good mornin', Mrs. O'Brien, and who is this handsome young man?"

"Morning, Mr. Koffy, this is Jimmy."

"What a fine head of hair he has." Mr. Koffy reached over and touched the mass of thick, loose ringlets. "Ahhh," he said with a sigh, and then chuckled low. "I remember when my hair was like that. What can I do for ya Mrs.?"

"I wonder … would you have a couple of daisies that we could have for fifteen-cents?" "Daisies, nooo! I have some cut mums, if you're not set on daisies, you're welcome to them. Fall is the season for mums ya know." Mr. Koffy hesitated only a second for Mama's answer, then added, "Let me show ya." Looking at Mama I beamed a smile of delight. I couldn't understand why she was so slow to answer. Mr. Koffy scurried into the back room of the shop continuing to talk loudly, so we could hear.

"My delivery boy ran all over Diamond Street last night trying to find this address. Someone was pulling a poor joke. Probably his hooligan friends." Returning to the counter Mr. Koffy heaved a sigh and continued, "Of course the boy never did find the house. Well, I should have known better anyway. Numbers don't run that high on Diamond."

Mr. Koffy emerged from the back room, carrying the flowers. The Mums were bundled in tissue thin paper. Lying then down on the counter Mr. Koffy pulled the crisp paper away. "As you can see, the flowers ended up looking pretty rough."

Mary and Richard peered over the counter to see. Jimmy stood on tiptoes straining to get high enough. "Wanna see. Wanna see the pretty rough flowers." Jimmy dug his feet in trying to scale the side of the counter. I grabbed him around the waist and lifted him up.

"Well, here they are, two dozen yellow mums. What do you think Mrs.?"

Mama looked at the flowers. She was running her finger across her lips. Every time she did that, we knew she was in a deep, decision-making thought. We certainly couldn't afford all those flowers. Mary, just tall enough to rest her chin on the counter top, watched the goings on intently. Mr. Koffy reached out in playful gesture and pinched her gently on the tip of the nose. Mary smiled back.

"They're more than I expected. I couldn't pay for two dozen, Mr. Koffy. I only have fifteen cents and… "

"That's all right. Take them. I'll probably end up throwing them out anyway. You can't sell flowers for full price looking like this. They were refrigerated all night, the flowers look fine, just the greens got messed up." As Mr. Koffy held the flowers up for us to see.

"They're beautiful, aren't they?" I hoped Mama would hurry and say yes before Mr. Koffy realized what he was doing.

"Oh yes! I never expected to get this many of anything for fifteen-cents. We're going to the Page Hill Cemetery. Bob's mother died last month. The flowers are for her."

"Yes, I remember." Looking up at the ceiling Mr. Koffy continued to remember, "Two baskets of gladioli and carnation mix, with fern and baby breath, and a white memorial ribbon with mother in gold. Yes … yes, I remember. Well, not another word. You just take these with you. Say, if you're going away up on Page Hill, you've quite a walk ahead of you. Here let me put them in a container. Lord knows they look bad enough without starving them too," Mr. Koffy darted again for the back room. We could hear him fumbling with things back there; then something metal dropped to the floor and bounced a couple of times. Mary and I looked at each other, and did our best to stifle a giggle. When he returned he was carrying a white papier-mâché container with water in it. After stripping off the wilted, broken leaves and cutting off the end of each stem, he placed them in the vase as though he had an exact spot for that particular flower.

"There Mrs., they'll stay fresh as ever in there. Kali, you carry them for your Mom." Eagerly I reach out for the flowers. "Careful, don't spill the water on ya," he warned.

"Thank you so much, Mr. Koffy." Mama placed the fifteen cents on the counter. Mr. Koffy hurried ahead to hold the shop door open.

"Give the mister my condolences," he said softly.

We were more conspicuous than ever now, with the big bundle of mums moving along with us. Mama led us to the fastest way off Main Street. "Lets cross at the corner. It'll be quicker. You know Daddy. He's liable to pop out from under a manhole cover. Come on kids, stay close crossing the street."

My nose was nuzzled up to one of the flowers, sniffing the fragrance as we walked. "Gee, I don't think they look bad Mama ... do you?"

"Mr. Koffy was just being generous. The flowers are beautiful."

Mama was right of course. I shouldn't have been surprised at our good fortune. She never had to try hard, or try at all, for people to do nice things for her.

The walk to the cemetery was long, just as Mama had warned, and the last two blocks were uphill. With each step, the vase of flowers got heavier and heavier. Soon I was stopping often to rest my aching arms. Mama suggested we trade jobs. When we reached the cemetery, Mary and Richard, still full of energy, bounded through the gate ahead of us. Mama and I were a little bedraggled, and glad that the hill climbing was over.

The cemetery was small, but well kept. Mama, lead the way to the far side of the grounds. Finally, she stopped. "Here it is." A plain small gray headstone marked the gravesite. Next to her was the grave of her second husband. We placed the vase of flowers on grandma's grave, and knelt to say a prayer. Richard and Jimmy were making a game of running between the headstones and over the graves. Mama wasn't happy with them. "This is not a park. Stop running and don't be walking over the tops of the graves."

Mama had always taught us to walk behind the headstone of each grave. That way we were walking at the foot of a grave and not across it. "Have a little respect for the dead. How would you like having someone walk all over your face someday?" Mama called the boys over and made them kneel. We said a silent prayer for Grandma.

"I want to look for one more grave before we go," Mama said. The surer she was of where she was going the faster Mama walked. Pushing the stroller over the grass was difficult, but I keep up. Then she stopped. The headstone was much bigger than grandma's. It read: Robert Thomas French, Beloved Son, July 3, 1934-August 15, 1938.

"Mama, why do they put year dates on the headstones," I asked.

"It tells the year the person was born and died. You can tell how old the person was when they died by subtracting the two dates"

"Well, all I get is four. That can't be right."

"That's right. Four is right."

"This person was a little kid?"

"This is Bobbo. Do you remember the little boy you played with you called Bobbo?"

"No."

"I guess you were too young. Bobbo was a neighbor of ours. You used to play with him … lets say a prayer for him first. I'll tell you about it later."

We both knelt down to say a prayer for Bobbo. Mary and the boys knelt with us. Older people died, not kids. Hearing that a small child was buried there, cast a serious note on all of us. After making a hasty sign of the cross, Mary stood up. She walked back to Grandma's grave, careful to walk behind each headstone. When she returned, there were four mums in her hand. "Here Mama, one flower for each year. Give these to Bobbo. Grandma won't mind."

Mama took the flowers from Mary, and laid them on top of the grave. We stood for a few seconds, looking in silence at the flowers, and then Mama broke the mood.

"Come on. Lets start back. We'll go through the park. We can rest there a minute n' get a drink from the fountain. I'm so dry I could spit cotton." Entering the park, the fountain was in plain sight straight. The kids, revived by the thought of a cool drink, dashed ahead. "I hope it isn't turned off. I don't ever remember being so thirsty," Mama lamented.

Mary was the first to step on the pedal at the fountain's base that sent the water bubbling into the air. The smaller kids struggled to reach the water with their mouths already puckered to take it in. We were not disappointed. The water was cool and delicious. We choose a park bench not too far from the fountain knowing well someone would need another drink before long. Mama lifted Johnny out of the stroller allowing him to scamper across the grass to Mary and the boys, who had already become involved in a game of jumping into the crisp, colorful leaves. Breathing a deep sigh, Mama settled sideways on the bench, a better position to watch the kids as we rested. We were both glad to be sitting down. Mama slipped her shoes off.

Surrounded by the many colorful trees in the park that day, it was hard to believe that in less than two months all the leaves would be gone. After falling gently to the ground, they would continue to fill our lives with a childhood delight. Raking them up in huge mounds was a yearly event that we all waited for each year. Kids on every street would spend hours raking, jumping and tumbling in them. After being reduced to a crumbled heap, the leaves would be raked up and burned. The air full of the smell of burning leaves signaled the end of another fall. The barren branches of the trees have always appeared to me as arms stretched upward in a gesture of prayer. Despite this pious image, it was depressing to see the trees denied their leaves and left with only an empty weatherworn nest or two. Soon even these small fragments of a warmer day would be snatched from them as well by the rambunctious breath of winter.

That thought always left me with a sad feeling until the day Aunt Katie suggested looking at it from a different angle, "Fall isn't necessarily the end of a season of growth, but for some just the beginning. The trees surrender all their leaves as a human mother watching her children leave home, one by one. For the children it's an exciting time to take their place in the world. All are part of the growing cycle that never ends. Trees and Mothers are of a noble design."

Sitting on the park bench, we were occasionally sprinkled with a leaf or two riding downward on a light current of air. The kids behind us were squealing with joy, diving head long, and bottom down, into the mound of leaves that they had labored to collect. Curious about my childhood playmate rose to the surface again.

"Mama, what happened to Bobbo?"

"There's not a lot to tell. It was a horrible thing. I don't even like to think about it."

"He was so little. How did he die? ...A car hit him?" I can tell it's difficult for Mama to begin. Little lines form around her eyes as she squeezes them closed while shaking her head no.

"When you were three years old, the city was doing some reconstruction on a highway, about three blocks from where we lived. They were using dynamite to break up big rocks. When those explosions went off, they rattled windows, and dishes in cupboards. On the days they were going to use the dynamite someone would come around and warn everyone who lived close by. We were warned that day. "You and Bobbo used to play in a sand box in the backyard of the duplex we lived in. His nickname was Bobby, but you never could pronounce his name right. It always came out, 'Bobbo'. Everyone thought it was a cute name for him. It even started to catch on. Anyway, the continuous vibrations were taking a toll on lots of things. Most of the damage was small like dishes or cracked windows. Two of our oldest elm trees were knocked over. Some sidewalks were left with cracks that are still there today." Mama reached down, and lifted a fallen leaf from the many that surrounded our bench. It twirled between her fingers like a propeller, perhaps giving her something to look at besides my intense gaze. This story is difficult for her.

"The sandbox that you both played in stood by the side of the garage in the backyard. It was put there to keep you and Bobbo safely out of the driveway. On the far side of the yard was a telephone pole that got weaker every time the ground shook. It must have loosened all of a sudden. No one ever noticed it until the day Mr. Ragen saw a slight movement with the last explosion. He was on his way to work, but before he climbed into his car, he scolded you both, and told you to go home and not play there anymore. You got up and ran in the house to me. Bobbo got up too and started for home. Mr. Ragen, thinking he'd chased you both off, backed his car out of the driveway and went on his way. Bobbo was kind of a stubborn little boy. All we could figure out was that he never went in the house. He must have gone back to the sandbox to play by himself. When Mr. Ragen got to work, it bothered him that he saw movement in the pole and tried to call his wife, but no one answered; he was too late. The pole had already come crashing down on that little boy. The poor little fella didn't have a chance. One of the climbing spikes on the pole…"

"The spike hit him?"

"He died instantly. Every time I think of you setting in that sandbox minutes before, my blood runs cold. Thank God you walked away when you did."

Mama looked straight at me, her eyes had a subtle, wet look. Rapidly rubbing her arms to brush away the goose bumps, she blurted out, "Oooh, it gives me chills to think about it." The thought of loosing one of her cubs was more than Mama Bear could handle.

It was a frightening thought, that I could have died that day with Bobbo. My Guardian Angel was working for me long before I knew I had one. Wishing we were back at Bobbo's grave again I would have liked a second chance to make that visit right.

Two weeks before Christmas of '48, Mama gave birth to Donald, the eight in our string of O'Briens. I was glad when she returned home. The thought of Christmas without her would be unthinkable.

CHAPTER 13
A Christmas Gift From Joseph

The earth is still, the stars are gone, the birds have fled in fear.
Man is angry once again, a storm is drawing near.

With a newborn baby in the house, it was important to keep the apartment warm all the time. Between school during the day and their jobs at night, Joseph and Andy were gone almost as much as Dad. It was up to Mama and me to see that the coalscuttle was always full. A small stove in the living room also had to be supplied with coal.

Money for Mama to run the house was always tight and by the end of the week would disappear all together. By winter's end, we could no longer afford coal. Mama would have asked for credit until she was so far behind on the coal bill she couldn't ask for more. For the remaining weeks of cold weather, Dad would tell Mama to send us down to the factory for a box of firewood. If we were lucky, he might have two boxes waiting for us. Many of the shipments received at the factory were in heavy wooden crates. One of Dad's jobs at the factory was to see that the crates were disposed of. Dad would pull the crates aside, saw them into smaller pieces, and they would be waiting for us in tall cardboard boxes. The wood was heavy and burned long and warm. Balancing the tall boxes of wood on our sled took all our efforts. One of us would pull and direct the sled while the other steadied the teetering cardboard tower. The factory was ten blocks from the apartment and if there would be a storm that day, we knew the job would be more difficult. It was disheartening when we'd accidentally dump a box. Throwing the wood back in was a rotten job, and if the box split apart, that was another problem. Making matters worse, our precious cargo would have to be dried out before it could be burned. Our hands would be frozen, and our feet numb from the wet snow; but Andy and I would get our blood pumping again with a short stop at the warm ol' post office. The wood-fetching job started out belonging to Joseph and Andy. Then it fell to Andy and me. When Andy began working a job, it was passed on to me with the help of Mary and Richard. Everyone did his share of the work when it was necessary. The wood was dragged up stairs and stored in our already crowded dining room. Mama didn't care. She was always relieved to see the wood arrive one more time.

Christmas Eve of '49, Mama and I received a very special present, a present that would neither break nor grow old. It wasn't the kind of gift to hold in the hand, but one to hold in the heart. The kids were down for the night, snug in their beds dreaming of Christmas morning surprises. Mama and I were in the front room wrapping the last few gifts, and were placing them under the tree. No matter how few presents there were, the beautifully decorated tree could cast a spell over its drab surroundings. This night even the tree was no match for Dad's anger. Suddenly, the serenity dissolved into a hell-raising argument from the moment Dad entered the apartment. He was so drunk he didn't even look like himself. His eyes never focused on either Mama or me as he began lashing out about something his twisted mind had conceived. The arguments that drew most rage from Dad were those accusing Mama of secretive dealings with other men.

"Where the hell were you this afternoon?"

"I was here."

"Like hell. I was here around one-a-clock and again at three, still no one here."

"We went to Woolworth's. I took the kids to see the Christmas toys."

"Did that take you all afternoon?"

"No, but shopping for Christmas dinner did. Where do you think we went?"

"Yea, that's why Mike at the butcher shop saw you 'cause you were shopping uptown.'"

"I went to the butcher shop to get you a cubed steak for your breakfast tomorrow. You're the one who wants the meat to come from Mike's butcher shop. It would be easier for me to buy at the grocer's, but we walk all the way down there just for you."

Dad grew silent for a minute. "'You have the nicest lady for a wife,' he says. What the hell do ya talk about when yer buying steaks?"

With a quick movement, Dad swings a foot out at the gifts beneath the tree. Two of them went flying to the other side of the room. Mama pushed Dad away. "Leave them alone, we don't have much and you want to destroy what we have. Get out of here." Dad stormed out of the apartment.

With his work finished at the Rialto, Joseph came home missing the blow up, only by minutes. He had planned to spend some of Christmas Eve with his girlfriend, Marion, but he couldn't ignore Mama and me being so upset. Calmly, he announced he was going to take us for a short ride in his car. "Come on, we'll take a few minutes and see how the better half of town lives on Christmas Eve." Mama hesitated to go. It would leave the kids asleep in the apartment alone, but Joseph persuaded her. "You know Dad won't have any place to go this late on Christmas Eve. He'll be back here before you know it. Let *him* watch 'em fer a change. Come on get your coat, you too Kali."

Joseph drove us up to the hill and slowly patrolled up and down the streets passing one beautifully decorated house after another. It was a breathtaking sight. Frosty lawns reflected by the lights, sparkled as if thousands of diamond chips had been lightly scattered about. Gleaming wreaths and strings of red, blue and green lights decorated homes, casting a cheerful glow into the night. Through the windows of several homes, we could see happy families gathered inside, these things really did happen on Christmas Eve. Everyone wasn't drunk and argumentative. It wasn't long before the tension of the horrible argument melted away. We looked forward to the next street, full of celebration, and decorated so grand. I sat in the back seat alone and whispered a silent prayer, "Please God, give us a home here someday."

By the time we returned home Dad was already there, asleep in bed. This was the worst Christmas Eve, and yet one of the best we ever had. Joseph put Dad in the background and made clear, the sparkle and joy of the holiday. He helped me to dare think, "Perhaps we'll have Christmas up on the hill someday, a Christmas not too far off." Joseph reminded us of the promise of peace on earth. I found it confusing, anticipating Christmas with one thought, and dreading with another. We all knew there would certainly be some kind of argument every Christmas Eve. It had become as traditional as Christmas itself. Mama would tuck her anger away, making sure the hard feelings were not carried over to Christmas day. Dad typically greeted Christmas morning as if nothing ever happened.

The year 1950 would be the last year of school for both Joseph and Andy. Joseph quit in January of that year because he felt he wasn't doing well and his interest in high school had become shallow. As a family, we didn't know yet of a plan he and Andy had been building on for some time. By February's end, Mama had reluctantly let Andy quit school too. Mama was against either of the boys quitting but they convinced her it would be better for everyone if they had full-time jobs. We didn't know that the jobs they had in mind were to join the service.

I was in eighth grade at St. Michael's and was heading for my first failure. Eighth grade was a culmination of everything that we had learned up to then. I, for some reason, had not accumulated quite enough. My absenteeism played a big part in my failure as well, I would never hesitate to jump at the chance to stay home and help Mama rather than go to school. My sliding though, one year after the other, was due for an about-face. In the past, little importance was given to what I wore to school as long as all the zippers zipped and buttons buttoned. My knack for accepting things as they were was to blame for my indifference. If she had known, Aunt Katie would have been displeased with the slight twist I gave to the advice she gave me on life.

The day would dawn, however, when matters of dress would become a great concern. Clothes the other girls wore were colorful and often new. It was easy to see by comparison my dresses were faded and drab. Shoes worn by all the O'Brien kids were pressed into service until the sole on one or the other pulled away and made a flapping sound with each step. Besides shoes, socks had also become a problem. The problem being we never seemed to have more than one pair at a time, and that one pair had to be washed out every night. In time, the holes in them would have been repaired so often the pucker from the sewing would rub blisters on our heels. Eventually Mama would buy us another pair, but only after the old pair had all but disintegrated. Socks gave me as much heartache in winter, as shoes in summer. A black smudgy ring would happen around their tops where my snow boots rubbed. It required something stronger than soap to wash that black mark off. Mama suggested that I add a little bleach to the water. She was right; they washed up like new. The warm oven door was a perfect place to hang them. There was one condition. Washing had to be done in early evening while the stove still burned the hottest. In the morning, they would be dry and ready to wear to school.

One time my nightly ritual of sock washing was put off too long. Late getting started on my chore, I haphazardly scrubbed them clean. Carelessly, too much of the magic solution had been added, and the rinsing had been done in haste. The next day that generous amount of bleach would raise up to haunt me, and at least half of St. Michael's eighth grade class.

That warm cozy feeling that was there when we went to bed would diminish through the night. Swiftly yielding to the prevailing chill of winter it was hard to remember how warm it had once been; there was no way my white beauties could dry in so little time. By morning it was obvious I had a problem. No time to make things right; school would soon begin. Time to hurry. As I trotted along the streets towards St. Michael's, the damp socks made my feet feel like two chunks of ice. It was good reaching the warm classroom. The tops of the socks had already frozen stiff around my legs, but it didn't matter. I wasn't late and in the more than adequate heat of the classroom, they would soon dry on my feet. The dryer my socks got, the stronger the smell of bleach became. My classmates, obviously offended by the pungent odor, were making faces and looking around to see where it was coming from. I felt like a giant bottle with "Bleach" written all over me in big letters. Ignoring what was going on, I tucked my feet in tightly under my seat; feet what feet? I didn't even own feet. The morning was almost over before that repulsive aroma finally disappeared. My peers never said anything to me; that was a good clue they knew who was wearing the bleach-smelling perfume. That night two of the whitest feet on the face of the earth climbed into bed. It was a lesson well learned, "don't *ever* bleach your socks in wintertime."

Being a cook for the priests, Aunt Katie was one of a group of women that worked as domestic help around Chipwey. When the seasons changed, and their affluent employers cleaned their closets of unwanted clothing, the housekeepers were given the liberty to discard them any way they choose. They all made sure these items got into the right hands. Remembering that Aunt Katie had many nephews and nieces, the clothing was sometimes given to her for us. The clothes were of very fine quality, better than we could ever afford. When shoes were given to me, they were usually too narrow although necessity told me to make them fit. I wanted to look like the other girls even at the risk of getting blisters. We couldn't depend on these donations to be given at the times when they were most needed. My inventive mother had become quit adept at sprucing up whatever we had on hand to a presentable condition.

One Easter Eve, after the kids had been scrubbed and put to bed, Mama and I remained in the kitchen alone. My bath was finished and the big tub stood in the middle of the floor waiting for Mama to take her turn next. Both feet drawn up on the chair; my arms wrapped around my legs; I sat snugly in my nightgown watching with interest as Mama worked feverishly over a hat that I had worn for three Easters in a row. It was a wide-brimmed straw hat; a ribbon circled the crown and hung down the back. The color was chipping off the brim, and the ribbon had the appearances of a snake that had gotten caught in a revolving door; it looked beat-up all right, but Mama had an idea. "Let's try some of this and see if it doesn't cover." Mama was excited as she applied a dark blue liquid shoe polish to the hat. Low and behold, it transformed the hat like new. Mama had washed the ribbon and ironed it smooth. Draped over the ironing board, it waited to be placed on the hat again.

"There, now set it some place safe," Mama handed me the shiny hat, "when it's dry we'll put the ribbon on."

The hat was sticky with the wet polish. Not wanting to disturb the perfect job Mama had done I reached for it with too light a grasp. "I have it! No, I don't! Yes, I do! No, I don't!" I could feel it slipping from my hand. I tried desperately to keep it from falling into the big tub of water, but it wanted to play a game of "you can't catch me," as it twisted around my arms and crawled up to my shoulder popping me square in the face. Then in happy glee, it did a graceful swan dive from my arm ending up floating in the bath water, bobbing up and down like a dark blue barge. To make things worse, my grabbing and fumbling left me with blue smudges on my arm, hands and nose.

"Oh, Kali, get it. Get it out!" I lifted the hat up carefully and held it over the tub as it continued to drip dark blue shoe die into the bath water. Now one might think all was lost, but not if one knew Mama. She blotted that old hat off and dyed it again. I wore it proudly to Mass that next morning.

I've heard adults say, "God watches out for drunks and children." That Easter I became a true believer in that saying because Easter Sunday morning was full of sunshine. If it had rained, the shoe die would have been sure to run.

St. Michael's is a cathedral-like church; the biggest of the three steeples house three huge bells that flood Chipwey every Sunday with their beautiful music. The ceiling inside the church rises to a towering peak, allowing exposed rafters to canopy over a thousand parishioners. The walls are adorned with beautiful stained glass windows. Statues of saints, elevated on wall pedestals, keep a silent vigil over their profound sanctuary. The main altar is straight up the middle aisle guarded on both sides by a huge white marble angel. The soft glow of flickering candles deepened the already angelic atmosphere.

The Mass attendance on Sunday nearly filled every pew. Walking up the aisle to Communion was like being on parade before the whole town, and as students of St. Michael's we were expected to go to Communion every Sunday. It was then I was filled with a self-conscious feeling. Generally, my hand-me-down clothes fit surprisingly well, but they didn't feel as though they belonged to me. I was sure everyone knew that we could never afford to buy what I was wearing. All eyes were certainly on me knowing I was parading around in someone else's clothes, and maybe that "someone else," was out there too. My brothers were buying all of their own clothes. Having a steady girl, looking good was important to Joseph. Andy didn't have a special girl. I think he liked them all.

That September, it was strange going back to school without Joseph and Andy. Joseph's job at the Rialto and Andy's at the bowling alley became their focus. They had willingly walked into the grown-up world leaving their schoolboy images behind. It was shortly after New Years of 1950 when I became aware of the plan my crafty brothers had been hatching for some time. I had taken Joseph's dinner to him at the theater many times before, and this time seemed no different than any other. Only a few scattered people were seated for the last show of the day. Entering the lobby, I saw that Joseph was in the ticket booth. Marion was squeezed in there with him and appeared to be very interested in something he was writing. Passing his sandwich, and a jelly jar full of hot coffee through the little window, I waited for Joseph to look up at me.

"Oh good. Kali you'd know this. What are the kids ages?"

"I'm 14, Mary is 10, Richard is 8, Jimmy is 6, Johnny is 3, and Donald is 1." I watched as Joseph wrote down the names and ages, wondering why he hadn't asked Mama for this information. What could it be for? Joseph was filling out his enlistment papers to join the Army. Joseph and Andy, despite Mama's objections, continued talking about enlisting. Joseph was only weeks away from his twentieth birthday, but Andy wouldn't be eighteen for nine more months. Mama Bear was clear on the subject.

"I'm not agreeing with all this, so don't ask me to."

"Why Mom? This is the best thing for us. There's no war. We can enlist and choose what we want."

"I just don't feel good about this."

Each of my brothers took their turn trying to convince Mama. Andy argued, "I can work for my high school diploma. I'll be going to school and getting paid for it."

Regardless of her opposition, my brothers were intent on their purpose. The more she resisted, the more determined they seemed to be as they quietly continued with their plans. Every so often, I would catch Joseph and Andy in deep discussion at the kitchen table. They drank their way through many cups of coffee as they mulled over the numerous brochures making decisions. With all the material spread out on the table, it looked as if they were planning a trip around the world. Mama walked around the kitchen pretending she was paying no attention to what they were doing; Mama bear had her ears tuned in, you can bet that.

Joseph had at least gotten to his last year in high school, but Andy didn't even have an eight-grade diploma. This was a stumbling block for being a pilot. Maybe if he couldn't fly them, he could learn to repair them. It would be one way of being around airplanes, and learn more about them. He jokingly referred to being a mechanic somewhat like being an airplane doctor, but that too would require schooling. For reasons of his own, he decided not to subject himself to a classroom; perhaps his dropping out of school left the bitter taste of failure in his mouth. The need to succeed in something was primary before going on to bigger things. By April, with the help of their recruiting officer, both boys had come to firm decisions. Joseph had chosen the Engineer Corps. After basic training, he would have to go to school for an additional three months to complete the course in Engineering. It would involve learning how to build bridges, roads and waterways, and learn the use of the different types of machinery for the work. Andy had chosen to enter the Army Infantry. He would have to learn to use various weapons. Although it wasn't his first choice, he was interested in learning to use firearms. Remembering how Andy maneuvered that empty beer bottles heist two years before, being a foot soldier was a good choice. While Mama still would not give her blessing, strangely enough, Dad would be the answer; at least they had his support. Dad ... the very one my brothers were trying to escape, would reluctantly agree to sign the papers that Andy needed because of his age.

Joseph and Andy talked about being sent overseas. Korea was becoming more of a problem, but it mistakenly wasn't taken seriously. Even Joseph and Andy tried to minimize the probability of Korea escalating to an all out-war. By the time they were past their basic training, they told Mama, the conflict in Korea would be settled. Knowing my brothers this may have been a ploy to keep Mama Bear sold on the stability of world peace. "Going overseas is more likely to be France or Germany. I think I'd like to go to France, or maybe Japan." Joseph said, his eyes wide and bright with the thought. The excitement of their plans filled the boys with the promise of marvelous careers creating a new life for them. In late June, they would head out for Fort Dix for basic training. They had four weeks to sow their remaining wild oats.

How fortunate Andy was, to be able to walk away from school and not be bothered again ever, with nuns, books, and exams, however, I would have to repeat eighth grade. The three months of summer vacation would give me time to accept my failure. It was comforting to think, next year I was certain to pass. I put any worry about school in my pocket for another day. Taking care of the kids with Mama for the summer was enough to occupy me.

Constantly playing games with babies kept me acting younger than my years. Other girls were beginning to notice boys; not me. I didn't care; I didn't want anything to do with boys. During the summer when Mary wasn't at home to go to the Saturday movies with me, I went with my younger brothers; Richard, Jimmy and Johnny. When the matinee ended, my brothers would find me and tell me that they were going home.

"I'm gonna stay and see the first picture again ... tell Mama." I would say.

It gave me such pleasure sitting in the theater for the second time around; more so than the first. The theater seats, cleared of all the noisy kids who attended the matinee, would now be filled with adults. Seeing the movie for a second time, I knew all that was about to happen. Now the game could begin, a game where I pretended that I was telling the whole theater the story. When they laughed, I thought that I told them the funny thing they saw, because I knew what was coming. I could soar to great heights on their roar of laughter or gasps of surprise. Pretending to entertain them was a most delightful trip to the Cloud. Could I be spending too much time there? That was the furthest thing from my mind. It was a good place to go. Unlike my older brothers, this was my only escape. I couldn't give it up for the world.

What a great idea, having three months for vacation from school each year, but this summer, saying good-by to two brothers at once would be filled with mixed feelings. After being at the Rialto for nearly three years, Joseph would say farewell to all the friends he made there. Mr. Kauffman was sorry to lose the best assistant he ever had, but understood and wished Joseph well. Joseph and Andy paid visits to different relatives to say good-by. Aunt Katie gave both boys a Holy Card; it would be easy to slip it into their wallets, and remind them to say a prayer now and then. Promises were made by everyone to write as soon as they could.

Joseph made a special trip to Hartford, to say good-by to Aunt Mildred and Uncle George. I would later be told by Mildred that Joseph felt if he didn't get away from home soon, either he or Andy would end up killing Dad. It would seem there was a lot more discord with home life for my brothers than I suspected. The days of June passed so fast it seemed in a blink of an eye that Joseph and Andy were going out for a final farewell with their friends. Joseph had a date with Marion; Andy went out for one last party. Some of Andy's friends were to follow in his footsteps joining the service too, but Eddie because of a bout with Rheumatic Fever couldn't pass the physical.

I was not able to go to the train station with Mama and Dad the day Joseph and Andy left. I had to watch the smaller kids at home. When Mama returned, she had that familiar worried look on her face. "We'll have to write to them often. It will help to keep them from getting homesick." All those weeks of planning had finally gotten Joseph and Andy what they wanted; independence and distance between them and Dad.

Three days after Joseph and Andy left for their basic training, all of Mama's nightmares came true. June 25, the conflict in Korea came to a head. With the impact of an overdue volcano, North Korea invaded South Korea. Members of the United Nations Security Council were asked to help the Republic of South Korea. By July 3, U.N. troops were engaged in military action in Korea. The war Mama feared had begun. My brothers couldn't have picked a worse time to enlist if they had tried. The conflict in Korea wasn't disappearing. Mama and Dad exchanged concerned words after they heard the news on the radio each day. Not quite understanding it all, I didn't want to think another war was possible. "Dad's reaction to the news always left him sputtering and spitting about something," I told myself. Everything will be OK. Despite my attempt to hold on to the upside of the situation, a little voice inside me whispered that this news was different. When Dad heard that U.N. troops were engaged in combat in Korea, he didn't seem to reach his usual level of calm. He knew things were bad, and would probably get worse.

CHAPTER 14
Mama's Fear Comes True

People say it can't be done, once started rain must fall.
But hold it back they will because they answer freedom's call.

With Joseph and Andy away, it felt as though half of the family was missing. It helped when Mama and I talked remembering how happy they were the day they left for Fort Dix. Our letters back and forth satisfied Mama that the family was still intact. The gentle way she folded every letter and placed it back into the envelope told more than words could say, how much she missed the boys.

Mama was forty years old and in the third month of her last pregnancy, though that didn't slow her down. We continued to take walks and shop for groceries together. Our Wednesday night band concerts were never missed either. We were getting to the concerts earlier than we used to. I think Mama had good memories of past concerts and felt closer to Joseph and Andy at the park; I believe this was true for me too. Despite the interesting lineup of talent the concert offered, my mind never failed to wander back to another concert night the year before when we met Joseph's new girl friend Marion, for the first time.

Joseph looked forward all day to the evening band concert. It was an ideal place to introduce Marion to all of us away from our drab apartment. Joseph was all smiles as he and Marion headed our way.

"Marion, this is my mom. And that's my sister Kali."

"Hi." Her voice was soft. Her short strawberry-blond hair was pinned back with a ribbon.

"That wild Indian over there is my brother Richard, and that one is Jimmy. Next to him is Johnny; the little guy in the carriage is Donald. Mary's on vacation with my Aunt in Hartford." Joseph said.

"How wonderful it must be having so many around all the time. I'm an only child, it gets pretty dull sometimes."

Joseph took Marion's hand, "See ya later, Mom."

"Nice meeting you Mrs. O'Brien. So long kids," Marion added waving back.

It wasn't hard to see they were very much taken with each other. Sure, I'd seen some schoolmates walking along together as boy and girl friend. Joseph and Marion were something different. There was no youthful self-consciousness, no feeling ill at ease about showing their fondness for each other. I had never been so close to young people who had this feeling radiating all about them.

"Mama, how long has Joseph been going with Marion?"

" ...'Bout a month, he really seems to like her."

"Yea. She's pretty."

I watched until the darkness of evening swallowed them up and they disappeared into the shadows of the crowd.

The band was playing the last song when we started for home. All their energy drained at last, the kids plodded along side the carriage. The night was pleasant for a change. A playful breeze cooled us as we ambled along. I was almost sorry when we reached the apartment.

"Kali, put the carriage in the storage room out back," Momma said, lifting Donald up to her hip. I started to do as Mama said when the sound of voices coming down the street drew my attention; Joseph and Marion were heading toward me.

"Kali, keep Marion company until I come back down? ...Spilled pop on my shirt ... gotta change." Placing his hand gently on Marion's cheek, he said softly, "I'll be back before you know it." Giving her a wisp of a kiss on the tip of her nose, he turned and dashed up the stairs.

Marion didn't say the word out loud, only shaped her lips to form the word "OK," as though it had a secret meaning.

We always asked our friends to wait on the street. The appearance of the apartment had lapsed into a condition none of us were proud of. That hole in the hallway wallboard was the first thing that company would see when the door opened. The day we moved in it was hardly noticeable. Three years later, it was now big enough to drive a Mack Truck right on through. After Jimmy learned to crawl he was attracted to the spot and picked at the plaster, sometimes stuffing it in his mouth until Mama or I caught him. This all eventually added to the size of the hole. We were all guilty of loosening the white stuff; a slight touch could bring a clump of it crashing to the floor. We hadn't painted anything since we moved there, and the walls had returned to its yellow grimy look. We never forgot the unpredictable roaches either, who could trust them to behave? Better to ask friends to wait outside.

Not knowing Marion very well, standing on the street alone with her was an awkward feeling. I noticed she was staring up at the sky with a far away look in her eyes. There was nothing to be seen but stars and a half moon.

"See that star up there Kali? It's that very bright one over there to the left. Joseph gave it to me and it's mine to keep forever."

I had seen things like this in the movies, but never thought there'd be a day when my own brother would give a girl a star. I looked hard at Marion's face. She gazed upward as though her star was going to hurl itself from the sky, drop into her hand, and she was going to be ready to catch it.

"Do you have a boy friend, Kali?" Marion asked her eyes still riveted on the bright dot of light.

"Uh-uh, not me."

"Well, someday when you find a someone special, you will understand how I feel tonight. No matter where he is, I can look up, see that star, and know he's thinking of me." Her attention was diverted only long enough for a quick look at me. Marion locked her eyes on to the star again. Our conversation made me uncomfortable; what do you say to someone in love?

Joseph bounded back out into the street. Marion reached up and straightened the corner of his collar. They smiled at each other. "Thanks for taking care of my girl, Kali. See you later." My head was full of thoughts of Joseph and Marion as I climbed into bed that night.

It's been a year since we first met Marion. I wonder, as my mind returned to the present, will Joseph being in the Army change things between them? Mama would also be aware of these memories and it could be why she grows restless, and decides to leave the concert early. Without fail, our walk would take us straight down Main Street. It was impossible to pass by the post office without running in to see if there was a letter from Joseph or Andy waiting for us. Then we walked to Nick's Barber Shop to see Dad. He'd be in one of two places; sitting in the big chair in the back of the shop talking to Nick, or outside standing next to the spinning barber pole watching people pass by. This time, Mama was able to coax a few nickels from Dad to buy us ice cream.

The warm summer evening, too much for our cold treat, added to the certainty of it's melting. Mama was doing her best to balance an ice cream cone and push Donald in his stroller at the same time. Little Johnny toddled alongside her doing his best to keep up with the sticky mess that was fast getting out of hand; it wasn't a bother that it was running down his hand and dripping from his elbow.

"Johnny, your ice cream is melting. Lick fast," Mama instructed.

Johnny did as he was told, but instead of faster, he licked harder and popped the ice cream right out of the cone. Looking down in surprise at the ball of ice cream that landed on his shoe, tears welled up in his eyes as he lifted his face up to Mama. Then there was a pitiful whine. Then real tears happened as he watched it slid down resting partly on his foot, partly on the sidewalk. Nickels were too hard to come by to throw the ice cream into the gutter. Mama reacted immediately. "Don't move, Johnny!" Reaching down she picked up the melting glob of cream, plopping it back into the empty cone. "Here, take mine." The tears ended quickly, Mama would take Johnny's ice cream as her own. Using her finger like a knife, she began to scrape away the dirt, flipping her finger behind her to cast off the unwanted cream.

Chipwey is no different from any other town. We have our share of pigeons perching on the edge of buildings and not caring where their droppings land. It just so happened, that all of this took place right by one of the bird's favorite perching spots. Mama flipped the ice cream behind her, acting on impulse. When it did occur to her, she peeked around to see what the consequences might be. Too late! A man walking a few steps behind us was in the wrong spot at the right time. When the ice cream left Mama's hand, it didn't land in the gutter where she intended it to, but continued on its merry way into the air then down, splattering on the sleeve of the man's shirt. By the time Mama looked behind her, the surprised man was glaring up to the edge of the building where an innocent flock of pigeons perched. He put his nose to the white spot on his sleeve as if to sniff it, took a handkerchief from his pocket and wiped it off. He looked up again. Mama had no choice but to start walking away pretending she was unaware of what had happened. Taking no notice of us, the man walked by still looking up at the pigeons. If it was going to happen again, this time he was going to see it coming. Mama couldn't control herself. Every time she thought of the man sniffing the white deposit on his shirt and looking up at the pigeons, she broke out in uncontrollable laughter. Though the whole thing was unintentional, we shamelessly let the pigeons take the blame.

It was good hearing Mama laughing so hard, distracted from her worries by the humor of it all. I believe if the pigeons knew what they had done for her, they would have forgiven us, because it had to be a first, using a real pigeon as a "Pigeon."

The day after Labor Day, I began my second year in eighth grade, and learned that I would be able to take final exams again in January. There was still a chance to catch up to my original class. I wondered, if I did manage to fail again, would I be allowed to quit school like my brothers? Staying home full time and helping Mama was a pleasant thought.

During the weeks that followed, Mama and I beat a well-worn path to the post office almost every day because of all the letter writing. We have rented the same box at the post office since the early thirties. Only a block away from his radio shop, it was convenient for Dad to pick up the mail for the family, and his business as well. Although the radio shop disappeared long ago, it remained part of his ritual to check the mail in his comings and goings. Box 182 is as familiar to all of us as our last name. In the past, the post office was a place Mama would take us. It had become more of a point of purpose for our walks than anything. By now with writing letters to Joseph and Andy we found ourselves there more often. The good old post office had been a port of comfort many times in the past. In winter, we used it as a warming up place and in summer, we could always depend on a cool drink of water from the small fountain tucked away in the corner.

One day a letter from Joseph told us he was coming home for a week. It would be a short break before heading out for Fort Belvoir, for his schooling in Engineering. Mama was disappointed that the boys were coming home at different times. "Andy is still in training. He's in the infantry." Joseph's answer was acceptable. Because of the three months of school, Joseph would be stationed safely in the country for weeks to come. This was a small comfort to Mama.

Though we saw quite a bit of Joseph during the day, most of his evenings were spent with Marion. I was surprised one evening, when two voices chattering with excitement entered the apartment. It was Joseph and Marion. I knew then how serious he was about her when he brought her into the apartment. Because Marion was going to be part of the family someday, it didn't matter if she saw everything. Maybe at this time in Joseph's life, material things didn't matter, only the people inside the shabby apartment counted. He wasn't ashamed of us.

"Where's mom?" Joseph started out through the hallway toward the bedrooms before I could answer him.

"She's putting Donald to bed," I call after him.

I gave the kitchen a quick check to make sure there was nothing embarrassing lying around, then greeted Marion. The radio on top of the refrigerator was playing too loudly to talk over. I reached up to turn it down.

"Wait, don't turn it down Kali, that's our song." Marion says, glowing with the same look she had the night she told me about her star.

Nat King Cole was singing, "Too Young." She motioned me to be still so she could hear. We didn't talk until the last note was played.

Joseph returned to the kitchen, "OK Mar, lets get going, they're waiting ... See ya later."

Mama entered the kitchen. "Boy, they come and go so fast. Where are they off to?"

"Some of their friends are taking them out for a little get-together. Joseph will be extra late tonight."

Several days after Joseph returned to base, Dad came home unexpectedly for lunch. He slapped a small bundle of mail down on the kitchen table. "Andy is coming home in two weeks." Mama pulled the letter from the already opened envelope. The expression on her face was enough to tell us it was true. With all of his basic and special combat training completed, he was coming home for five days. Then he would be shipping out for overseas duty, and that meant Korea.

The news over the radio on September 20 saying that UN forces had arrived at Inchon, Korea, upset both Mama and Dad. It took the UN forces two weeks to reach the 38th parallel and accomplish the surrender of North Korea, and four days after that to capture the South Korean capitol Seoul, from the North Koreans. In late October, under the command of General Douglas MacArthur, the troops took Pyongyang, the North Korean capitol. Everyone was so sure this victory meant an end to the conflict, and we were sure it meant a short stay in Korea for Andy. Mama and Dad were overjoyed. The danger was passing just as the boys had told Mama it would.

It was an overcast and gloomy October day when Andy stepped from the train into Mama's open arms, then stepping back to take note of Mama's girth.

Mama replied, "It's seven months already," patting her stomach; but for Mama the sun couldn't have been shining any brighter. We had seen Andy in uniform only in a photograph he sent us. Seeing him right there in front of us, it was quite evident he had changed; he looked so grown-up. "Why he's downright handsome," I thought. "But I won't tell him that, he'll just get conceited." It was hard to believe he was the same person that traveled the back alleys of Chipwey, rummaging through dumps. On the way home Mama and Andy walked arm in arm as Andy talked continually about his training.

"You should see me tear down an M-1 'n rebuild it. I was one of the fastest in our group."

"What's an M-1?" Mama asked.

"An M-1 is a solders' best buddy." Mama looked puzzled.

"My rifle," Andy said laughingly.

"You take 'em apart and put 'em together?" Richard asked.

"Only my own. And with no parts left over." Andy laughed again.

Overflowing with enthusiasm, Andy continued to talk. His bubbly conversation lasted all the way home and up the two flights of stairs. It was a good thing that he joined the Army. Andy finally seemed happy with his world.

When Dad came home that night, he shook hands with Andy. Things were so different. As two ordinary guys getting together, they exchanged stories. Dad's story of how he tried to enlist during the last war, but was turned down because he had too many children, surprised all of us. There was an air of respect in Dad's attitude, as he listened to Andy with interest; this attention from Dad was a first for Andy. Those five days of Andy's furlough went by fast, but not so fast that he didn't get to see all of his old friends in town. During the day he was all ours, at night, there was time for parties with his friends.

The closer Andy got to the end of his leave the more I noticed a slight change in him. As I stood at the sink washing dishes one day, I could see him from the corner of my eye. He was sitting at the table, quietly smoking a cigarette and drinking a cup of coffee. He seemed to be lost in his own "Cloud." It wasn't the first time I caught him in such deep thought. I walked over to him with the coffee pot.

"Is the coffee OK?" Andy gave a little jump. "Yeah, Pigeon."

"How 'bout a little more?"

"Okay. I see you drew KP today."

"I have KP every day Andy, remember?" Andy reached out and smacked me on the behind.

"Smarty," he said.

When the day came for Andy to return to base, we all walked down to the train with him. Dad had said his good-by to Andy the night before, and reported to work like any other day in order to avoid an emotional good-bye. I had my customary care of Donald in his stroller. Mary and Richard took charge of Andy's duffel bag, pulling it along in the beat up old wagon as if they had a load of gold. The train station was on the opposite side of the tracks, so we had to travel through an underpass that ran beneath all three sets of tracks. Despite the little lights on the walls that illuminate the tunnel, it was still a long spooky walk even during the daytime, but it was fun to read the walls. They were marked with things like: "Kilroy was here," and "V for Victory;" even the old "F" word was scribbled several times. Being very proper, we made believe we didn't see that.

As we stood on the platform waiting for the train, the conversation took a very interesting turn.

"Hey Mom, you ought have a phone. Why don't you talk to Dad about it?" Andy asked.

"I've been thinkin' about that too. Tomorrow I'll go down to the phone company and talk to them. We really should have one now."

When the time came for Andy to board the train, Mama did well and held back the tears beautifully. The recent turn of events in Korea was encouraging for her. We took turns hugging Andy, with Mama going back for seconds.

"Be careful, God Bless you and take care of yourself."

"Don't worry Mom, I'll be OK. Things are looking good over there. I'll probably be back before you know it. Just keep the mail flowing and I'll be fine."

Mama kissed him one last time. Andy boarded the train as it began to roll. We waved, and watched until the last car snaked around the far curve out of sight.

On the way back home, I asked Mama more about getting a phone.

"Do you think Dad would let us?"

"Let us? If we need one, we'll get one. I think he already knows what we should do. Supposin' something should happen to one of the boys? I just knew Andy would be headed for Korea. We'll get the money somehow! We need a phone!"

A week later, we had a telephone just as Mama wanted. Dad agreed that it was a good idea. Its place of honor was on a stand in the dining room; it sometimes was difficult, keeping the kids from using it as a plaything. This required a constant watch to make sure one of them wasn't standing mute as a boot, listening to the voice on the other end. The operator saying, "Number Please," repeatedly, was just enough to keep little ears listening. The newness eventually wore off.

One day when Mama was using the phone, she heard a familiar voice ask for her number.

"Carol, is that you?"

"Yep, I'm your friendly neighborhood operator. Isn't it something, having a phone? We're not supposed to talk to subscribers. My supervisor is coming." Carol had been talking in a hushed tone. Now she raises her voice and loudly announces, "Number please." We felt very proud having a cousin who was a telephone operator. Our phone number was easy to remember and full of lucky numbers, the little tag read 1711.

Our letters to Andy continued all while he was on his way overseas. Traveling by boat, we didn't know exactly how long it would take him, but when he arrived, there would be several letters waiting. Andy's first letter was a relief to us all. We were glad to know he had made it across safely. We laughed when he poked fun at how seasick he had gotten. However, the laughter soon died when we learned one day that Chinese troops entered the Korean conflict and pushed UN troops back to the 38th parallel. The war was again in full swing and our Andy was right in the middle of it.

Four days before Christmas Joseph finished his engineering courses. He called Mama on the phone and told her that he had passed third highest in his class. He would be home for a week's leave and then he too would be heading for Korea. Mama was grateful she still had Joseph for a while more. Joseph and Mama talked about Andy, where he was, how bad things looked. Joseph remembered how he and Andy met for the last time on the base at Fort Dix. I listened to their conversation as Joseph told her of that parting. Andy was packed and ready to ship out. Joseph walked Andy as far as he could, then they parted. "We were walking together through the barracks talking, and we came to a fork in the road. We shook hands … said our good-byes. He went one way and I went the other. I turned around on last time to see him hurrying off with the duffel bag slung over his shoulder." Joseph was moved by his own words.

About eleven o'clock, Dad woke me and told me it was Mama's time; he and Joseph were taking Mama to the hospital. Sharon was born just before midnight on New Years Eve. We were one O'Brien short at Christmas, but we had a brand new baby sister to bring in the New Year. There would be no more babies for the O'Briens; Mama called Sharon her "change of life" baby. The last of us to be born, now gave Mama nine diamonds. Sharon's birth couldn't have been timed any better since Joseph was scheduled to leave on New Year's Day. The next day, Joseph and Mama said a tearful good-by from Mama's hospital bed. Taking one last look at his new baby sister, Joseph returned home to grab a bite of dinner, which I had tried my best to make as Mama would have. After dinner when Joseph was packed and ready to go, I found him in Mama's room. He was examining the contents of a small tray that rested on her dresser. The tray held an assortment of different size safety pins, buttons and the remnant of a rosary that had found it's way into the hands of one of the inquisitive toddlers.

"You need something Joseph?"

"I was looking for a medal or something to take with me. Does Mom have anything like that?"

"Here's a small crucifix … came from the broken rosary. Will that do?"

"Yea. That's good." Joseph slipped it into his pocket.

Joseph had a 1:30 train to catch that afternoon; time was running short. Dad and all of us kids accompanied him to the train station. We kissed and hugged him, promising to continue our letters. As with Andy, we didn't start for home until the last of the train disappeared around the bend, out of sight.

Mama spent the usual six days in the hospital. When she came home, we thought Sharon was quite unique; after all, three boys had been born in a row between her and Mary. In no time, Mama was back in the swing of her household duties, and worrying about the boys. Joseph had convinced her that because he was in the construction end of the conflict he would probably see little combat. Andy was over there for three months, already.

With Joseph coming home and leaving, and Sharon being born, Christmas vacation from school disappeared quickly. Regents' exams were bearing down on my classmates and me. Sister Agnes worked overtime with us. Regents' exams were put together by members of our religious order and were tough to pass. These exams came twice a year and could unnerve the best of students. For the few of us below a passing average, even ordinary school exams could turn our minds turned to mush.

Nothing was permitted in the classroom with us but a pencil, pen and a bottle of ink; even sister's desk was stripped of everything. When sister opened the big sealed envelope and distributed the exam papers, a silence fell over our normally busy classroom. Sometimes she would walk up and down the aisles observing everyone. I knew when she was near; the large rosary around her waist would make a soft rattle. Sometimes, when she passed me by, Sister pointed to an answer on my paper that was incorrect. I had better give that one a second consideration. The exams lasted three days and when report cards were given out, I heard the sweetest words from Father Kelly. "Good work, Kathleen." Hurrying home, I held fast to the book with my report card safe inside of its pages. My marks wouldn't be in the headlines of tomorrow's paper, but I had a passing grade in everything. Now my thoughts turned to how on earth could I ever pass first year high in just half a year's time? Oh well, I'd just put that worry in my pocket for another day; the important thing was, I was now in high school.

As the days rolled by, I settled down in my new surrounding. Thing were to my liking, except for one small problem; Albert, the class clown, took a liking to me. I couldn't make him understand that the feeling wasn't mutual. Albert was attending St. Michael's as a tuition student from nearby Morgan. There was no parochial high school in Morgan so he came to St. Michael's. The courses there were geared for those heading to college. Albert, however, didn't seem to be college material as he sat in his seat making all kinds of strange noises trying to break up everyone in the room. He wasn't a very tall boy, and that in itself wasn't bad, but the appalling grin he had on his face most of the time, was. It turned my stomach. He had dark brown tight wavy hair that the boys made fun of behind his back.

It was hard for me to feel sorry for Albert. To me, it seemed that he brought this kind of thing on himself. He thought everyone was laughing with him, but I knew they were laughing at him; I was embarrassed for him. Albert's favorite sound was putting his hand under his armpit making it sound like someone breaking wind. Everyone else would giggle and laugh. I couldn't understand why Sister never corrected this behavior. It was as though she turned a deaf ear to it, and maybe that had more truth in it than I knew, she may have been hard of hearing. When school was over for the day, I'd start for home fast before this Albert person could catch up with me. It was strange, but the more he pursued me the more I tried to avoid him … or was it the other way around? Either way, he was making my life miserable. Notes that Albert left on my desk were always the same, "Meet me at the Chocolate Bar after school." My answer was always, "No!" I was constantly blaming Mama for my not being able to go; I had to be at home after school and help her with the household chores. Once this magic excuse was found, everything settled down. I had to rely on my own ability to handle Albert; this time, there wasn't a big brother around to bail me out.

We continued writing on a regular basis to my brothers. I loved the short visits we had through our letters. One corner of the envelope had the words Air Mail above a ribbon of red white and blue, and the writing paper was so thin it was almost transparent. This was the official lightweight paper for writing letters headed overseas. Mama said it was important to be able to get as much mail on one flight to our fighting forces as possible; all this had to do with keeping morale up for our fighting men. One day I heard Dad talking about the little attention the conflict was getting from the people in the United States.

"Just wait and see, when this thing drags on for years they'll wake up. When we've lost so many of our boys it'll be too late. Police Action, bullshit."

We wrote Andy and Joseph every chance we got. We didn't wait to hear from them. We would write just to keep the mail flowing at a good pace, just as Andy wanted. We made sure Andy was kept abreast of what was happening with Joseph. Andy said he was going to keep his eyes and ears open. He thought there might be a chance that one day, he and Joseph would run into each other. Andy never wrote in detail about the fighting he was in; perhaps that was deliberate, and perhaps it was censorship, but whatever, the less Mama knew, the better it was. It would be like him to protect Mama from worrying. His letters were always short, except for one that he wrote while he was on R&R. In that particular letter, he told us how cold the winter in Korea was. He often mentioned names of his buddies. That included half of the army, for he referred to everyone as his "Buddy."

One time he made light of an incident with a U.S. tank that had wandered into a rice paddy where it stalled and started to gurgle as it sank into the soft wet ground. The crew from inside came out and began the struggle to free the metal monster. It was clear with each gurgle it wasn't going to be easy. Andy and his buddies sitting on the sidelines gave out with smart remarks. In the end, Andy and his buddies were told to help them release the gargantuan thing from what would have been its watery grave. It took half a day, but they finally did get it out. Andy said he had never been so cold and wet in all his life; it was only a continuation of the bitter cold that our forces endured.

Listening to every news broadcast on the radio and reading between the lines in Andy's letters, we could tell that the going must have been rough. There were times he had to scribble off those precious few lines using the back of his helmet for a desk. We learned later that some of the time his hands were so frozen it was difficult just to hold the pencil, when he could find one. We didn't care about the quality of his writing, as long as we heard from him. At least he was all right up to the date of his last letter, and then the worrying would begin all over until the next letter came.

He wrote of being on some kind of point system. When a soldier had spent a certain amount of time at the fighting lines, he would accrue points that would eventually allow him to take a break from active duty. Going to Japan for "R&R," was something every soldier welcomed when the time came. While browsing through the shops in Japan, Andy came across something he thought I would like; silk lounging pajamas. In one of his letters, he told me to send him my size; Of course, I couldn't have been more pleased. The next letter out, I did just that. Weeks later, on one of our many trips to the post office, we found a pink slip with our mail, it told us there was a package to be picked up at the postage window. The man took the slip of paper and returned with a tattered looking box. Peeking out of a crushed corner was a bit of the contents, something silky and soft, my pajamas had arrived. They were a dazzling shade of blue that I had never seen before. When we reached home and were able to take a good look at my pajamas, we found them more splendid than could be imagined. The blouse had a high oriental type collar, the buttons down the front were loops that hooked over tuffs of material I called soft buttons. On the front of the blouse, two large dragons curled their yellow and green bodies up to the shoulders. Their open mouths revealed a very threatening set of teeth. The back of the blouse had a picture of the snow-covered peaks of the highest mountain in Japan. Now I could see why they appealed to Andy. They were truly beautiful. A note tucked into the pocket of the blouse read: "For being a good sister."

Everything settled into a kind of pattern for a time. Letters out and letters received were the focus of our lives. In school, classmates who never gave me a second look before, were now stopping me and asking how my brothers were doing. I felt good. For the first time I was recognized as part of school like everyone else, but as I had observed many years ago, when good things happen, watch out. Often, some mean thing is lurking just around the corner for you. I must keep my head, and not get too proud. Then, I might fool whatever it was that played that dirty trick on me.

CHAPTER 15
A Fateful Message

Some will fall, but rise again to carry out the deed.
Some will fall, become the earth, to nurture morrow's seed.

After the Christmas break, the whole high school buzzed with plans for the upcoming prom. Girls were accepting invitations to the dance everyday. The words, "Snow Ball" were cleverly worked in as the theme. I knew the probability of Albert asking me to go to the dance was high, and so I tried to avoid him but my plan was doomed …

"Boy you sure walk fast," he giggled. "I've been looking for you after school, for days. How is it I miss you?"

"I have things to do at home you know." I knew what he was leading up to.

"Well … how about going to the prom with me?"

"I don't think I can go. It means getting a dress and everything. I'll let you know." I was a coward not to come right out and tell him, "I don't particularly like you, get lost." I would suffer for that lack of backbone., although it did get Albert out of my hair for the moment. He would gladly wait for my answer.

When I told Mama about my prom invitation, she was more excited than I was.

"I don't want to go to any old prom, what can I tell him,"

"Oh Kali, go. Make some memories of your high school days."

" …But I don't want to go, besides where are we going to get a gown?" I cleverly threw the stark reality of our lack of funds right back at her; "a gown meant money, and there was hardly enough for food let alone a dress for a stupid dance. "

"I'll ask Vera if she has one you can borrow. She was in a wedding not long ago. It should fit. You're the same size."

Vera was a neighbor who lived in an apartment over the Belmont Bar. Mama was sure to get her to loan us a dress, or Vera was bound to know someone who would have one. I was crushed, betrayed by my own mother; like everything else she told me to do, I obediently went along with the plan. Holy mackerel! I was going to the prom and didn't even know how to dance.

Vera was more than happy to supply a dress. She had several for us to choose from. One look at the gown and I was caught up in the excitement of wearing that mass of white netting covering a deep pink skirt. The right sway on the dance floor would certainly send it flaring out for miles. This would be my first gown. I could picture me twirling and whirling around the dance floor like Ginger Rogers. I was under the spell of the romance of the dance. Suddenly there was no thought of how I felt about going on a date with Albert. "Besides," Mama said, "you're only going to a dance, not getting married." Dancing would come naturally. "Just follow the boy," was her only advice.

The night of the prom Albert arrived at the apartment right on time. I wasn't too happy about him coming into the apartment to pick me up, but Mama said it was definitely not right to meet him out on the sidewalk. Albert looked quite sharp in his dark pants and white sport coat. The big smile on his face told how pleased he was with himself as he handed me a small flower box with two gardenias and one red carnation inside. When the lid was lifted, I breathed in the most pleasing fragrance. Mama pinned the corsage on the shoulder of my coat. "Try not to touch them too much when you pin them to your dress. These flowers don't like to be touched," she whispered. Gardenias were very appropriate for me. Mama helped Albert pin the red carnation on his lapel. He did look very nice.

Outside Albert had a taxi waiting where his best friend Francis, and his date were waiting for us. Soon our coach and four were hurrying along taking us to St. Michael's, and to our first prom. As the evening wore on I became more impatient with dancing, Albert would dance every dance he could, but I wasn't doing very well. I wasn't able to relax long enough to forget myself, and Albert's arm around me made me uneasy. He and I changed partners with Francis and his date for one dance. Francis was good company, and so easy to be with. In his capable hands, I could have been dancing like a movie star before the evening was over. We talked and laughed as we danced and I was really beginning to see the reason for the whole evening. It was disappointing that we swapped partners only once, and though it was a bit unethical for the occasion, Francis continued making faces over his date's shoulder, trying to make me smile back. I did encourage him, and felt I had defiantly come with the wrong partner. Albert could see the joking going on between Francis and me and would whisk us off to another part of the dance floor. It was no use; sooner or later, Francis and I would lock eyes and grin at each other again.

When the prom ended, I was left alone with Albert and couldn't wait for him to take me home. Francis and his date had gone off to a party. Albert asked me to go to a party someplace where the others were to meet, but I would have nothing to do with it. Going to a place where there would be drinking was about as inviting to me as having a second date with Albert. I was ready to go home and told Albert so, but he wanted to go someplace for a while and thought going for a soda would be more to my liking. "Well, I'll have to ask my mom. I was told to come home right after the prom." It was a lie, but getting away from Albert wouldn't be easy. We climbed the stairs to the apartment. When we reached the door, I told him to wait there. Mama was sure to be in bed, and this would give me the opportunity to talk to her alone. I groped along the dark hallway heading for Mama's bedroom, but I was counting on the darkness to cover my conversation with her. Slowly I pushed the bedroom door open. Mama's head suddenly popped out from around the door. I knew she was in her nightgown, because she stood completely concealed behind the door except for one hand and her head. "Mama he wants to go for a soda. Say no, say no." Before I knew what was happening she was pushing me back, away from the door, "Yes go ahead it's all right, its all right." What was the matter with her hadn't she heard me? She should have said no, but here she was almost kicking me out of the house! Turning, I was shocked to find I was slammed up against Albert. He had quietly followed me to the bedroom door and was waiting to hear for himself what Mama was going to say. I was trapped again. How much of the conversation between us had he heard? Embarrassment gave way to a growing anger. Why should I be in this situation? I didn't want to be with him. Why was he still here?

We descended the stairs, and I hit the sidewalk at a very fast pace. Albert had to quicken his step and I heard him say, "Geezze, you walk so fast." He took me to the ice cream parlor; I don't remember if we even had a conversation or not, though I'm sure we did. I was so angry my gardenias were all wilted, and turning brown from my body heat. I don't think we spent more than 15 minutes there, but I had done all that was expected of me; now home. Our "good night" outside the door was as stiff as a frozen flounder. I thanked him politely and then closed the door slowly. I heard the door latch, then footsteps going down the stairs, slowly at first then picking up speed. He was gone at last, and I'd never let myself be talked into something like this again. The next time around I would probably be expected to give him a good night kiss, oh brother!

The following Monday Albert acted as if we were going steady. I continued to turn a cold shoulder to him, but like our ol' stove, he was made of cast iron. Accepting the prom invitation, I had undone the hard work of my ignoring him. I would have to start all over. One day as I was leaving school, Albert thrust a note into my hand and disappeared down the stairs. The note read: "Meet me at The Chocolate Bar for a soda and come alone ... understand?" This meant, of course, not to bring any of my brothers or Mary with me. Reading this made me angrier than the night of the prom. "Do you understand?" Who did he think he was ordering around? I crumpled the note up and tossed it into a wastebasket. "I hope he grows roots waiting for me."

Albert must have decided to let things cool off for a while after that. He left school each day walking with Francis and gave me no notice. Had it finally gotten across that I had no interest in him? I would have enjoyed walking with Francis, but because the boys were good friends, this was not possible. There was one class when Francis and I were together and Albert was somewhere else. Francis chose the seat behind mine, and would whisper funny comments to me as he crunched down behind me out of view from Sister. One day I heard him quietly whisper that my hair was very pretty, and had a lot of red in it. It was the nicest thing a boy had ever said to me. That was as far as it went. Perhaps Francis was trying to remain a loyal friend to Albert. My resentment toward Albert grew; he was messing up my life trying to make something happen that never would.

Mama thought I was being mean to Albert, but she didn't have to be with him. It made shivers up my arm to think of him only holding my hand. Mama had no idea that I secretly liked Francis, and in my frustration, all I could do was concentrate on the important things in life, like writing letters to Joseph and Andy. Joseph and Andy had done well keeping in touch, until a time when three weeks passed and we had heard nothing from Andy, it worried us.

School was out for the day. Time wouldn't be wasted sauntering along in conversation with someone when Mama could be sitting at the table reading a letter. Swinging in the door, I found Mama sitting at the kitchen table; she was stressed and pale.

"We just got word that Andy has been hurt. He's in a hospital!"

"Hurt? How?"

"I don't know every detail, only that he suffered a severe concussion."

"What's that mean?"

"It means a head injury. I knew it. I just knew something would happen to him."

We found out later through the Red Cross that Andy was hurt when a hand grenade exploded near a foxhole he was in. He was found unconscious, bleeding from the ears, and mouth. He had numerous shrapnel burns but was expected to recover. Mama was grateful to the Red Cross for getting the information. A special trip was made that night to the post office to mail two hastily written letters. For now, nothing would be said to Joseph about Andy. There wasn't much to be said anyway until we knew more about Andy's condition.

Less than a week later, I received a letter from Joseph. Usually Joseph would say "hi" to all of us in one letter, but this time I had a letter of my own. Joseph spoke of the cold, and how tired he was every night. He told me to be good, and stay in school and try to graduate, for Mama if not for myself. Reading between the lines, I got the impression he knew he had disappointed Mama when he quit school, with only a half year to go. He closed his letter this way: "*Kali*, you're the oldest one home now. It's up to you to watch out for Mama. Take care of her until we are home again. Keep saying your prayers for all of us over here. We need them.

Your Loving Brother,

Joseph"

Easter came during the month of March this year. Andy was still recuperating, but there was nothing more that to be done for him that wasn't already being done. During Andy's recovery, Dad took Mama to the movies every Sunday without fail, hoping it would lift her spirits a little. There was some resistance at first. She didn't think she should be enjoying a movie when Andy was hurt, so far from home. Dad's persuasive way won out, and reluctantly she went. One movie that they saw was a comedy called, "Ma And Pa Kettle." When Mama came home, she was still laughing over that silly movie. She told me that Dad shook the walls of the theater with his robust laughing.

At last, the day came when we received a letter from Andy, it was short, but he was writing again. Joseph would be celebrating his twenty-first birthday on April 4. With things the way they were, a birthday wouldn't have much significance for him this year. Mama and Dad planned to send Joseph a telegram wishing him happy birthday from all of us. He had to know we didn't forget. The telegram was sent on April 2 to be sure he would get it on time.

The following day I bolted through the door mindful that it was Joseph's birthday; maybe there'd be a letter.

"Any letters, Mama?"

"No. Nothing."

The snow had melted off early leaving behind an unusually mild April. Mama had firm convictions that the sooner windows could be opened throughout the apartment, the sooner the germs of winter colds would be swept away. Several windows were open, including in the kitchen, where Mama had just thrown the laundry basket in ahead of her. Laundry day had kept her busy taking clothes on and off the clothesline since midmorning. Lowering herself on to a chair, she heaved a sigh of relief that the job was finished for now.

"You must have been awful busy today. You haven't even combed your hair."

"I did, but the wind ... it's made my job harder all day. At least it's warm out or I'd be frozen by now." Mama tipped Sharon's empty bottle of baby oil upside down to drain the last drops to her dry hands. Resting her head against the back of the chair, she pushed her tousled hair from her forehead. Taking the hairbrush from the shelf, I offered to brush the tangles free. The gentle pull of the brush was soothing to her. .

"Your hair is getting long."

"Uh-huh."

It wasn't long before I had fallen under the spell of the brush too; the way it cut little furrows in her wavy hair, stretching each lock out straight then the sudden snapping back into the wavy ridges of before. Gray hairs are noticeably invading her chestnut hair, but I say nothing of them. It was time to relax. Sharon was sleeping in her bassinet in the next room. Donald played on the floor nearby. Mama could use this moment to recover before the rest of the kids clamored through the door. She closed her eyes in complete surrender as the brush moved through her hair. The serenity lasted for a couple of minutes, but was shattered by someone knocking on the door. It startled both of us.

"I'll get it Mama. It's probably some kid looking for Mary or Richard." It was a young boy wearing a Western Union hat, and an anxious look on his face.

"Your name O'Brien?" He made little eye contact as a pencil was thrust out to me.

"Yea."

"Telegram. Sign Here,"

I tucked the hairbrush under my arm, signed a paper on the clipboard, and in exchange he handed me a yellow envelope. The young boy darted briskly down the stairs.

"What is it," Mama called impatiently.

"Just a second,"

Holding the envelope out to her I was thinking, "Could Joseph's telegram be coming back to us for some reason? Now he won't get his birthday greeting on time."

Mama snatched the telegram from my hand and tore it open. The envelope drifted to the floor as she read the telegram. A few silent seconds passed then, "No … No!" Mama stared at the telegram in her hand. Rising to her feet, she slumped back down in the chair. I stood watching confused, but expecting her to say something. She said nothing. Her arms went limp to her sides, the telegram tight in her hand. Trying to stand again, she slipped from the chair to the floor landing on her knees. What in the world was happening? Helplessly I watch her crumple to the floor. I rushed over to her.

"Mama! Mama, what's the matter?" Her fingers were tight around the crumpled telegram locking it in her fist. Whatever it said, it had to be awful. Grabbing her by the arm I tried to help her back on the chair. "Mama, come on. Sit back in the chair. Come on! Stand up!" She had no strength to rise on her own, and wasn't even aware I was talking to her. "Get to the front room," I thought. "The couch in there will be a good place for her to lie down." Straining against her weight, I gave one strong tug. "Come on Mama let's go in the front room." Slowly she rose to her feet. The hallway stretched out in front of us. "My God, it must be at least a mile long. Will I ever make it?" I thought.

Looking through to the other end of that long dark corridor, this helpless feeling was strangely familiar. I was not only afraid of what was happening now, but what might be at the other end when we got there. All that was missing was, the rumble of a train from overhead. Mama was far from steady as we both started through that damn long hallway. I had her arm around my neck as we moved; her body pressed against the wall for support. Then with no warning she buckled, slid down the wall dragging me with her. We end up in a sitting position on the floor.

"Stand up, Mama, please stand up." Frustrated and angry I tug on her. Why can't I keep her going? She is on her feet again. The pile of plaster we have torn from the hole in the wallboard is of little concern except that it crunches beneath our feet. All that matters is getting her through the hallway. We're almost halfway now, when Mama tears from my grasp and lands in a kneeling position on the floor. I can do no more than what I've been doing; tug her to her feet again. The end of the hall is but a few steps away. Just ahead is the doorway to the front room. Mama collapses again. Straining, I help her up for the third time; my breathing is too labored to talk. My heart is pounding from the struggle, and fear of the disaster still unknown to me. I can only press forward.

A quick glance around the room, and I feel I'm seeing the room for the first time, the way it really is. The look is bleak and barren; I never notice it that way before. There is no warmth or comfort to offer Mama here. The few pieces of scratched furnishings look pitiful and dilapidated. The worn linoleum floor covering adds to the cold dreary look. Dad's chair is worn and dirty. His table with the two little doors stands barren, emptied by young undisciplined hands. Where are the precious papers now? My beautiful horse clock is tarnished, with one leg missing. Our well-worn lumpy couch over by the window is the only welcome thing in sight. The open window beside the couch allows a breeze to blow into the room that gracefully pushes the curtains inward.. "The breeze will be good for her," I think.

We make our way to the couch. Sitting down, Mama begins to cry and holler out, "Andy. I want to see Andy! I want to see Andy!"

Something has happened to Andy. Had he gotten worse? Could it be that he...? No time to wonder, Mama has wrapped her arms around herself, closing up in a ball. It was frightening watching her rock herself back and forth, then suddenly become silent. Leaning on the arm of the couch, she stares intently out of the window as though the breeze was drawing her outward, just like the curtains. Could she be thinking...? Quickly I slammed the window down, trapping the curtains beneath the sash.

Mama started crying again. I felt helpless, but I could do nothing for her. At least she was crying and not just sitting there. Stepping back, a ways in front of her, afraid to take my eyes away, I prayed. "God help me! What do I do? Please, what do I do now?"

The telegram, Mama had let go of the telegram. It was lying beside her on the cushion all crumpled up. I read it and discovered that it wasn't about Andy, but Joseph. It said that Joseph had been killed in action on March 22, 1951. In my shock I blurted out, "Joseph, not Andy!" Mama stopped crying, creating a deafening stillness. That brief moment filled me with dread. Looking up she stared at me, her cheeks glistening from the tears. My words took a few seconds to make sense to her. Reaching out for the telegram she snapped, "What? Let me see that." I handed the paper to her regretting that I had spoken without thinking. It could set her off in a way I couldn't handle. A cold fear gripped ever bone in my body. I squeezed my hands together until they hurt. My eyes burned into her face, I must be ready for the unexpected. She read the telegram again and then pitifully called out, "Joseph, my first baby, not my *first* baby." The telegram dropped from her hand to the floor as her body slump backward against the couch. Gathering her apron in her hands, she sobbed into it.

Someone entered the room behind me. I was hoping for a miracle, but it wasn't Dad. It was Richard and Mary.

"What's the matter Kali? What's wrong?"

I handed Mary the telegram. "Go get Dad. He's probably in Nick's barbershop. Tell him to come home, now! RUN!" Mary dropped the telegram. She ran from the room. I was satisfied she was the right one to get Dad. If anyone would have him here soon, it was Mary.

Little Donald, who was just beginning to walk, had finally managed to work his way through the hallway and peek into the room around Jimmy and Johnny. The three of them pile up in the doorway not daring to enter the troubled room. They're just little kids, but their presence is a comfort; at least I don't feel alone. When Mary returned to the apartment, I felt the world had been lifted from my shoulders. Dad made his way through the hallway, with tear filled eyes. Crossing the room, he reached out for Mama. She was on her feet in a second. They ran toward each other meeting in an emotional embrace. Mama was safe now. I headed for my bedroom.

Lowering myself on the bed completely exhausted. No tears came, but my heart ached; not for Joseph, but for Mama and Dad. I could feel their anguish over this unbearable thing that had happened. Dad and Mama Bear had lost a cub. We kids had lost a friend, a brother, a valiant defender. It can't be true. Dad was still consoling Mama as the last glow of day faded. He had gotten her to lie down on the bed and sat beside her. The telegram was on the bed, as Dad talked softly to her. Dad told me to call Aunt Hanna and tell her what had happened. My eyes took in the number tag on the front of the phone; 1711, so much for lucky numbers. I hoped Carol's voice would be on the other end of the line. I wasn't disappointed.

"Carol, something awful has happened."

"I know, Kali. My friend at the telegraph office called me. I knew before you did."

"Well … I was gonna call Hanna and… "

"I've called Mother already, she knows. She'll call Aunt Katie and tell her; Mother will call Mildred too. How's your Mom doing?"

"Not too good."

"Is your Dad there?"

"Yea."

"OK! Mother will be down to see you first thing tomorrow. If you need anything call and let us know."

"OK Carol … thanks."

The next day when Hanna did come to see us, she thought Mama needed a doctor. "I'd have a doctor look at her. She's not sleeping or eating, and now she's not crying either. That's not good if it goes on too long," Hanna cautioned Dad.

Of course she was right, the next day found Mama no better, so Dad called a doctor to the house. The doctor said she was suffering from shock and told us to watch her closely. She was a hair's breath away from a nervous breakdown. The doctor left some pills that would help her to rest. Mildred agreed to take Mama back to Hartford with her for a while, until Mama got stronger. Mildred refused to stay in our bug riddled apartment, and a change of scenery for Mama wouldn't hurt. Sharon and Donald went with Mama to Hartford; I stayed home to take care of the rest of the family. Dad came right home almost every day after work. I wasn't used to the small size our family had shrunk to. The once crowded apartment seemed spacious and empty. So much so, that even the echoes of happier times were gone. First, we kept Joseph from finding out about Andy being hurt, and now we had to keep Andy from finding out about Joseph. Would our lives ever return to normal after this strange turn of events?

Two weeks later when Mildred brought Mama and the two babies back home, we could see Mama was a little better. She was glad to see all of us again, and hugged us so hard. Mama wasn't perfect yet, but she was on her feet. She drank coffee but still only picked at solid food. Mildred had made Mama talk; unlike the rest of us who treated the subject of Joseph's death like taboo. It was good to make her talk about it Mildred said, even though Mama would start crying every time. Mildred said, "Be patient. She'll be able to talk about it without crying. It will take time."

We were getting things in the mail often, things from the government about Joseph. The day that Mildred brought Mama home, there was a small pile of mail waiting for Mama. Among the array of different size envelopes was a small package containing Joseph's personal effects. A jack knife, a comb, a picture of the Sacred Heart creased and rumpled almost beyond recognition, and the small crucifix from the broken rosary that Joseph had taken from Mama's dresser last New Year's Day. There was no wallet.

"Do you recognize any of these things, I don't!" The sight of the articles seemed to agitate her. When I saw the little crucifix, I knew.

"Yes," I said softly. "This is the crucifix from your dresser."

"I don't recognize that. How do we know these are his things? They could be anybody's. Where's his wallet?"

Mama also learned from the mail that day, that she was the sole beneficiary to Joseph's insurance. "I don't want any money. There isn't enough money in the world to pay for this." Mama was stubborn about the money. I was glad Mildred was still there to talk to her. Mildred gently scolded mama, telling her that this was something he left behind for her. "Use the money like Joseph would have wanted you to," she said.

"I can't think about money now. I can't think about anything except that Joseph won't be coming… "

"Uh, oh, she's gonna start crying again. Mildred! Stop pounding away at her," I thought. Mama didn't cry, she hesitated and glanced up at the wallpaper on the kitchen wall. The bright colors of the little cups, saucers and teapots had faded long ago. The grease-stained wallpaper was an agonizing reminder.

Then she finished the sentence, " …home. What home? This pig sty isn't a home!" Mama slammed a chair into the table. Angered by her own words she left the room. Mildred followed Mama into the bedroom. When Mildred returned to the kitchen, I was still upset at Mama's outburst. "She's lying down now," Mildred explained. "But she'll be all right. Your Mom has a lot of thinking to do." Mildred made tea for Mama and stayed with us a few hours more until Dad came home. Mama was doing better, but I truly doubted that she would be the same again.

She walked as if she were in a dream, and rarely smiled. When she did it was a halfhearted smile that never reflected in her eyes. Dad said it was the medication to help her sleep that made her act that way. Mama would need more than just medicine to get through this ordeal; something that would give her some peace of mind. What that something could be was beyond me.

Eventually Mama stopped taking the medication, and decided it was time for her to go grocery shopping with me. Up to now, I had been doing a light shopping as we needed things, but day-to-day buying was costing us more. We needed to shop the way we used to, enough to last a whole week. I was glad something normal was happening; still it was too soon for Mama. It was nothing but a constant battle trying to get through the stores, with well-meaning people approached her with their condolences. We decided thereafter I'd do the shopping by myself with the aid of a grocery list. One day after I'd finished the grocery buying, I hurried toward home with the wagonload of groceries when I spotted Marion. It had gotten so repetitious and uncomfortable talking about Mama to everyone that I didn't want to talk about it anymore. Marion was different. I was glad to see her but she appeared uneasy as we talked.

"Kali, I have some pictures of Joseph that I thought maybe your mother might... "

"No, she doesn't need them. Keep them Marion. They'll just make her cry." My answer was quick, without thought. "Well ... if you change your mind ... you can let me know. Tell your mom I was asking about her." I felt bad about my response, but I thought I would save Mama the pain of looking at those pictures taken only months ago.

Mildred did say it wasn't bad for Mama to cry, but I felt so helpless when she did. I was holding on to my own theory that if Mama wasn't crying she was getting better.

When I returned home Mama was waiting in the kitchen. I began placing the canned goods on the shelf in the cupboard, gabbing away about the shopping trip. Mama sat in a chair listening. When I told her of my conversation with Marion, she jumped up from the chair. Her reaction was so sudden. "No, don't tell her that! I want those pictures. I want every picture of him I can get!" The angry tone startled me. The expression on Mama's face was pure anger; I had done something very wrong. I tried to choke back the tears that refused to be held back. At last no longer able to, I fled from the kitchen to the bedroom, crying harder with each step. I buried my face in the bedding, asking myself when this sort of thing was going to be over. Then I felt two hands lifting me up. Mama was sitting next to me, and drew me close hugging me tightly. "You've wanted to do that for a long time haven't you?" she said. "I've been worried about you and Mary both. She hasn't cried yet either. It's all right to cry honey." I hugged Mama back, and for the first time in weeks felt she was the mother again, and I the child. It was comforting and safe snuggled into her shoulder. Though Mama thought that I was crying about Joseph that wasn't how it was. I had spent so much time trying to mother everyone; I foolishly thought I could do no wrong. By some magical appointment, I was an adult, but now something did go wrong. Hearing Mama's angry words was like a sudden spanking. I was still just a little girl after all. We sat on the edge of the bed for a time hugging each other, then Mama wiped my tears away, and we both returned to the kitchen.

I continued stacking the groceries in the cupboard until Mama came up from behind and hugged me. She kissed me on the cheek and said, "Remember how Joseph used to do this to me whenever he came home? Sometimes I'd be standing at the stove cooking his supper, or maybe at the ironing board pressing a shirt for him, remember?" I did remember, but for some reason told Mama that I didn't. Maybe I was still a little angry with her for making me feel bad, and maybe I didn't want to talk about Joseph any more. "Oh you must remember," she continued. "He hugged me this way all the time. I can feel his arms around me, like he was here now." Mama was remembering good things about Joseph for a change. Her voice was soft, contented.

One day I was left to watch the small kids while Mama and Dad went to the Red Cross; they were trying to get Andy home on an emergency furlough. Because Joseph had been killed and Andy injured, the lady at the Red Cross thought there was a good chance, especially since the

Doctor recommended it. Again, the Red Cross came through for us. Andy was granted a 30-day furlough, and was on his way immediately. He was able to hitch a ride on an airplane that was returning stateside; at last Andy was to have his first long trip in a plane. As the military winged Andy closer to home, we waited excitedly for his return. In no time, it was the day for Andy's train to pull in at the Chipwey train station. Dad wasn't with us. He always seemed to be missing at times like this. Perhaps he knew he couldn't cope with the emotional part of it all. This time he thought it best to go on to work as usual; he would see Andy at lunchtime. We started out that day with our parade of little people running far ahead of us, each one eager to be the first to set eyes on Andy. Little thought was given to the rain that threatened that late April morning. Only one thing concerned us; how close was Andy now? We hadn't gone but a block when we heard a train whistle. "That's the train. He's here and we're not there to meet him. Hurry everybody." Mama quickened her steps to a trot as we headed down the street for the railroad underpass. At the far end of the street, we saw a lone thin figure. It was Andy; he had already walked the underpass by himself. Walking slowly with a duffel bag thrown over his shoulder, his hair fell across his forehead from underneath the hat, pushed to the back of his head and obviously not regulation. The beard on his face and his badly wrinkled uniform indicated a trip with few pauses. When he saw us, he let the bag drop to the sidewalk, and stood waiting for us. Mary and Richard were the first to greet him; Mama was close behind with Donald in tow. I quickened my steps, but I was carrying Sharon and was the slowest of all. Mama threw her arms around Andy to give him a big hug. Realizing how weak he was, she released her embrace and slipped her arm tightly around his to give him support. Mary, Richard and Jimmy took charge of the duffel bag as we began the walk back home.

"Who's that," Andy said in a thin voice as he craned his neck to see Sharon?

"That's Sharon, your new baby sister. Remember, I wrote you about her? She was born on New Years Eve." Mama's voice had more life to it than we had heard in a month.

I was smiling a proud smile until what I saw next almost took my breath away. Andy looked up at me, and as our eyes met, I could see that this person was much older than I remembered. It appeared that we had gotten our Andy back twenty years older than when he left us eight months ago. His mischievous dark eyes, a trademark of his energy and life, were dull and weary. His thin and wiry frame was much too delicate. Korea had pushed him through a knothole and then showed him things that had taken a horrible toll. His gray pallor and feeble smile were proof enough of that. For me this awkward moment had gone on long enough. I broke it by holding Sharon up so Andy could get a good look at her, hoping my stunned expression had not given me away.

We had asked the Red Cross not to let anyone tell Andy about Joseph, and apparently, they complied with our request.

"How are you doing Mom," Thinking that his leave was because Mama was sick, "Did you get a leave for Joseph too?"

"I'm doing OK, but it was because you were hurt that we were able to get one for you," Mama explained. Andy didn't question it further.

Andy was not to know about Joseph yet. We had all been warned to say nothing. Mama and Dad would determine when the time was right.

That night we had a celebration dinner, and a sedate, but welcome feeling of jubilation filled that scruffy old flat on Albany Street. Mama cooked a big meal with Andy's favorite chocolate cake for dessert. We kept Andy well supplied with milk. A cold glass of milk was all he could think of for months. After dinner, Dad sat and talked to Andy for a short while, but Andy wasn't holding conversations very well. He still appeared to be restless and disoriented; some things that should have been familiar to him would elude him for a few seconds then he would remember. In the midst of our joy and celebration, he asked that heart wrenching question again, "Did you get a leave for Joseph, too, Mom?" Mama calmly gave him the same answer. It was amazing that she could be so strong when the situation called for it. Twenty-four hours earlier she would have been reduced to tears at the very thought. After the first night, my parents agreed that we would use every bit of the time we had to let Andy adjust. Good wholesome meals and rest were priority now.

Our only problem was, if Andy wanted to visit his friends, there was no way we could get to all of them and swear them to secrecy. We didn't want him to find out that way. When it was time for Andy to know, Dad was the one who would tell him.

The first day Andy spent at home, he slept on and off. By the third day, he was sleeping the whole night through. His color was returning and soon he was talking more, asking questions about his friends. A week into Andy's furlough, Mama and Dad knew he was becoming impatient to see other people. Andy himself had decided that now was the time to tell him about Joseph. After dinner that night Dad took Andy to the Belmont Bar around the corner. "Let's go get a beer, come on just you and me," Dad said as he corralled Andy around the shoulders with his arm. Entering the bar, they found it almost deserted. It was dinnertime; most everyone was home with their families. Dad had planned it this way so he and Andy could sit at the bar without fear of something being said out of turn. Dad and Andy sat at the far end, quite secluded from the others. They talked with the bartender, whom dad had confided in earlier, as they leisurely drank a glass of beer. All was going well; soon, Dad would take Andy back home, and on the way would tell him. Two men entered the bar. When they realized Dad was sitting with our returned Andy, they shook hands with him and told him they were glad to see him home again. A third man entered and did the same only this one added, "Sorry about your brother." He gently patted Andy on the shoulder and walked away. Andy asked, "What's he mean?" There was no answer. Money was thrown down on the bar. Dad motioned Andy to follow him. Once out on the street Dad was aware that the moment of truth had arrived. "Andy, Joseph didn't make it. It happened last month. Mom took it real hard... " Andy didn't say anything he only listened as they walked slowly back to the apartment.

We were nearly finished with the supper dishes when we heard the door open. Looking over my shoulder, I saw Dad enter the kitchen. He had that scowl on his face that always camouflaged his feeling so well; Andy retreated to his room. We didn't have to ask. We knew Andy was now aware of everything. Dad said something to Mama, and then left the apartment again. Not more than five minutes had passed when Andy entered the kitchen.

"Is there any coffee left mom?"

"Yea Andy, want some?"

"Naw," apparently changing his mind, "I think I'll go outside and sit for a few minutes."

Andy grabbed a book of matches from the table and pulled a cigarette from the pack he carried with him. He left the apartment never lifting his head up or looking at us straight on. I looked at Mama trying to understand what was going to happen next. Mama whispered to me, "Go, and stay with him." I followed Andy down the two flights of stairs. He sat down on the big step outside the apartment. I sat down on the opposite side of the step so he wouldn't be too aware of me. I felt he didn't want anyone right now. We sat in silence for a while. He didn't look left or right only ahead out into the road.

"Wish I knew what he's thinking about." I found myself staring at the red embers on the tip of his cigarette growing brighter and longer with each puff. Then he flicked the cigarette into the street. It hit the pavement throwing a shower of sparks into the air. He instantly lit another. It was a new experience for me to see Andy smoking openly. Knowing our Andy he had probably been smoking on the sly for years. What did it matter, he couldn't get any more grown up than now.

The night was one of the darkest nights I had seen in a while. The streetlight that stood a few feet away was throwing off a dirty kind of glow. There wasn't the slightest movement to be seen anywhere; to me, it was like the end of the world with Andy and me the only two people alive. I felt awkward having no way to remedy things, and so I did what came natural for me, I spoke.

"Boy this old town stinks …. Wish we didn't live here."

"Yea? Well, it's a lot better than some places I know." His voice was tainted with anger. Though I didn't feel it was directed at me, I did know it was the wrong thing to say. Why didn't I keep my big mouth shut? Without warning, Andy stood up and walked away leaving me sitting there. I ran up stairs and told Mama he was going for a walk. "Stay with him. Go on, follow him." She pushed me toward the door. I ran back outside, and caught up with him at the corner.

"You don't have to come with me, Kali. I'll be OK," he said as he flicked a cigarette into the road. I hung back until Andy got some distance ahead, then I followed. We walked up Gardner Street, stopping in front of the apartment house where we once lived. He lit another cigarette, took a long puff on it, lifted his head to blow the smoke out. He paused when he spotted the fire escape above where he and Joseph had spent many August evenings long ago. The smoke was released with a gush of breath that I could hear from several yards away. The cigarette was dropped to the sidewalk, and mashed into the cement with his foot. The distance between us shortened as Andy's pace grew slower. I didn't want to get too close, each time this happened I stopped letting him get the lead again. Andy looked back at me only once, giving me no more notice. He walked as though he hadn't a care in the world. He even stopped often to browse at things displayed in store windows. Andy's walk took us down one side of Main and up the other, and finally headed for home.

"Mom, is there any coffee?" Mama jumped up eagerly to do what she could.

"Sure, do you want some?"

"No, I think I'll go to bed," he said in afterthought. "Night."

"Goodnight Andy." Mama's voice was soft. She reached out holding him close for a moment then gave him a goodnight kiss on the cheek. Andy hugged her back, and then walked the hallway to his room. Andy was hurting deep inside, and we could do nothing for him. Nothing could change what had happened to Joseph, and no one could help Andy through his pain. Strangely enough, something good was coming out of Andy's struggle. Mama had grown stronger by turning from her own grief to her concerns over him.

Mama was doing household chores again and able to care for Sharon, so I returned to school. I had been out of school for a full month. Andy and Mama had time to talk and visit with little interruption while the rest of us were in school. Sharon and Donald were the only ones not going to school yet; Sharon was still sleeping most of her day away and Donald was no trouble. Every day when school let out I was impatient to get home. Andy would be there. One day as I entered the apartment Andy and Mama were seated at the kitchen table. He had a cup of coffee in front of him and crushed a cigarette in an ashtray as he talked. Beside Mama on the floor was a basket, full of wet clothes waiting to be hung on the clothesline. I approached the table. Mama looked up at me and gave me a look that told me not to interrupt. I pulled a chair from the table, sat down and listened.

" …So by mid morning we were still advancing forward. Boy, you talk about the cold, my fingers were frozen from holding on to my rifle. We came to an open stretch of terrain that was covered by heavy enemy fire. The problem was to get all of us on the other side of the open stretch of ground with as few casualties as possible. There's so much going on in a situation like that. It doesn't matter how many people are around you, you feel like you're all alone. It's up to *you* to make sure you're going to make it.

"I was crouched down getting ready for my dash to the other side. My buddy Lee was somewhere behind me. Lee was a tall lanky guy. We always warned him about getting low enough and kidded him about even if his head was low enough not to forget about his butt, 'cause he towered above all of us. I didn't know how far behind me he was, but then that wasn't the most important thing to me then. I made a quick sign of the cross and said a fast 'Hail Mary,' and took off. I dove for the cover of a tree. I stopped for a second to catch my breath, tying to get used to the idea I made it, when it occurred to me to see how Lee was doing. When I spotted him, he was sitting in the middle of the opening, just sitting there with his legs out in front of him like a little kid getting ready to catch a rolling ball. He was hit in the chest. He raised his arm out as if he was trying to grab something and then dropped it. He must have been in shock or something. His eyes were open, but he wasn't aware of anything. I lay on my belly and crawled out to him. I never hugged ground so close in all my life.

"If you can imagine yourself in the middle of a bunch of angry bees and you don't know from what side you're gonna get stung, that's how it feels." Andy took another puff on the cigarette. "Lee was an easy target. I was scared he was going to get it again. Then it happened ... another shot. I knew it was too close to be good. The bullet caught him in the jaw jerking his head to the side. He fell backwards like a rock. I crawl out to him just far enough to grab his ankle. Slowly, I shifted my body backwards to the tree, dragging Lee inch by inch. By some miracle, we made it, by then Lee was out. He was so still ... I wasn't sure he was breathing ... I didn't get a chance to find out. Someone else came slamming into us. I heard him say, 'Keep going soldier, he'll be taken care of.' I grabbed my rifle and took off as I was told. The next cover I found was a hole in the ground. I dove in and the next thing I remember was waking up in the hospital with the biggest headache I ever had in my life. I never found out if Lee ... made it or not."

Andy blotted the cigarette in the ashtray and fell silent. Mama lowered her face into her hands then looked up at me with moist eyes. "How awful," she said. Andy rose from the chair, walked to the kitchen window, and stood looking out into the courtyard. No one said anything more, but I felt a lump crowding my throat.

Andy's leave was nearly over when he began to resemble his old self. The sparkle that was his alone had returned, to a degree, and the ashen tone of his skin had become nothing but a memory, but one thing didn't change; that often quiet seriousness that was so contrary to his personality. Andy was in better shape than when he first arrived home, and it helped Mama to realize that we still had many things to live for. After all, she still had eight diamonds left to fill her life.

It can only be imagined how difficult it was for Andy to go back to know he was headed for Korea again. He had lost a brother, and had been injured himself. It had to be difficult to return to that place of death and uncertainty but he never let his feelings show. After all, he was a master by now at keeping things under control. Andy would have to endure nine more months of Korea before he'd be sent home for good.

After an emotional good-by, with all our promises to keep writing and praying for him, Andy boarded the train. It wasn't until he was out of sight that Mama showed any sign of tears. Determined not to let Andy see her that way, she was learning how to control feelings as well. I couldn't help wondering how he would look the next time we saw him. As the sound of the train grew faint, we began a quiet march back to the apartment. The mood was reflected in the smaller kids too, as they shuffled along in unnatural silence. It was then that I became aware of something; Andy had never once called me Pigeon. There was a feeling I'd never hear it again. It made me sad. I had gone through the portal of a small but meaningful change. After everything Andy had been through, it was possible he didn't even remember he once called me Pigeon. I like to think he did remember, but decided it was time to put it tenderly away, where all childhood memories go.

CHAPTER 16
Home On The Hill The Hard Way

The battle's won, but left behind such devastation here.

What keeps the hand of God in check? Instead, he sheds a tear.

The punches we were taking lately were different from anything we had experienced before; I found myself doubting that things would be normal again. From the oldest to the youngest of us, we had learned to survive the hard times. This time, our world was inside out, how were we supposed to react about what we heard and saw? If there was a ray of hope in all that had happened, it was when Mama started talking about buying our own home.

The thought of having our own home seemed too much to ask for, but that was about to change. The thought of having Joseph's wake in our own home gave Mama a reason to accept the insurance money. To live in our own home had been on my mind and in my prayers for so long I felt responsible, not for the joy that teased our feelings, but for the bitter way it came about. I pushed my guilt down deep inside.

Dad had his problems too. He had no desire to live in any other town. Moving to a house was fine; moving out of Chipwey was not. Looking for a home in Hartford was Aunt Mildred's brainstorm, and

Mama liked the idea that it would get Dad away from his drinking cronies. Dad didn't need a ton of bricks to fall on him, Mildred, his enemy of many years, had a hand in this. Every day an irritable, sulking Dad drove Mama to Hartford where a Realtor took them to view houses for sale. In spite of his unspoken protests, I felt that Dad would soften as time went on and that things would work out. House shopping had gotten Mama up and on her feet early. By eight o'clock every morning, she and Dad were on the road headed for Hartford. As time went on, I could see her enthusiasm was being drained away every time she returned with nothing to show for her efforts. The houses she liked were too costly, and those that she could afford were so run down she wouldn't even consider them. This house would have to be special, it was out there somewhere but there wasn't much time left to find it, and finding it would only be the beginning. There would still be many preparations before Joseph came home.

One day, Dad refused to go to Hartford anymore and reported to work as usual. Mildred picked Mama up that day continuing the search for a suitable house. When she returned, Mama announced that she had left a fifty-dollar deposit on a house. I should have been excited, hearing that the searching was over; instead, my instincts were telling me something was bothering her. There wasn't the slightest glimmer that she was pleased. Later that evening, while Dad was out of the apartment, Mama and I talked about the house.

"Is the house close to Mildred's house?"

"No." Mama replied. Both of her hands were resting on the back of a chair, her arms drawn down straight and tense, she took a deep breath "I'm not sure I'm doing right."

"Getting a house?"

"Not this one."

"Aw, no."

"The hardwood floors are buckled in every room in that place. I won't spend Joseph's money on a piece of junk."

That night, Dad came home with his usual brown bag under his arm. He was in a dark sullen mood. He had been drinking, though far from having overdone it. Without a word, he pulled a bottle of beer, and two small packages from the bag. I was swimming in a river of confusion that night with the unrest I felt from both Mama and Dad. I stayed tuned in to their conversation and this time I didn't care if I was caught listening or not.

Dad's feelings of resentment had grown stronger. The trap door had sprung closed. There was no way out. This was a feeling totally unfamiliar to him, the man who always took pride as having full control of the family. The money was in Mama's name only, and for the first time Dad would have to go along with decisions made by someone else. It was too bad he didn't know of Mama's troubled thoughts.

He poured a glass of beer, sat down at the table and opened the two packages; one of cheese, the other of hard salami. He nibbled on the cheese, and meat, and sipped the beer. Mama entered the room. "Bob, will it be worth it to fix hardwood floors in a house?"

"Why don't you ask Mildred, she knows everything? You're running the show. You tell me," he snarled.

"What do you mean running the show? I just want what's best for everyone. This isn't a 'show'! We're trying to get ready to bring our son back to a decent home. How DARE you refer to it as a "show?" Are you saying you don't want to move?"

"I don't want to move to Hartford and you know it. Now leave it alone." Dad's voice could shatter glass when he was angry, and normally Mama would have walked away to keep the peace. Not tonight.

"Oh, you want to stay here. You want to have your son brought back to this hellhole? Isn't this beautiful? Isn't it great?"

As Mama screamed out, she walked into the hallway. When she neared the hole in the wallboard she began to tear away at it. It frightened me to see her dig into the plaster. We kids had been scolded countless times for knocking bits of plaster from that gaping cavity, and there she was throwing handfuls of the stuff to the floor, one after the other. "By all means' lets stay here it's a beautiful place to live." Moving through the hall Mama disappeared into her bedroom as a cloud of white plaster dust swirled in the air behind her. Mama had doubled the size of the gaping wound in the wall. Barren of plaster, the thin wooden strips underneath looked like the side of a great beast that someone had blown a hole in, revealing the frail bones of its rib cage.

Dad counted on keeping all of us fearful of him, and up to now he had succeeded. Just two weeks ago, I had turned sixteen, but was still scared silly of him when he started yelling in that deafening tone of his. Tonight I forgot myself.

"Why don't you leave her alone? She's been through enough already!" My outcry could have been the last straw to Dad. There I was poking my nose into adult business again.

With a thunderous scowl, Dad continued to chew on the salami staring at the table in front of him. I ran through the hallway to Mama's bedroom and burst into tears. Mama was sitting on the edge of the bed, and already had her arms open to me as I rushed to her side. "It's all right honey it's all right." There was an unexpected sound of assurance in her voice. She should have been in tears, but she had somehow taken charge. I nestled into her arms. "I'm not really upset, I only did that to let him know everything isn't gonna be his way anymore. It's all right, it's all right," she said repeatedly. I had intended to console HER, but Mama Bear had finally come of age, saying what she felt, regardless of the consequences. She did her best to comfort me, but it was too hard anymore for me to guess what was going to happen next. I continued crying on her shoulder, holding on for dear life. Mama had no rest that night trying to decide about the house. The next morning she made a phone call to the agent and canceled the deal. Something in the back of her head kept telling her, "This is not the right house."

Another week had slipped through our fingers. Our time was growing shorter. We had one month left to get a house ready; there was so much to do before the funeral. Mama's spirits had taking another beating. She was back to square one, but Dad shed no tears over her decision. He almost had both feet out of Chipwey, and that was as close as he wanted to come.

Dad knew Mama could resume her trips to Hartford at any time; he had to act quickly. If he was going to find a suitable house here in Chipwey, it had to be now. The next day, Dad came home from work at lunchtime, but not to have lunch. He would spirit Mama away in a mysterious fashion telling me to stay with the small kids. Judge Horn had come up with a solution for Dad.

After retiring from the bench years ago, the Judge had returned to his law practice with the title of "The Judge" still hanging on. He had taken on the noble task of defending the poorer class of people. Anyone who went to him with a rightful cause was never turned away. In his time of desperation, Dad enlisted the help of The Judge to tell him what homes were available in town. The Judge told him of a house up on the hill that needed some work on the outside, but was a good buy. The previous owner had bought the house on speculation, remodeled it inside and ultimately ran into financial problems. To avoid his creditors, he packed up his family and stole away into the night. That was a year and a half ago. The abandoned house was now the property of the City of Chipwey. The asking price was only the amount of the back taxes. The situation was tailor made for us. It would permit immediate possession. Dad had gone ahead alone to look the house over, and couldn't wait for Mama to see it.

When Mama and Dad returned home, Mama had changed; it was as though a bright light was shining out of her every pore. There was an air of excitement in her. This was more like it, more how I expected it to be.

"Where did you go?" I asked.

"We were looking at a house."

"Did ya like it? Are we gonna get it?"

"We don't know yet."

"Where? Where is it?"

"On the hill where I grew up as a little girl."

"Where Grandma Desmond used to live?"

"It's right next door. Our old house isn't there anymore. It was torn down long ago. There's a grassy yard there now, for a more modern house. This house is right at the foot of the woods." I felt Mama's eyes riveted on my face, reading my every reaction.

"When will we know; what do we do?"

"Dad and I have to go to City Hall in an hour to talk to someone. We have to find out more. Keep your fingers crossed."

When the kids were told the good news, they were jumping up and down with joy. As far as we were concerned, the house that Mama had been looking for had been found. There would be a whole world of trees to climb, and woods to hike and explore, and a big yard to put up a swing. Could it all possibly come true? By the end of the week, Mama and Dad had signed the papers for our new home on Monroe Street. For better or worse, it was all ours. The best part, there would be money left to buy furniture, and still money leftover for Mama to put away in the bank.

With only a scant three weeks to get ready it was going to be close, but all that mattered to Mama was the wake would be held in our own home, and what a special home it was. As a baby, Joseph had spent many days with his Grandma and Grandpa Desmond in the old homestead up there on the hill. It was a kindly twist of fate that Joseph would return home for his final rest to this happy, familiar place from the past.

The day the final papers were signed, Dad drove us up to the hill for the first time. The three huge maple trees that stood in front of the house completely concealed it from the road. The house had two stories plus an attic, and sat high on a grassy hill, up and away from the sidewalk. A porch with several posts missing from its railing stretched across the front. The clapboards on the house were a dirty gray, and the paint was peeling from years of neglect. One lone rose bush and a plump green bush, that we came to call the prickly bush because of its tiny thorns, were growing in the side yard of the house. The stairs from the sidewalk to the porch were natural stones and though a bit too high in places for the little ones to climb, it didn't stop them from reaching the top. We swarmed up to the porch like a plague of locust.

There was a new front door, which stood out against the run-down condition of the outside walls. The large window in the center of the door allowed us a peek inside as we waited noisily for Mama and Dad to catch up.

"Hold on. At least wait 'till we move in to bust the door down," Dad said with a laugh. We could hear the key slip into the lock, and turn. Dad pushed the door open wide. The heavenly odor of fresh paint came tumbling out around us. An enclosed staircase to the right of the door led to an upper floor, and to the left a good-sized living room with a flat, hardwood floor. We won't call it a front room any more. Mama says the proper name is living room.

Bursting with excitement, the kids spread out in all directions; I followed Mama and Dad. The house had been locked up for so long the smells of new wood and fresh paint had been trapped inside. We entered a kitchen that was so big it would have made up two rooms of our apartment. Boxes stacked at one end of the room contained red and white floor tile that was left behind. Laying the floor tile would be Dad's first job before we moved in.

The kitchen cupboards were the color of the cream, and unlike the apartment cupboards that loomed up to the ceiling, these were low for easy reaching. A counter supplied plenty of space to fix food. Two bright, cheery windows above the kitchen sink looked out on to the Simons' side yard, where a line of pine trees grew. Beyond that, a grassy covered yard where Mama's old homestead once stood. Birds constantly chirped and flew from one tree to another. Screams of blue jays echoed from the treetops, reminding me of the pinewoods at Barter Lake. This was the dream kitchen that I was so sure would never be ours.

A bedroom off from the kitchen would soon be furnished with bunk beds for my four brothers. A bathroom strategically located next to it was fully equipped with at last, a bathtub and sink. The tub stood on legs that looked like lion paws, and Dad proudly announced that he already had plans to put a shower in there. No more galvanized tub bathing or cleaning up in a kitchen sink, we were going to live like other people. The second floor had three more bedrooms plus a smaller room that would be Sharon's. A fold-up ladder pulled from the ceiling allowed us to investigate a dusty attic.

Exploring the cellar was a little frightening that first day. Johnny and Jimmy refused to go down there, but that wouldn't last long; in the days to come, they'd be running down quite willingly for apples stored there. I have to admit it was unnerving, the dirt floor and willowy cobwebs that float back and forth at the slightest draft, did give a tingle to the spine. As one would expect in a cellar, there was a menacing-looking furnace. Some of us had never seen a furnace up close before, with its wide girth, and bloated pipes. They appeared as huge arms holding up the floor above as they rose upward into the darkness. Not far from the furnace was the less threatening coal bin, big enough to hold a ton of coal. Mama was delighted with this dank old cavern under the house. She said the cool temperature made it ideal for preserving and storing food.

Everyday Mama, the kids and I hiked up the hill to the new house. Floors were scrubbed and rooms dusted in readiness for our move that coming Friday. Dad did as he said he would; he laid the kitchen tile, put a portable shower in the bathtub, and added a door to an upstairs bedroom. As we worked inside the house the kids spent their time outside covering every inch of the backyard and woods. Mary had already climbed half of the trees there. It was the first time there was something better to do than eat. When they did take time to eat, they had their peanut butter sandwiches on the cool grass of their own backyard.

One day as the kids played outside, Mama and I were finishing up the last room. All that remained were the cupboards and the kitchen sink. I wiped the cupboard shelves down as Mama cleaned the sink and the two windows above it. We had been chatting about this and that as we worked, when I became aware that she had grown quiet. She was staring out of the window. What was she was looking at so intently? As beautiful as they were, there was nothing, but the line of pine trees standing one level above our house. They were on a shelf of earth held back by a gray cement retaining wall.

"What's out there?"

"I was just looking at that wall. Papa built that wall years ago."

"Grandpa Desmond built it?"

" ...Better than forty years ago." Mama smiled. "He did everything very well. He was a good carpenter. His hands were his best tools. Imagine that wall is still standing strong as ever." Mama wiped her hands and walked out to the side yard. I followed her. She walked up to the wall and looked it over as though she had lost something, and was searching to find it there. Although it was still sound, the wall showed its age with a few cracks here and there. I know walls can't talk, but this wall was speaking. I stood a few steps behind Mama, watching. She reached her hand out to the rough gray barrier, hesitated for a second, and then tenderly laid her hand against it. One would have thought it was made of a delicate glass and would break if she pressed too hard.

"It's like touching the hands of my father. Papa's wall." It wasn't unusual to see a glimmer of a tear in Mama's eyes these days, but this wasn't the look of sadness. Something had definitely directed Mama to this place, back to this street, hurling her back in time. She had come home again.

"We were meant to have this house. It's like coming back home isn't it?" I asked.

"Ya, but ... doing it the hard way." Mama put her arm around my shoulders and together we walked the length of it out to the sidewalk. There it joined up with another wall, one that had no cracks in it at all. When we returned to the house and our cleaning, Mama continued talking of her happy days growing up in the house that once stood next door. I was glad that Mama was able to talk of these memories, and her curly headed first-born son who broke the hearts of all who met him. Her eyes reflected a warm calm feeling that had been missing. After their long absence, smile lines were collecting again at the corners of her dark brown eyes. Mama wasn't thinking only of the loss of a son, but was given the gift of a visit from her father. A little more peace of mind was Mama's by simply laying a hand on this plain, but faithfully strong, old gray wall.

Our last day in the Albany Street apartment couldn't come soon enough. The kids were giddy and uncontrollably alive. This would be the first night to sleep in the new house. It was all so overwhelming and easy to forget how we came to such good fortune. Mama on the other hand never forgot, and was a constant reminder pulling me back to the stark meaning of it all. That week Mama and Dad shopped for new furniture for the kitchen and living room. Packing up our belongings from the old apartment took no time at all. Only our clothes, dishes, pots, pans, beds, and two portable closets would move with us. Mama enjoyed throwing out all the jelly and mayonnaise jars that were used for glasses. She would have a set of matching glasses now. Most of our old furniture was left behind, sold to Foot's Second Hand Shop. We were saying farewell to all of it forever. Our dining room table, ol' elephant legs, was sold too along with our faithful kitchen stove.

By the time we moved in, we had a new white stove. It was fascinating that we didn't need matches to light it. We had but to turn the knob and the gas burner lit, just like Aunt Mildred's stove. A new automatic washing machine was placed in the far corner of the kitchen; the wringer washer was in our past too. The appliance that made the biggest hit with everyone was the refrigerator. It held more than the old one ever could, much to our delight. The first meal that Mama cooked on the stove was fried potatoes. It was only fitting that as true Irishmen we would christen the new stove with a feast of potatoes. Mama had bought a fifty-pound bag of them, and a bushel basket of apples. There was a secure feeling in seeing food bought in such quantities. They were immediately stored in Mama's cool dungeon below the kitchen.

The next morning we awoke to delicious smells of the breakfast that Mama had gotten up early to prepare. We would have pancakes, bacon, eggs, toast, orange juice and coffee, a king's banquet. As Mama stood in front of her brand new stove cooking, the kids seated themselves around our new kitchen table. Dad was the last one up that morning as Mama and I finished placing the food on the table. When Dad walked in the room, he paused to look at the scene before him. "For Krips-sake! This is the first time I've seen everyone with a clean face at the same time!" The kids looked back at Dad with smiles beaming from their well-scrubbed faces. The night before was the first time everyone went to bed clean as a whistle; we had a *real* bathtub now.

The days for us school-going people went on as usual despite the hustle and bustle that flooded the house. It was the second week in June and we were all having final exams at St. Michael's. It felt hopeless for me to take exams, having been absent for three months. I went through the motions anyway and did what I could. I will have to repeat first year high again next year because I didn't pass all subjects. There was always next year; I stashed one more problem in my worry pocket.

Six men swarmed over the outside of the house, replacing porch railings and painting the woodwork white. Two days later when they completed the job of installing the shingles over the gray clapboards, the front door no longer looked out of place. I'm a little ashamed to say that during this metamorphosis I became completely swept away by all the excitement. This was as good as any trip to my Cloud-cuckoo land had ever been.

With all of us pitching in extra hard, we pushed on at a steady pace to ready the house. Mary and Richard raked the front yard and made everything neat. The sidewalk and stairs were swept clean, and the bushes were trimmed. Outside of rescuing one or two of the kids who had climbed too high in a tree, the days passed without event. Everything was ready, and we were two days ahead of schedule. Mama, Mary and I took time now to write Andy and let him know all was going well at home. As the day of Joseph's arrival came nearer, a somber atmosphere filled the house. Mama was reading herself for the hardest time of all. Joseph's Funeral."

CHAPTER 17
Peace Of Mind For Kali

__The Dove returns and brings to man, hope and love and song.__
__But who will heed the message, and for just how long?__

Kali rises from the glider, stretches and yawns; can it be that she's been reminiscing out on the porch all night? The first glimmer of daybreak is hard to believe, it seemed like a short time since Kali first stepped out of the house. Behind her, the screen door opens. Helen steps out into the cool morning.

"You up already," Helen asks?

"Couldn't sleep; it's beautiful out there, huh?"

Sitting down, Kali curls her legs up and scrunches up in the corner of the swing; maybe her mother can be enticed to sit too. She will say nothing about the sleepless night spent on the porch; no sense in troubling Helen about that. Mother and daughter sit together on the glider saying very little. The delicate smell of the nearby pines surrounds the porch as strands of light from the yet unseen sun reach for the treetops.

"The sun is a kind of miracle, isn't it Mama?"

"It'd be a cold world without him."

The screech of the blue jays, the clamor made by scores of robins and their fledglings, slowly builds. The tranquil morning is no more; it lends a comforting feeling of home and family. There is a temptation to stay here surrounded by things so ordinary and to forget that this is the start of one very special day, Joseph is coming home.

"Those jays are loud."

"I remember waking up every morning to them when I was a girl." Helen gently squeezes her daughter's hand, and watches the quick departure of a jay that, in spite of its wide wingspread, easily passes into the tight cluster of pines. "So little has changed after all these years, and yet so much has happened.... " Helen slowly rises, tightens her robe tie, and takes a deep breath. " We'd better go in ... 'n start breakfast."

The house will be full of people coming and going this morning. Before leaving for the station, household chores must be done; beds made, kids fed and dressed, and the kitchen straightened again. The living room had been cleared of unnecessary furniture the night before, to make way for the coffin. Except for the news to keep in touch with conditions affecting Andy in Korea, the radio had remained silent for days. Happy sounds from the radio, and the new television would not be heard until the funeral was over.

It was decidedly best not to take the smaller children to meet the train. Aunt Hannah lived just over the hill from the O'Briens. It would take no time for her and Carol to pick them up and return home. Lined up for final inspection Mary, Richard, Jimmy and Johnny, were dressed in new clothes bought for the wake, and the funeral. Their faces didn't reflect the spit and polished looks they wore. Smiles, teasing and jokes didn't abound this morning. The solemn group filed into the back seat of the car. Not one of them squabbled or fussed over who would set where or who stepped on whose foot. Helen, dressed in the proper color of black, sat apprehensively in the front seat next to Bob. As the car inched its way down the hill, everyone one seemed to be locked in thought. Bob never did talk much when he drove the car. Helen stared straight ahead, not really noticing anything. Jimmy and Richard, with grave expressions, sat stiffly with arms folded. Johnny fingered the buttons on his new suit jacket pleased with their smooth feel and shiny surface. Mary didn't even complain about the tight fit in the back seat. Trying to pull as far as she could into her own space, she rode with forehead pressed against the car door window, not caring that her head was making small bounces off the glass.

When the park came into view, Kali spotted a sign jutting up from the patch of green grass by the curbing. The sign reading "VFW," is a reminder of a first experience; shoveling snow with her two brothers. She smiles to herself until she sees another house coming up fast. The trees around the house, now heavily laden with huge maple leaves, are remembered as stripped of their foliage and outlined in freshly fallen snow. The happy glow of Christmas lights shimmers around the front door of the house, and through the window a quick image of people joyfully celebrating the holiday. The words to a prayer returned like an assassin to the scene of the crime, "Please God, give US a home here someday," Those were hard times, but at least the family was together then.

"Is this how life is? If you get what you pray for, do you have to give something up? Is our God a bartering God?" Kali closes her eyes and scolds silently, "Stop, stop, stop!"

The house is soon out of sight as the car turns on to Main Street. Next is the post office. Helen can't resist. "Maybe there's a letter from Andy," She is hardly audible, but Bob has heard. "I'll take a look later." He says softly.

The car makes a rumbling noise as it moves over a bumpy metal grid, then on to the bridge that spanned the railroad tracks. It was a mere six months ago that Joseph left from this very place; it felt like years. Bob parked the car where the family would have full view of the train when it arrived. A military car parked in front of the station, waited with a uniformed man behind the wheel, and three others in the back seat. Mr. Upright, the Undertaker, and his five assistants waited near the hearse that was parked close to the tracks.

"Now stay inside the car." Bob looked over his shoulder addressing his order to the kids in the back seat. Judging by the crowd that had gathered on the platform, it was clear why Bob wanted it that way. There must have been more than twenty, maybe thirty, people there. Perhaps most of them were just curious, but it would be more fitting to think they had all gathered to welcome Joseph home.

The whistle of the train was coming closer, announced the train's arrival.

The car windows rolled down for ventilation on this warm morning allow an old man passing by to poke his head in, almost into Helen's face.

"It's too late for tears now, Mrs. O'Brien," he blurts, then promptly moves away.

"What's he mean? It's my fault?"

"Ohhh, don't pay any attention, the old fool doesn't know what the hell he's talking about," Bob grumbles.

Helen's sobs are lost in the overpowering roar of the train as it clatters by, gradually slowing down. The train engine hisses, breathing heavily like a runner taking advantage of the brief stop, knowing well the running would begin again. The huge door of one of the train cars pushed open. A large object concealed under a blanket-like covering is just inside the door. When removed, the covering reveals a glossy gray coffin. As if a silent signal is given, the men on the platform lower their heads, pull their hats off and hold them close to their chests. A large freight cart wheeled to the open door of the train transports the coffin to the back of the hearse.

Sergeant Burney, custodian of the coffin for the last miles of its journey, drops down from the train car. There is a short conversation between him and Mr. Upright. Six men slide the coffin into the hearse and close the door. Bob follows the hearse back to the house.

Passing over the bridge, the cars have a clear view of the station below. The O'Briens could see the impatient train engine on the track spinning its wheels and spewing heavy billows of white steam, straining to gain momentum. As it moves from the station, the crowd on the platform is breaking up, spreading out in all directions.

Joseph is home at last.

When the hearse reaches the house, the coffin is readily moved up the steps, across the porch and into the living room. Four soldiers unfold a large American Flag, and drape it over the top of the coffin. One of the soldiers immediately takes up his post at the front door standing guard with a rifle. The four would take turns in three-hour vigils every day until the morning of the funeral. Their moves were performed with an air of well-disciplined ceremony.

When Sergeant Burney entered the house, he introduced himself and shook hands with Helen and Bob. Bob settled himself on the arm of the couch behind Helen, and both listened intently to the Sergeant. He glanced often at Bob, but mostly looked straight into Helen's face as he talked, maybe trying to be sure that she understood all that he was saying. He told Helen and Bob that Joseph had been caught in a sudden, heavy attack, forcing Joseph's regiment, into an a head-on battle. One lone bullet found a vital spot on Joseph's body; there was no lingering pain or suffering. He was neither dismembered nor disfigured in any way. As she listened, Helen occasionally dabbed her eyes with the wadded up handkerchief. These were hard words to hear, but it did offer some comfort in knowing.

After minutes of conversation, Sergeant Burney took what looked like a jewelry box from a small satchel he carried. He opened it, and handed it to Helen. She gazed at it for a few seconds then took it from him. He cupped Helen's hand between both of his in a sympathetic handshake, shook Bob's hand again and then left the house. The jewelry box that the Sergeant gave Helen contained a Purple Heart Medal. It was set on top of the coffin next to a picture of Joseph.

Shortly afterwards Aunt Mildred arrived. It appeared an unspoken truce was happening between her and Bob. This wasn't the time to harbor bad feelings against old enemies. Bob did leave the house shortly after, but only to check on the mail at the post office as he promised Helen he would.

It was mid-afternoon before the house felt calm again. Anyone who had a service to perform had come and gone. Only the statuesque guard and Mr. Upright remained.

As Mr. Upright was about to leave, Helen had one last request of him. She asked if he would consent to open the coffin and make sure that it was really Joseph in there. The weary looking woman stood close to the coffin stroking it gently.

"It would be better to remember your son the way he was." Mr. Upright moved his hand across Joseph's face in the picture that stood on the top of the coffin. "It's been three months ... too long now. You don't want to remember him that way." Reluctantly Helen gave in; the coffin would remain unopened.

After Mr. Upright's departure, Kali went to her room to lie down for a time. Her lack of sleep from the night before had caught up with her. Blessed sleep would give some release from the nagging gilt that refused to go away.

Mildred had told the smaller boys that they could go out to the backyard, which they were happy to do. It would be several hours before the wake that evening, and it was a good time for Helen and Mildred to catch their breath. The two sisters sat at the kitchen table sipping their tea as they opened Sympathy cards.

"I've never seen so many cards." Mildred said.

"They started coming in the day the newspaper printed when Joseph was coming home."

"Here's another with a Mass card. You'll need thank you notes for all these. When things settle, I'll help you."

Busy opening envelops, neither woman noticed that Mary had slipped into the room by the coffin. Both were startled by the sound of crying; they found Mary leaning against the coffin crying bitterly. Mary had finally faced the truth. It was easy to say Joseph was gone when there was nothing more tangible than a telegram to make it real. Her period of denial was over. Mary was inconsolable, and was taken to Aunt Hannah's house to be quieted down.

The first evening of the wake, many of Helen and Bob's acquaintances paid their respects. All family members living in Chipwey were there also. Aunt Katie arrived later that night, Carol's family arrived after that; Carol stayed behind looking after the two smaller O'Brien children. Later that evening, Carol would take her turn to come to the house. Helen was comforted by all of them being there. The traffic in and out of the gray-shingled house on the hill was constant that first night. When the last few people had left, including the sentry at the front door, family members gathered in the kitchen. It was a private time for conversation over coffee and sandwiches. Mildred was in charge as usual. Kali took advantage and slipped away to her room. No one would miss her now, and there was a need to be alone for a few minutes.

In her bedroom, Kali sits on the little bench in front of a table that will, in the more peaceful weeks ahead, be a dressing table for her and Mary. Helen has promised to make a pretty organdy skirt for it later on, for now the brush, comb and hand mirror rest on the bare wooden tabletop. Kali stares at, but doesn't really see the pink orange tree blossoms pictured on the back of the hand mirror. Then a familiar voice calls out, "Can I come in?"

"Carol, you're here." Carol enters the room and seats herself on the edge of the bed.

"Congratulations on your engagement. Lets see your ring." Kali takes Carol's hand and looks at the ring. "It's beautiful. I can't imagine you being married."

"Mother can't either. She's still not sure my choice is the right one." Carol chuckles, but notices Kali's response is flat. A moment of awkward silence follows. "How come you're up here by yourself? Are you okay?"

"Guess so."

"Is it all starting to get to ya?"

"Not all."

"What then?"

"How much do ya know about ... God?"

"How much do ... what's the problem?"

"How much do ya know about God?" Kali insists.

"We're on good terms if that's what you mean."

"If you get something ya pray for, do ya have ta give something up?"

"You're describing a pack rat, not God," Carol chuckled. "Kali, what's cookin'?"

"For the longest time I've prayed that someday we would live up here on the hill. Here we are. But Joseph is gone."

"So you think… ?"

"Last time I prayed for a home I was in the back set of Joseph's car. See what I mean?"

"You think God's a spiteful God? None of us know how long our lives are going to be. We have to take it as it comes." Carol moves from the bed, sits on the bench beside her cousin, places an arm around Kali's shoulder. "You got it all wrong. If you ask me, He's a very sympathetic God. Think about it. Maybe this house happened for another reason."

"What?"

"Could be this house carries a message that says, 'Joseph is with me now, and this is his wish.' No matter what, this home will always belong to your family. Doesn't that sound like Joseph?"

"Do you really think so? If that were true… "

"I don't think you're powerful enough to change people's future. Come on powder your nose, comb your hair. Let's go downstairs."

"Okay. You go. I'll be right down."

Carol walks to the doorway, and looks back at Kali, "You ought to do something with that imagination of yours; it's a doozie." Kali grins sheepishly. Carol smiles back, then gestures to Kali to come downstairs.

The next day food from people in the neighborhood began to arrive at the house; many of them were not well known to Helen or Bob. The new neighbors, respecting the delicate situation at hand, had put off welcoming them to the neighborhood, but with these kindly gestures, nothing more had to be said. The O'Briens had never seen so much food in the refrigerator at one time. Helen's brothers, and sister would attend the funeral after traveling from Buffalo. Tomorrow after the funeral, family members would gather at the house where a reception was planned.

The second day of the wake Sister Anne, who had taught Joseph his uncompleted last year at St. Michael's, arrived with the entire class. Later that night, Father Kelly arrived and everyone knelt together to say the rosary. Joseph's two best friends, Bosco and Crud approached Helen. Both boys had graduated from High School the week before as Joseph might have, had he stayed in school. It was plain to see they were both shaken. The boys didn't stay at the house for very long. Marion, Joseph's girlfriend, arrived that night too; she remained with Helen for a time.

The last person to arrive was Mr. Kauffman. Helen was glad to see him. Friends of the O'Brien family, including Mr. Kauffman, ended up in the kitchen with Bob for a drink, a typical Irish tradition at a wake. By evenings end, most of Bob's cronies had joined him there too. Helen was truly touched by so many people remembering Joseph. Even Bob's closest friend Louie, with his pitted bulbous red nose and all, was appreciated.

The next morning, the sentry at the front door, who had become so familiar a sight, was noticeably absent. This was the morning of the funeral, and everything and everyone would move to the church. Many people attended the funeral Mass, and some of them made the three-mile trip to St. Michael's Cemetery. The officer who had talked to Helen two days before was at the graveside too. He and seven armed soldiers stood at attention. They stood with feet spread, and rifles held butt down. They looked like wooden soldiers. With all crowded around the gravesite, Father Kelly said the final prayers then blessed the grave with holy water. It was hard for Kali to concentrate on the prayers Father spoke now. She kept thinking about something that he said in church; it was so true of Joseph, and all the men who had died in every war. "Greater love hath no man than this, that he lay down his life for his friends." To Kali the words were so moving, she would never forget them. There was even a small touch of irony in this.

Kali was jarred from her deep reflections as the crack of the seven rifles vibrated the ground beneath her. Four times, the officer barked the order out; four times the rifles fill the air with an ear shattering sound. Then the bugler played a slow mournful Taps. The flag was lifted from the coffin and folded in the traditional triangle fold of the military, then handed to Helen. The crowd began to drift back to their cars. Everyone was going away. With his arm wrapped around Helen, Bob started to walk her back to the car when, without warning, she collapsed. She almost dropped to the ground before being caught. Sergeant Burney helped Bob guide Helen back to the car. Helen never let go of the precious flag.

The day that Kali had been dreading for so long was over. The time for adjusting was all that remained. Each one would have to deal with that in their own way, in their own time. Of everyone, it would be hardest for Helen. She had just given one of her diamonds back to the earth.

CHAPTER 18
Diamonds Are Forever

Heavy hearts beat slower now, longing to be healed.
Make pledge this day, forget them not,
All Children of the field.

Through his last winter in Korea, Andy received letters from home at a steady pace. For Christmas, Helen sent Andy a package containing soap, a razor with extra blades, and a familiar taste and smell of home; a fresh batch of peanut butter cookies. In a letter to Kali, Andy asks her to drop a line to a couple of his buddies because, "These guys don't get any mail. It means a lot to get those letters," he wrote. "You don't feel home is so far away when you can hold something in your hand from home." For six months, Kali wrote the two men, until they began to split up. It was an exciting time knowing they were completing their tour in Korea, and were being sent home. By Memorial Day, Corporal Andrew Terrance O'Brien had left Korea, and was stationed on a base on home soil.

If only Andy could have been home for Memorial Day, it would have made the celebration complete. But it was good knowing that Andy, who had learned to be such a good survivor in his younger days, had made it through his biggest survival test of all, and would be discharged in eight weeks. Andy would have a lot to catching up to do when he came home for good, including a trip to the cemetery. For the family, there weren't many trips to the cemetery during the winter months because of the heavy snow. When spring finally fought her way through, she flourished with unusual vigor. Evenings were sill cool, but days sparkled and blossomed with warmth. The lilac bushes had all they could do to support the huge, purple blooms that bent many branches to the ground. Lilacs would be plentiful this year to decorate graves.

The activities of the day would start with a parade down the flag lined Main Street. Memorial Day had always been a day of patriotic speeches and remembering for Chipwey. This year it had an added profound meaning. The country was still fighting the Korean War. Nearly 300 citizens from Chipwey were now involved in the conflict, and that was of great concern. Many of the speeches delivered from the bandstand that day spoke of sacrifice, dedication and not forgetting the lessons of the past. One such speech given by Judge Horn was a reminder to support those who were still carrying on the day-to-day fighting.

Everyone wore a red poppy with a red, white and blue ribbon attached to it. They were given out by the VFW and had the word "Remember," printed on it. That simple flower filled everyone with the glow of being part of something special. Though there remained an occasional look of subdued pain on Helen's face, she had learned to smile again. Mourning and sadness were being replaced with acceptance and the drive to carry on.

After the parade and speeches were through, Bob drove the family to the cemetery. People milled between the headstones, searching out graves probably not visited since last year. It was traditional on Memorial Day to honor the graves of all veterans with new flags. Popping sounds filled the cemetery as the flags tugged against the pull of gusting spring air. A new flag snapped proudly in the wind for Joseph. Flowers adorned so many graves the cemetery resembled a field that spring herself could have planned. Kali and Mary carried two huge bouquets of lilacs for their mother. Flowers were never just placed on Joseph's grave and that was that. Helen was always concerned; had she put the flowers in the best place? Before leaving, the cemetery the lilacs would be moved around several times, sometimes only a fraction of an inch.

It had been a good day of celebration for Chipwey. By noon, the crowds had gone to their homes or to picnics. Then without warning, the day that seemed to take so long to come began slipping away with the first signs of a setting sun. Early evening found Sharon fast asleep in her bed, tuckered out from the busy day. Helen, sitting on the porch glider, was squashed in the middle of her still very lively brood. The small group gushes with verbal energy as they examine an impressive cache of crystals in a handkerchief cradled in Helen's lap. The aftermath of a spring thaw was one of the best times to search for these small odd shaped stones. The kids looked forward to going into the woods, and several trips had already been made to the thinking rock. The trip would always include a story of bygone days. The gasp of wonderment each time someone found a diamond was music to their mother's ears; more satisfying than the days of hunting diamonds alone.

"Look at this one Mama it's almost perfect." Jimmy holds up a small, but well shape diamond he has taken from the handkerchief. His enthusiasm rocks the glider from side to side.

"Take it easy, Jimmy. You'll dump the whole bunch." Mary scolds.

"It's all right. I got a good hold… " Helen says, "and Look at this one. If only it didn't have that brown spot it would be perfect."

"Kali did you write Andy … we could find diamonds in our woods?" Johnny asks.

"Yeah, I wrote him. He knows,"

"I wrote him too," Mary adds.

A whistle from the street below silences the chatter on the porch. Kali raises her hand and waves; it's David, a newcomer to the block. If someone was out on the porch, David always gave out with his familiar wolf whistle.

Mary cranes her neck to see. "Who is it, Kali?"

"Who do you suppose?" Kali speaks softly so as not to be heard.

"Hi David." Mary yells, as she jumps up to get a look at him.

"Hello beautiful." David says pointing a finger at Mary. "Were you all at the parade this morning?"

"Yea." Kali and Mary answer in harmony.

"Pretty nifty, huh? Well … don't eat too many hot dogs. See ya later." David waves again, then he continues on his way.

"Kali's got a boy friend," Richard sang out.

"Maybe he's my boyfriend." Mary coos.

"Oh keep quiet, both of you." Richard was turning into a big tease these days, and Kali didn't take well to being teased about such things.

"Kali's got a… "

"Richard, I'm gonna strangle you. He can still hear. Shut up!"

"Shhhh, stop arguing." Helen scolds.

"Well, tell him to mind his own business."

"Kali's Got… "

"Richard! Stop now. That's enough." After a second of hesitation Helen asks, "Is he?"

"Is he what?"

Helen looks at Kali and grins. Kali rolls her eyes, "Mama!" She says, "Oh for heavens' sakes." Kali jumps up and moves off slumping down on a section of the railing away from the glider. She is relieved that the talk has returned to the diamonds.

From where she sat, Kali could see her father alone in the living room. He is seated in his recliner smoking a cigar, watching television. Being Bob's decision, it couldn't be anything but an RCA TV.

Kali studies her father, sitting comfortably, viewing a boxing match. Beside him on a table is an oversized ashtray for his cigar. Among a small stack of electronic books, one book in particular tells of the recent advances of colored TV.

"Dad is different now. It's been a whole year," Kali thinks.

Bob rises from the chair and walks to the screen door.

"--Fights are over. Movie is coming on in a few minutes. Are we gonna have a little popcorn, Mom?"

"Yep. We'll be right in."

As if propelled from a slingshot, the kids stampede into the house leaving behind a disheveled heap of shoes and socks on the porch. Scattering themselves on the living room floor like rag dolls, the boys quibble over who will occupy which spot. Then there's a brief exchange of head bopping with a throw pillow. "Come on kids. Be quiet. We want to hear the movie." Mary, always agitated with their boyish nonsense, didn't want to miss one syllable of the Hoot Gibson Western that was about to begin.

On the porch, Kali hangs back. It would be a crime not to straighten out the array of shoes and socks before going inside. The corn popping in the pan, and the aroma filtering into the air around her, makes this a most satisfying part of the day.

The sun has almost disappeared creating a time that is neither dark nor light. As a soft breeze slides past, the leaves on the big maple are making that rustling sound. Kali pulled her sweater around her to block the cooling air, and continued to straighten up the porch. Stuffing socks into the shoes, she lines them up against the porch wall. All that's left on the glider is the handkerchief containing the diamonds. Carefully she opens the folds, and studies the shiny treasure; her thoughts turn to Joseph.

"Leave it to you Joseph," Kali whispers, "not only to give us a home, but one with diamonds in the backyard. You may not be here, but you're still taking care of us. We'll never forget what you've done for us. We have something now that no one can ever take away. Not just a home of our own, but also our togetherness as a family. Even Dad is better."

"Kali, the movie has started, and your popcorn is waiting," Helen calls.

"O.K., be right there, just straightening up the porch."

Kali approaches the screen door, and then pauses. Each face inside is aglow from the eerie light emanating from the television. By now, everyone is drawn into the movie, and has their bowl of popcorn. How many times before had this scene repeated itself? The radio was the entertainment then, and Bob was missing many of those times. Now Kali's family was looking more like a real family. With so many good changes this past year, she wondered, "what if it was to all to suddenly disappear?"

No. It was time to remember what she had learned. Life is always changing, and change isn't always sad. Accept as best you can things you can't change, and keep your heart as a storehouse of faith.

"Kali."

"Coming, Mama."

Wrapping the diamonds back up in the handkerchief, Kali casually drops them on the glider then turns and walks away. Glancing back, she smiles, "The only diamonds that matter now are already inside the house."

Kali opens the screen door and steps inside to join her family.